OLD MENDIP

OLD MENDIP

by
ROBIN ATTHILL

BRAN'S HEAD

This Book
is dedicated
to the memory of
my Father and Mother

First published by David & Charles 1964
This edition published by Bran's Head Books, 1984

ISBN 0 905220 55 2

Printed at the
Hunting Raven Press, Frome,
for
Bran's Head Books,
45, Milk Street, Frome, Somerset.

Contents

List of Illustrations

PLATES

7

List of Illustrations

LINE-DRAWINGS IN TEXT

List of Illustrations

MAPS

NOTE TO THE THIRD EDITION

Old Mendip was first published in 1964, with a revised edition in 1971. In the last 20 years a number of important changes have occurred, and it has seemed best to leave the main text of the book unaltered and to add an Epilogue in which it has been possible to comment on some of the major changes and alterations, with special reference to the railways, Wookey Hole, and Fussells of Mells, and so bring the book up to date.

Ashwick, July 1984

Preface

This book is concerned with what John Aubrey, the Wiltshire antiquary, called 'the art of local memory'. It is not a guide-book to Mendip, and as far as possible I have made no attempt to deal with aspects of Mendip that are already dealt with in well-established guide-books: the towns and villages, their architecture and their industries, the scenery above and below ground. Instead, from the landscape and its buildings, from written records, and from the lips of its inhabitants, both past and present, I have tried to recover something of an older Mendip which is still everywhere visible to those who have eyes to see.

I have sometimes been asked why there are so many ruined houses all over Mendip. To answer that question fully, one would have to know a great deal of history—social, political, religious and economic—more in fact than an amateur could hope to learn in a lifetime. But it is not difficult to learn enough to begin to be aware of some of the questions posed by any square mile of the countryside. Who built this wall? Why is there a double hedge down this hillside? Why is there a stile at that bend in the road? Why does that stream pour through a broken dam in the deserted valley? The answers may not be easy to find. The wall is there, perhaps, because in that particular parish the Mendip common was enclosed in the years immediately following an Act of Parliament in 1773, and the Award will show to whom the allotment was made; the double hedge may mark the line of the old road before the local Turnpike Trustees built a new stretch of road, perhaps in 1811; the stile may well mark a footpath which is still a parish boundary following the line of the Roman Foss Way; the broken dam may once have contained a small reservoir, which supplied power to an edge-tool mill which was closed down before the first six-inch Ordnance Survey map was published in 1886.

Preface

None of this information is likely to be found in any guide-book: some of it is buried in the Journals of learned Societies, or in old topographers' tomes, or in documents deposited at the Somerset Record Office; some of it is available to a limited public in the invaluable series of Village Histories compiled in 1953 by the members of numerous Women's Institutes. This book of mine has come to be written very largely because of the innumerable questions to which I have had to find out the answers for myself, and because, in the course of lecturing to W.E.A. classes and other adult groups, I have found a widespread interest in just the sort of problem I have been delving into for my own satisfaction. Furthermore, I am continually amazed at the untapped sources of information which one is liable to come across. I have seldom come away from giving a lecture without having acquired some new and interesting piece of information which has enlarged and deepened my own knowledge of Old Mendip; nor is it always possible to remember accurately where one has picked up some vital clue which has helped to solve some particular problem or to fill in a gap in one's interpretation of the palimpsest of the countryside. In unspoken gratitude to many friends all over Mendip, I can only put on record that this book, like the melancholy of Jaques, is 'compounded of many simples', assembled over a period of around fifty years in which I have known and loved Mendip.

CHAPTER ONE

Hazel Manor

I dwell in a lonely house I know
That vanished many a summer ago . . .

ROBERT FROST: *Ghost House*

Hazel Manor was burned to the ground one winter's night in March 1929. We watched the glow in the sky away to the west, without knowing that it marked the destruction of our first home on Mendip. The fire brigade, too, watched helplessly; for apart from a rain-water tank and a pond in the farmyard there was no supply of water available to tackle such a conflagration. Boring had been undertaken, but the only visible result was several hundred feet of circular sections of Mendip rock lying about in one of the fields. One piece has served me as a door-stop for 40 years, and there were pieces still lying about when I last went to look at the ruins. For Hazel Manor has never been rebuilt.

It is not even mentioned in any guide-book or history of Somerset: such parts of its story as I have been able to piece together I have gropingly compiled from a fortuitous series of hints—a detail from an old map; the reminiscences of a very old lady whose father arrived on Mendip in 1854; a single reference in Humphreys' *Somersetshire Parishes*;[1] and my own childhood recollections of some ruins in the shrubbery, which may conceivably be the remains of an Elizabethan manor house—beyond which the darkness descends.

I have said that Hazel Manor was my first home on Mendip. It was only a temporary home, for my father had come to take charge of the estate for the Hills, and while the farmhouse which we were to occupy was being got ready for us, we lived for several months in a corner of the big empty Manor which had been shut up for the winter. They were impressionable months: I was just six years old, it was the first home I can recollect with any real distinctness, and it was the only large house which I have ever lived in. Of course it was not really a large house except to a child's eyes. The Hills had bought it as a shooting-lodge, and only came there for a month or two in the summer and again for the autumn shooting parties, but it had something of the atmosphere of a much larger country house with its library and billiards-room and servants' hall. We merely occupied two small rooms on the ground floor and two bedrooms up above. The other rooms were all shrouded in dust-sheets. Beyond the green baize door in the hall was the servants' wing in what was obviously an older part of the house, and right at the top were their bedrooms, swept and garnished and empty, with sunlight streaming into the arid air, and butterflies pattering despairingly against the window-panes.

Our rooms looked north, across a little ha-ha which separated the lawn from the field round which the drive swung in a great semicircle. There was practically no view, for the house was set back about a quarter of a mile from the northern escarpment of Mendip, a site that was doubtless chosen for practical rather than for aesthetic reasons. To get the view, one took the Channel Walk, a grass border lined with shrubs and leading away from the house: at the end, a gate led into an open field, and there below lay the valley, with Blagdon lake cradled in the green hills that tumbled away towards Dundry, behind which one guessed at Bristol; to the west, across the glistening Severn, were the piled Welsh mountains; to the east, where now the Chew Valley lake lovingly follows the contours of the land, was rich pastoral country, and beyond the plume of smoke that marked Pensford colliery was the Lansdown ridge, and the upper terraces of Bath; eastward again the eye picked out the conical spoil heap of Camerton, the unfinished tower of Downside Abbey, and the Westbury White Horse. Yet from the house itself one was completely shut off from the magnificent panorama.

The front door looked out on a courtyard, enclosed on two sides by grey crenellated walls: beyond this there were coach-houses and kennels and stables, above which there were men-servants' quarters which were always known as 'the bothies'. The square walled garden was always full of the scent of sweet briars, and beyond it, paths wandered through shrubberies, past a wooden summer-house which was to me a place of particular horror, for once the gardener had hung there the bodies of a couple of grass-snakes, which glistened in the sun and wriggled ominously in the faintest breath of wind.

Nearly 40 years after the fire I went back to look at the ruins and to remind myself of what had once been a well-appointed and well-loved home. At first sight, approaching from the half-mile drive of straggly beeches, one was hardly aware of what had happened: the gardener's cottage was still there, the grey-walled garden was still there, the outbuildings were in use as part of a farm; but the walled garden contained only the tortured earth of a pig-run, the once carefully tended shrubberies and winding paths were a tangled wilderness, and Channel Walk was blocked from end to end.

Except to one who had actually known the house, the ruins could make little sense. I know now why the sites of abbeys and castles, neatly patched and labelled by the Ministry of Works, so often fail to give any conception of what the original buildings must have been like. Some grey walls still survived from what was the oldest part of the house, but the main block was no more than mounds of rubble, where it was only just possible to trace the ground plan of the rooms which I knew as a child. The most spectacular relic stood by itself—the red-brick chimney and part of the wall of the drawing-room, with the hearth-tiles still showing. I remember that drawing-room. Mrs Gathorne Hill had complained that all the living-rooms looked north and had no sun, and when she was asked where she wanted her drawing-room, she stood in the courtyard and they planned round her there and then. It was a light, sunny room, parquet-floored and fragrant with bowls of lavender and roses, and now the stark red-brick chimney alone survived:

> And thorns shall come up in her palaces,
> Nettles and brambles in the fortresses thereof.

I always took Hazel Manor for granted: I felt a genuine affection for the place because it was my first home in Somerset, and because of my family's fealty to the Hills. But the house apparently had no claim to architectural distinction, and no history. I had always been told that it was a nineteenth-century shooting-lodge which perhaps incorporated an earlier farmhouse, but a passage in Morris's *Directory of Somerset* for 1871 raised all sorts of questions and set me thinking along very different lines:

Hazel Manor

Hazel Manor House is an ancient Gothic building which has been lately restored by Adolphus Ennor Esq., the lord of the Manor. The Hall and library contain fine oak ceilings with cross-bars or Oxford beams, and in the staircase is a fine oriel window of stained glass with the family arms in the centre. The grounds are tastefully laid out; the buildings covered with ivy and there are some remains of the old manor found. The founder of the manor is unknown but it formerly belonged to Billingsley Wilkins Esq.

Who was Adolphus Ennor? and Billingsley Wilkins? and what was 'the old manor'?

Neither the Court Rolls nor the Ministers' Accounts at the Public Record Office in London contain any reference to the manor of Hazel, nor does the Manorial Register. On the other hand, in the *London Gazette* for 28 February–3 March 1697-8 and again for 15–18 May 1699 there appeared advertisements to the effect that 'The Manor of Westharptree and Hasell . . . late the Estate of Harry Roynon Esq., is to be Sold by Virtue of a Decree of the High Court of Chancery.' There are also two voluminous sets of Chancery Proceedings from the Elizabethan period relating to Haysell or Hashell Manor and lands in Hasell, in which Francis Roynon was involved with George Bredyman and William Leversage.[2] The Roynons were a Hampshire family who had established themselves at Compton Martin. Collinson describes a memorial stone in the chancel floor of Compton Martin church with the inscription:

'Here lyeth the body of George Roynon, gent. the last of the house of Bigfold (i.e. Bickfield). He deceased 9 August 1637, aged 79.'[3] Earlier still, Roynons had owned Tilly Manor at West Harptree in 1476 (16 Edward IV), and also Emborough, before it came into the hands of the Hippisleys in 1570 (13 Elizabeth 1). Roynon is still a north Somerset name; there was a family of that name living in a cottage on the Hazel Manor estate in 1918.

By 1700 Hazel Manor was passing out of the hands of the Roynons after at least 150 years: there is no evidence of a large house on the manor, but there must have been a house of some sort there. One can only conjecture that it fell into ruin after 1700 to become the 'remains of the old manor' referred to in 1871. There is no building on the site in the Ubley Enclosure Award of 1773, but by 1817 'Hazel Farm' has appeared in the first edition of the Ordnance Survey, with a half-mile avenue leading to it, and the

1. (*above*) Hazel Manor about 1900 showing the Gothick windows and the crenellations in the forecourt. 2. (*below*) The ruins of Hazel Manor in 1964

3. (*above*) Ruined cottages at Leighton on the main road between Shepton Mallet and Frome. 4. (*below*) Pillar Lane between Radstock and Frome, which once led to the mansion of the Bampfyldes at Hardington

Hazel Manor

Ubley tithe map of 1839 recorded the owner as Charles Wilkins, one of the family established at Twerton on the outskirts of Bath. At first I assumed that Charles Wilkins was the father of Billingsley Wilkins who had preceded Adolphus Ennor as 'Lord of the Manor', but an examination of the land tax assessments at the Somerset Record Office showed that Billingsley Wilkins Esq. was almost certainly a fictitious character, invented by the compilers of the 1871 *Directory* from an amalgamation of the names of the two previous owners of the property; for from 1781 to 1817 'Hazel Farm' belonged to John Billingsley of Ashwick and his widow, and thereafter to Charles Wilkins, who finally sold the estate, comprising 1,058 acres, in 1849. The catalogue of the sale, however, raises yet another problem, for the map included with it shows that the house which the 1817 O.S. map calls Hazel Farm, and which I knew as Hazel Manor, was in 1849 called Ubley Hill Farm;* but much more important is its description as 'a House fit for the residence of a Gentleman', and as such it was purchased by the Ennors.

Nicholas Ennor, father of Adolphus, who arrived on the scene about 1854, was a Cornish mining engineer; he came to Mendip from the Brendon Hills in West Somerset, together with James Payne of Tiverton (1802–1882), his steward, who was to look after the Hazel Manor estate for him. Nicholas Ennor's mining activities on Mendip are fully described in J. W. Gough's *The Mines of Mendip*.[4] In 1857 he got possession of the mineral rights of Priddy minery, where he established the St. Cuthbert's leadworks with the intention of reworking the old slags which lay there. Almost at once he became involved in two expensive lawsuits: the first was against his rival, Barwell, of the adjacent Chewton minery, who was attempting to contain all the surface water there and to prevent its natural flow towards Priddy minery. Ennor, however, won his case, and Barwell was restrained from diverting any more water, but Ennor himself was then sued by the owners of the paper mill at Wookey Hole for causing the pollution of the headwaters of the river Axe, and was himself restrained from allowing any of the water used for sifting and cleaning the lead, preparatory to smelting, to run away down neighbouring

---

* Two other farms have now acquired the names of Hazel Farm and Ubley Hill Farm; the 1817 O.S. map erroneously gives the name of Ubley Hill Farm to two different farms, about a mile apart.

17

swallets. Few of those who in their season enjoy the somewhat limited facilities for bathing and skating offered by the two bleak little pieces of water known vaguely as Priddy Pool are likely to be aware of the passionate and costly litigation which went to provide them with their sport.

At this stage Ennor seems to have lost heart, for in 1862 he sold out his interest to the newly formed St. Cuthbert's Lead Smelting Company; but it was during these difficult years, when Nicholas Ennor was trying to establish himself on Mendip as a prosperous industrialist and a landed proprietor, that the restoration of Hazel Manor described in the 1871 *Directory* was carried through, and the grounds 'tastefully laid out'. Deep in the shrubberies I remember some vast piles of masonry, vast at least to my childish eyes. I now wonder if they were 'remains of the old manor' or artificial grottoes, a *nouveau-riche* hangover from the eighteenth century, a minor folly in keeping with the crenellations on the courtyard walls, and the Gothick windows which were moved across from Fernhill Farm. The Ennor régime, however, did not last long, for by 1880 they had sold Hazel Manor to the Hills, and moved away from Mendip—except for Adolphus's brother Albert, who was rector of Ubley from 1874 to 1893.

The story of the Ennors and their connection with Hazel Manor was told me clearly and circumstantially by the late Edith McLaughland, who was born in 1880, the grand-daughter of the Ennors' first steward, James Payne. She showed me a postcard of the house as it was before the Hills altered it by adding the drawing-room wing: half the façade is covered in ivy, as in 1871; there is some half-timbering at one end, the Gothick windows, the courtyard crenellations—but for all its air of sham romanticism and its rather pathetic attempts at grandeur, it was a house without distinction and without apparent charm. The sale catalogue of 1924, however, when the Hills disposed of the Hazel Manor estate, shows pictures of a very much more imposing mansion. The Gothic windows had been removed and dormers added, while the splendid new drawing-room dominated the courtyard.

This was the house which I remember so vividly; but of all this nothing whatsoever remains today. The site, cleared and levelled, is occupied by modern farm buildings. Hazel Manor has finally disappeared from the map.

CHAPTER TWO

The Lost Villages

In succession
Houses rise and fall, crumble, are extended,
Are removed, destroyed, restored, or in their place
Is an open field. . . .

T. S. ELIOT: *East Coker*

Why, then, should one bother about Hazel Manor? Why interest oneself in the patchwork history of an undistinguished nineteenth-century shooting lodge, let alone expect to interest anyone else? Apart from purely personal and sentimental motives—what one might regard as an act of local piety—there grows a conviction that this is the stuff of which local history is made, and the more the patchwork is studied, the more clearly some sort of pattern begins to emerge, a picture of the way in which life was lived in one's own locality.

For a house, even in ruins, is a focal point of individual human existence: here, people like ourselves have lived and loved and died. There is a reason for the situation of every individual building in the countryside—and for its disappearance. There was a cottage in a field near Kilmersdon with its back to the road, placed clumsily askew; or so it seemed until I realized that an older road wound steeply down the hillside *in front of* the cottage. The hollow way still visible in the field was the old coach road from Trowbridge to Wells, and preceded the new stretch of turnpike road which was only cut about 1830. Or there was the cottage at Charterhouse where old Mercy Green used to live when I first came to Mendip: nobody lived there after she died, and I watched the grass grow on the thatched roof, until the roof fell in and the walls crumbled, and now there is only a grass-covered hummock in the little enclosure by the roadside, 'where once the garden smil'd'.

19

The Lost Villages

Sunk are thy bowers, in shapeless ruin all,
And the long grass o'ertops the mouldering wall.

I fondly used to believe that Goldsmith was using his poetic licence to describe *The Deserted Village*—that it was perhaps a local phenomenon of the eighteenth century in specific areas directly affected by the Enclosure Acts or by a despotic landlord. Only gradually have I come to realize that this wastage of houses has been a perennial and universal phenomenon: it is not only the present age that has demolished so many houses and allowed so many more to fall to ruin. In some sense the English countryside has always been 'a garden and a grave'.

Fifty years after Goldsmith's poem was written, Cobbett rode through Windsor Forest on his way to London. He eagerly took the opportunity of inveighing against the new enclosures and houses that were springing up here and there all over 'this execrable tract of country'. While 'these *spewy lands* and *gravel*' near London were being enclosed and built on, good lands in other parts were in Cobbett's eyes being neglected:

> The farmhouses have long been growing fewer and fewer; the labourers' houses fewer and fewer; and it is manifest to every man who has eyes to see with, that the villages are regularly wasting away. . . . In all the really agricultural villages and parts of the kingdom, there is a *shocking decay*: a great dilapidation and constant pulling down or falling down of houses.[1]

There are few 'lost villages' in the Mendip countryside in the sense that Professor Maurice Beresford uses the words in *The Lost Villages of England*.[2] In Somerset the conditions most favourable to the disappearance of medieval villages were less likely to occur than elsewhere. The Black Death was a ubiquitous disaster. It often resulted in the wholesale enclosures of the early Tudor period, when sheep farmers found that wool was a more profitable commodity than corn, and proceeded to seize and enclose for pasture the fields that had lain inadequately cultivated in the years of depopulation that followed the Black Death, evicting if necessary the inconvenient survivors who clung with peasant stubbornness to their native heath. But these conditions were more usual in the wider arable landscapes of the Midlands and north-east England, notably in the Yorkshire and Leicestershire wolds where Beresford estimates that there were ten per cent more villages in medieval times than now. There were also few large estates on Mendip whose Georgian landlords might have wished to move villages to suit their personal fancy; the later enclosures (1770–1830) were mainly concerned with bringing into cultivation the Mendip commons.

The only two lost medieval villages specifically mentioned by Beresford were on the southern flanks of Mendip: Horseley lay near the head waters of the Brue, Spargrove on the little river Alham between Batcombe and Milton Clevedon. At Horseley the only surviving building is a farmhouse incorporating some of the fabric of the church in an ecclesiastical-looking barn; the very name has disappeared from the map except for Horseley Farm two miles away to the south, though at Batt's Farm the legend *Church* is marked in Gothic letters. Spargrove still figures on the map, though here too there is only one inhabited building. In 1623 a branch of the Bisse family was established here, which suggests that Spargrove was a cloth village like its neighbour, Batcombe, where the Bisses were noted clothiers. The old manor house, dating in parts from the sixteenth century, is now used as farm buildings: the site was moated, and the tithe map of 1843 shows several ranges of buildings—the stables are dated 1749—with surrounding lawns and paddocks. A portion of the large field designated as The Park is marked off as glebe (1 acre and 13 poles), and this is the traditional site of the village church which was dedicated to St. Lawrence.[3]

Both these sites have yet to be excavated and explored; so has Holcombe, where the situation is different in that a new village with a new church (1885) has grown up half a mile or so away from the site of the old village. Here, on the edge of the deep wooded combe from which the village derived its name, stands the old church, which has recently been restored, and the burial ground: its most notable monument is a memorial slab to Captain Robert Scott, whose father lived in the present manor house in his capacity of manager to the local brewery. Nearby there is one farmhouse, the old rectory and an uneven hillside with some tell-tale fruit trees—the supposed site of the lost village. Legend asserts that the village was wiped out by the Black Death;[4] the old church is locally known as the 'Plague Church'; and when some abortive excavations were being carried out on the site by the Downside Archaeological Society, inhabitants were heard to express their anxiety that if graves were found and disturbed, the amateur archaeologists might 'let the germs out again'. Beresford gives a warning against blindly accepting any story of the Black Death, which is regularly trotted out by local tradition as the reason for a village's disappearance: only careful examination of poll tax and other returns for the relevant decades of the fourteenth and fifteenth centuries can decide each individual case. From whatever cause, however, the old village of Holcombe decayed, and by 1800 a new village had grown up nearer the coal workings on the edge of the Nettlebridge valley.

There are two other places on the eastern fringes of Mendip where the churches stand alone and the villages have disappeared. At Babington, near Mells, the exquisite little Georgian church built in 1743 stands on the lawn of Babington House, for long the home of the Knatchbulls: this is a case where the village may possibly have been removed by the landowner when he was rebuilding his house and enlarging his park; but if so, where did the village go? Furthermore, the rebuilding of the church almost on the scale of a proprietary chapel suggests a scanty population by the middle of the eighteenth century. At Hardington, also between Radstock and Frome, the church stands a little distance from an unclassified road, more or less in a farmyard, surrounded by ranges of farm buildings and by the surviving fragment of what was once the mansion of the Bampfyldes. It is a charming little church with a roof of stone tiles, Cotswold fashion, and an unrestored Georgian interior: plaster roof and walls, box-pews, a double-decker pulpit with a clerk's reading desk, a hatchment of 1640 and the Bampfylde arms. It may in fact have come to be regarded as the family chapel of the big house, for although the Bampfyldes continued to live there until well into the nineteenth century, Collinson describes Hardington as 'almost depopulated' in 1791, and the 1801 census returns show only four inhabited houses: here at any rate was one of Cobbett's villages 'wasting away'.

Another possible site which has still to be investigated is at Egford, on the road from Mells to Frome. Twenty-two families were recorded here in the Domesday survey of 1086. Melting snow at the end of the arctic winter of 1962–3 revealed patterns on the ground suggesting the lay-out of a medieval village. A large stony mound may mark the site of the church, or possibly the manor house, but the site is awaiting fuller investigation by the Frome Society for Local Study. The site of the medieval village of Marston Bigot, two miles south of Egford, also showed up quite well in the melting snow.

Frome East Woodlands, on the other hand, was a comparatively new village that grew up, as its name suggests, in a clearing on the edge of the Forest of Selwood, and still snuggles under the shelter of Longleat woods. The church was built in 1712–14, but only its classical tower survived nineteenth-century rebuilding; the 1817 Ordnance Survey map actually marks it as 'New Church'. It is a large building in proportion to the number of houses anywhere near it, but when I commented on this to a woman whom I met in the road, she replied, 'Oh, but there used to be many more houses; I can remember cottages all the way down to the farm'; and this was confirmed by the 1817 map. It was this map which also drew my attention to Leighton, now a small and straggling hamlet on the main road between Frome and Shepton Mallet. The old map marks it with houses lining both sides of the road for more than a quarter of a mile. The ruins of some of these are still visible, and the sites of others, with the enclosure walls of their gardens, and lanes leading through into the fields.

The 1817 map is indeed an absolute essential for the local historian or for anybody in any way concerned in discovering what the Mendip countryside was like 150 years ago. The original drawings from the first survey of the area, dated 1808–11, are preserved at the British Museum. This first edition of the one-inch Ordnance Survey map is a thing of beauty in itself, and gives a fascinating picture of the late Georgian countryside; there is scarcely a mile where there is not some detail to interest even the most casual observer—an alteration in the line of a road, an avenue that has disappeared, a mill, a turnpike gate, a variation in a place name or even a name that has now disappeared (like Lechmere Water, an old name which has a good deal more charm than the modern Emborough Pond). Above all, one gets a much clearer idea of the shift of population by observing the rise and fall of hamlets and villages, the disappearance of individual houses, the absence of building where there are now long ranks of nineteenth-century miners' houses or post-war building estates. In fact the changing pattern of the buildings in the English countryside, so accurately described in the lines from T. S. Eliot's poem quoted at the head of this chapter, can be most vividly studied in the whole series of maps published by the Ordnance Survey over the last century and a half.[5]

CHAPTER THREE

The Lost Houses

Houses live and die: there is a time for building
And a time for living and for generation
And a time for the wind to break the loosened pane.

T. S. ELIOT: East Coker

When Cobbett wrote in 1822 of the 'great dilapidation and constant pulling down or falling down of houses,' he was referring to the disappearance of farmhouses and labourers' houses. The latter were as anonymous and unnoticed in their decline and fall as were their owners, 'each in his narrow cell for ever laid', in country churchyards 'where heaves the turf in many a mouldering heap'; the farms at any rate often perpetuated the names of their one-time owners—Clavey's and Dunford's, Blacker's Hill and Phippen's, Mitchell's Elm and Hillier's Down, to choose at random a selection of local names from a single piece of the map. But it is the disappearance of the larger houses, sometimes without a trace, and certainly without any adequately recorded history, as in the case of Hazel Manor, that is the most surprising phenomenon.

I am the more concerned with what might be called the middling houses. The larger and more notable houses in the Mendip country have been adequately photographed and described, and we can be sure that posterity will have a record of them, whatever fate awaits them. Mells Manor and Harptree Court, Gournay Court and Ston Easton Park are already fully dealt with in guide-books or architectural studies; even Dr Whalley's fantastic Mendip Lodge, which was demolished in the post-war years, is splendidly described by Vincent Waite in *The Mendips*.[1] The Ministry of Housing and Local Government and the National Building Record have now between them taken cognizance of this problem, and it is unlikely that any houses of genuine architectural or historic interest will henceforth be demolished without an accurate record of their appearance being preserved. Hitherto it has often been impossible to get any idea at all of what a house looked like, even when it has been pulled down within living memory: sometimes folk memory can be tapped, occasionally an old photograph or print is unearthed. Indeed the postcard and the battered sale catalogue of Hazel Manor which I have been lucky enough to find may well be the only surviving records of the appearance of a large house that was still standing less than 50 years ago, and it is essential that any such records be copied (I have always found the owners agreeable and co-operative), and copies then deposited with local libraries and with the Somerset Record Office.

There is hardly a parish in which there is not some memory or vague written reference to the disappearance of a middling house, or to the remains of some grander mansion fallen upon evil days. Cobbett himself, during his famous description of his ride down the valley of the Wiltshire Avon in August 1826, marks on a map 'the spots where *manor-houses*, or *gentlemens' mansions*, formerly stood, and stood, too, only about *sixty years ago*'. He estimates that in a distance of about thirty miles, there were formerly fifty mansion houses of which only eight survived in his day. At Milton, for instance, 'there are two mansion houses, the walls and *roofs* of which yet remain, but which are falling gradually to pieces, and the garden walls are crumbling down'.

Mendip is dotted with such sites, and I have spent many pleasant days searching for ruins, or trying to interpret them and piece together their history. Although this process of demolition, decay and disappearance is a centuries-old phenomenon, demolition at any rate has taken place very much more rapidly in our own day owing to social changes and to domestic problems. These have rendered the maintenance of such middling houses uneconomic to their owners, while they are often too small or too old-fashioned in their lay-out to be adapted for use as schools, old peoples' homes or business premises. Even since the last war, apart from Mendip Lodge, the following houses, all situated within five miles of each other on the north-eastern flank of Mendip, have been demolished: Woodborough House, South Hill House (Radstock), Chewton Priory, Charlton House (Kilmersdon) and Ashwick Grove.* Cer-

* There is another Southill House at West Cranmore, and also another Charlton House just outside Shepton Mallet.

tainly not all these houses were architecturally significant, but there is something rather sad about the comparative youth of some of the victims; sometimes little more than a century of living before it was time for the wind (or the bulldozer) to break the loosened pane.

Woodborough House, between Radstock and Peasedown, was basically a solid eighteenth-century house, and is described by Pevsner.[2] Here lived the Squire Purnell who figures in the pages of Skinner's Journal. By 1832 'the said Justice who knows neither Law nor Justice' was upwards of 80 years old, and was one of the many targets for the misanthropic rector's shafts of bitter invective: in Skinner's jaundiced eyes he is a 'mock Magistrate, made out of a petty-fogging Attorney'; a 'Wretched miser'; 'if ever there was a muck-worm, this is the creature'.[3] Later, Woodborough was the home of the Beauchamps who owned several of the local collieries, and for a few years before its demolition it served as the local headquarters of the National Coal Board.

South Hill House, Radstock, was demolished recently to make way for the new Norton-Radstock Technical College. A square early Victorian house, it was for many years the home of the McMurtries, a notable local family of Scots descent, several of whom served the Waldegraves as agents for their Somerset estates or as general managers of their collieries. James McMurtrie (1839–1914) is a name that constantly recurs in local history records, whether he is being lowered precariously into the lately rediscovered Lamb Leer in June 1880, excavating the *agger* of the Foss Way at Clandown, or entertaining the Somerset Archaeological Society to lunch on the lawns of South Hill after a descent into Ludlow's pit at Radstock. This was a gala occasion: 145 members were taken down in carefully cleaned cages with the sides boarded, and the roadways underground were brilliantly illuminated by some thousands of candles, placed on either side about a foot or eighteen inches apart.

The Waldegraves themselves lived at Chewton Priory for just a hundred years. 'Priory' was a courtesy title, for the house had little more claim to ecclesiastical origin than Beckford's Fonthill Abbey, but it could at least claim to stand on the site of an ancient Benedictine house later occupied by the Carthusians. When a new house came to be built there at the end of the eighteenth century, it is said that hardly a fragment of the old Priory remained. A rockery to the west of the house was, however, said to have been composed of stones from the ancient building: traces of the high-raised causeway connecting the Priory and the parish church are also alleged to be visible. Pevsner's statement that 'the house was built for the Waldegrave family in the Gothic style shortly before 1791' is misleading.[4] Collinson describes it as 'a very neat seat . . . built in a very elegant Gothick stile of architecture', and belonging to Richard Jenkins Esq.[5] When Earl Waldegrave recently demolished the Priory, it became plain that the front block of the later Victorian house had engulfed the earlier and much smaller house. It was not until 1858 that the Waldegrave family acquired Chewton Priory. Frances Lady Waldegrave, whose brilliant and fascinating career is ebulliently described by Oswald Wyndham Hewett in *Strawberry Fair*, had decided to sell Harptree Court, where the family had lived for half a century, and to buy this 'architectural nightmare at Chewton Mendip' to provide herself with a house for her visits to her Somerset estates.[6]

Chichester Fortescue (whose home it was to become five years later when he married Frances Waldegrave) came down to inspect the Priory. He found the situation, the ground, the trees very good, but was rather staggered by the house which he described as 'so whimsical—bad architecturally': not that it can have been any worse than the monstrous Victorian pile that engulfed it. The rebuilding was completed by 1864, and the first house party was held in the following year, with Edward Lear as one of the guests; three wings in all were added, and the house became the scene of the wonderful social gatherings described by Hewett, at which ambassadors and diplomats, and literary and artistic celebrities, figured, until the villagers hardly bothered to turn out to cheer the arrival and departure of the distinguished guests. 'We have been immensely happy here', wrote Lady Waldegrave in February 1868, 'in spite of all sorts of little worries, broken chillblains, Mendip mists, East winds, weak eyes, etc. etc.' When she died in 1879, she was buried in Chewton Mendip churchyard, in the shadow of the sublime tower on whose summit a man with a telescope had been stationed to give warning to the bell-ringers, both at Chewton and at East Harptree, of the approach of the carriage which was bringing her to Somerset for the first time, as a radiant bride, in August 1844. The memorial tablet in the church, erected by her husband, who survived her, movingly pays tribute to her brilliance and to her nobility and beauty of character. 'She made herself a much loved home at Chewton Priory in this parish with him who inscribes on these walls her dear and honoured name'; but of that much-loved home there survives today only 'the situation, the ground, the trees very good', and the Gothick lodge erected by Richard Jenkins Esq.

Charlton House, a mile west of the village of Kilmersdon, had a much longer history. On the death of Gabriel Goodman, a Bristol merchant, in 1679, the manor of Kilmersdon was divided between his two daughters: Charlton came to the elder, Sarah, who had married James Twyford, another Bristol merchant. About 1685 he moved to Kilmersdon and began to build a new manor house at Charlton. Details of the house were given in a letter dated 25 February 1683, from Goodman's old bailiff, who was now serving his Trustees. It is a delightful letter, quoted in full in Hylton's *History of Kilmersdon*. The faithful old servant is loud in his loyalty to the old régime, and disapproves heartily of 'new improvements' such as sowing 'parsley-seed, clover-seed, Tray-foyle, Turnips, Buckwheat and several other fantasyes, which I doubt will not pay half the charges. . . . I have left Mr. Twyford to his own quarters, and have Betaken myself to a Little Cottage, where to live private.' He describes the new building for which 'Order is Taken', and in a Decree of 1694 it is referred to as 'a new built Genteel Mansion house' with a new Stable, Coach-house, Dove-house and several other new built Outhouses, orchards, gardens and fishponds.[7]

It was from this house, nearly a hundred years after it was built, that Ann Twyford married Thomas Samuel Jolliffe, who in 1787 proceeded to acquire the other half of the manor by exchange for a Sussex property, and in 1791 moved to Ammerdown where the present mansion had been built to the designs of James Wyatt, in a newly created park. Charlton House thus became a sort of dower house, occupied by various members of the Jolliffe family from time to time. By 1826 it was in a state of disrepair, and was modernized with a casing of Bath stone and alterations to the floors and windows so as to leave little of the older house visible: the stables, however, and the ornamental water on which the site still looks down were part of the original design.[8] For many years one could drive through the hamlet without even being aware of the big square house hidden behind a thick curtain of trees on its little bluff above the lake: its entrance was unobtrusive, and the fanciful pillared gateway and lodge on the Kilmersdon road was merely a façade, as latterly the drive was not used. Finally the protecting screen of trees was cut down, and the stark ruin of the house stood reproachfully on its terrace, uncompromisingly conspicuous even from beyond the Foss Way. Gradually the eyesore was demolished, the ruins were levelled, and today a small modern house occupies the site.

The situation at Charlton is one that must have been repeated all over the country: Gibbon in his *Autobiography* describes the situation at his family's home at Buriton in Hampshire, where 'an old mansion, in a state of decay, had been converted into the fashion and convenience of a modern house'. The result was an imposing Georgian façade tacked on to a low rambling Elizabethan building. If the old house was not to be incorporated in a new fabric, and a new and more fashionable house was built upon a nearby site, the old house was generally demolished; though sometimes it was allowed to decay picturesquely. At Orchardleigh, nothing remains of the original house down by the lake, pulled down when the present house was built in 1855–58. At Hunstrete, and perhaps, as I have suggested, at Hazel Manor, ruins of the older house survive as ornamental features of a romantic landscape setting. It was doubtless the presence of genuine Gothic ruins of abbeys and castles that inspired the sham castles and artificial ruined follies of the Georgian period. The situation at Kilmersdon was perhaps unique in that both the old and the new mansions survived, little more than a mile apart, both of them to outward appearances being houses of the Regency period.

Almost all the houses so far referred to in this chapter survived into the present century: it is now time to consider some of the nineteenth-century demolitions and rebuildings.

At Chilcompton, there were at one time no fewer than three large houses, of which only one survives today. This is the old manor house of the Stockers, now the Manor Farm, close to the church; here too was the manor mill, showing clearly the site of the original settlement in the combe.* The later village has straggled, first up the hill towards the railway which arrived in

* The village is recorded as Comtuna (Compton) in Domesday Book: the later name Childecumpton (1227) perhaps indicates that the manor had been lopped off as the portion of a younger son or 'childe' of noble birth.

1874, and then along the main Bath–Wells road. When Collinson says that the village is situated partly on the great turnpike road to Wells and Bridgwater, he is referring to the older through road which dipped into the valley from Norton Down and climbed again towards Old Down.

The Manor Farm is a late Tudor building, long and low, with mullioned windows; Collinson calls it an L-shaped house, though there is actually a break between the two ranges of buildings: the smaller range, formerly the dairy, is now a separate house. The big house bears the date 1612 and the Stockers' arms; and the initials A M S (Antony and Margaret Stocker), and the date 1611, are still to be seen high up on the gable of a splendid stone barn. There was also a small park, whose memory survives in the name of one of the fields near the house.

Half a mile up the valley the stream tumbles pleasantly over a series of miniature cascades beside the village street: here stood Norton Hall, the home of the Tookers. Although right in the middle of what we now know as Chilcompton, by virtue of its situation on the east bank of the little stream, the house was in the parish of Midsomer Norton. It was demolished about 1875, soon after the arrival of the Somerset & Dorset Railway, which emerged from Chilcompton tunnel to sweep in a spectacular curve high up above the village. From the railway one looks down, across what appears as park on the 1817 map, to the levelled terrace where the house stood. The lodge that marked the entrance to the park was standing until a few years ago—a curious survival, for the old road on to which the carriage drive debouched had been replaced in the 1820s by a new and easier graded stretch of turnpike road; the lodge itself, a little two-roomed house with a tall chimney, nestled right into the railway embankment, and must have quivered continually to the pounding of the heavy freight trains which woke the night echoes, or to the roar of the holiday expresses hurtling down the Mendip gradients from Masbury to Radstock.

Old prints of Norton Hall survive: it was an imposingly symmetrical house, dating at a guess from about 1700, with mullioned windows and semicircular hood-moulds on the string-courses above them. The front consisted of seven bays, including a two-storeyed porch, probably a later addition, with three bays on the return, three storeys and a stone-tiled roof behind a parapet:

a solid and comfortable-looking country squire's house. Across the road was a row of stone-built tenements known as the 'bothies' and by tradition the living quarters of the domestic servants. Yet it seems unlikely that there was no room for servants in such a fair-sized house. Bothy is a Scottish word, but in pre-war days many English country houses had a range of buildings where unmarried gardeners and other outdoor servants lived—as at Hazel Manor where the 'bothies' were the men-servants' quarters above the stables.

The Tookers were settled at Chilcompton from the seventeenth century at any rate: in 1674 John Tooker of Norton Hall went into partnership with John Salmon of Holcombe to dig for coal in Stratton parish;[9] there are Tooker memorials in Chilcompton church dated 1712 and 1714; James Tooker—presumably the same James Tooker who was High Sheriff of Somerset in 1765— was one of the original proprietors of the Somersetshire Coal Canal by reason of his interest in the local mines, and about the same time his name appears as one of the Trustees of the West Harptree Turnpike Trust which was established in 1793, along- side other local squires such as Bampfylde, Hippisley Coxe, Horner and Jolliffe. Although it is only a few years since the last piece of the Tooker estate passed out of the family, it is more than a century since any Tooker lived in Chilcompton; the last re- presentative was Hyde Whalley Salmon Tooker, a Whalley who was authorized by licence to take the names and arms of Salmon and Tooker as their heir and representative. After that the house declined in fortune: it was at one time the Frome Deanery School —one of the old prints is ponderously inscribed to the Rural Deans and the Decanal Board of Education—and was finally occupied by a local wheelwright, nicknamed 'Squire' Purnell.

Two links with this vanished mansion can still be seen: in the nearby Norton Hall Farm there are some pieces of old panelling which by tradition derive from the Hall; and the pineapple-topped stone gateposts, which figure conspicuously on the old prints, now stand beside the road from Norton Down to Mid-somer Norton. They belong to another Norton Hall, previously known as Norton Down House, which was rebuilt and enlarged in the 1870s, so tradition says, with a good deal of the stone from the old Hall. The new Norton Hall is described in an 1883 *Directory* as 'a modern Gothic residence', but it incorporates an earlier

5. (*above*) The lodge gates, the only surviving feature of Charlton House, near Kilmersdon. 6. (*below*) Detail from the barn at Manor Farm, Chilcompton, built by Antony and Margaret Stocker in 1611

7. (*above*) Norton Hall, Chilcompton which was demolished about 1875.
8. (*below*) The entrance front of Hill Grove in 1964

building which was added to about the time when it was acquired by the Beauchamps.

Of the third great house in Chilcompton nothing whatsoever remains except the elusive memory. Even its site presented a mystery for a long time. This was surprising, because an article in *The Downside Review* for 1884 describes it as a 'Caroline mansion' standing 'close to the stream towards the upper part of the valley', and living in the memory as 'a remarkably fine old house, somewhat in the style of the Maypole hostelry in the early editions of *Barnaby Rudge*'.[10] There is no sign of any such house on the 1841 tithe map, and no local tradition of its whereabouts. Fifty years earlier, however, it was described by Collinson as the ancient house of the Werrets; he mentions some curious painted glass in one of the windows, and the date 1636 on a wainscot.[11] This completely vanished, but convincingly documented, house particularly intrigued me, lying as it were beneath the grass almost at my own door.

I finally solved the mystery in the library of Longleat. The property of the Stockers had eventually come into the hands of the Thynnes, and a 1734 survey of the Manor of Chilcompton describes a property of 55 acres called Kelsons, which includes Werrets Wood of 8 acres, and also refers to a close of one acre 'by Werrets Orchard'. A map of the Manor dated 1784 shows exactly where this close was situated, and the Werrets' house (alias Kelsons) must have stood on the site of the house in the deep valley just below Chilcompton station. In the latter part of the nineteenth century this was an edge-tool mill; with the building of the railway along the hillside and the damming up of the stream to form watercress beds, the old field boundaries have been obliterated, but from the station platform one still looks across the little valley to what Collinson called 'some romantic shaggy rocks', clothed with the last remains of what was once Werrets Wood.

At Holcombe there is no such problem to solve, for although the manor house was demolished 90 years ago, both its site and its appearance are fully documented. The present Holcombe Manor, which stands in the middle of the village, was formerly known as Holcombe House, and is a solid square late Georgian house, built by one of the family of Ashman Green who owned the brewery in the village, and later, as we have seen, occupied by Captain Scott's father, the last manager of the brewery. The old manor house, however, was out in the fields, half-way to the old church, where we have assumed the original village stood. There is a sketch of it in the 1884 *Proceedings* of the Somerset Archaeological Society, reproduced in Wickham's *Records by Spade and Terrier*: it looks like a sixteenth- or seventeenth-century farmhouse, long and low, with small two-light mullioned windows, gables and buttresses—a rambling old house with no two rooms on the same level, as one description says.[12] It belonged to the Salmons, who were at Holcombe from at least 1630: William Henry Salmon (who had married Mary Tooker of Chilcompton) bought the Manor in 1734 and the house remained in their possession until it was pulled down in 1880, the year before the Squire's death.[13] This seems to have been a premeditated gesture, as if the Squire clearly foresaw the end of his line—his daughter died only 14 years later—and wished to tidy up everything before his own death. He did this effectively enough, for today there is only a level field in front of the Holcombe Inn, where the 1840 tithe map shows shrubberies and lawns and outbuildings grouped round the manor house. By his gesture, however, the Squire shored some fragments against his ruin; for the furniture and the fittings were sold room by room from the old house, and as this was before the days of predatory dealers and the modern craze for antiques, many of the village people were enabled to buy relics of the family who had lived among them and ruled them for 250 years. There must be many such surviving fragments in Holcombe homes: I know of one magnificent stone fireplace built into a post-war house after being ejected from another house as too cumbersomely old-fashioned. There is indeed something rather touching about this vicarious existence of the older houses after their demise and disappearance: if one knew where to look, there must be a number of such posthumous survivals, for old builders and landlords are likely to have been thrifty with good worked stone or even with wooden fixtures such as window-frames, doors or staircases and panelling.

But if the houses have vanished, often leaving no more than a vague memory behind, what of the families who built them and lived in them, and loved and died there? 'Where is Bohun? where is Mowbray? where is Mortimer? nay, which is more and most of all, where is Plantagenet? They are entombed in the urns and sepulchres of mortality.' So wrote Sir Ranulphe Crewe in 1625. And in terms of our own Mendip countryside, where, we may well ask, are the families whose houses we may look for in vain today? Where is Chichester? where is Werret? where is Tooker? where is Salmon? Entombed like their more notable forerunners or contemporaries—Newton and Scrope, Rodney and de la Mare, Hungerford and Gournay—in Somerset tombs and sepulchres of mortality: like the Leversedges of Vallis, of whose ancient manor house, with its mile-long avenue leading to the very outskirts of Frome, only a sixteenth-century range of building survives, alongside the shell of the magnificent fifteenth-century hall, with its fine open timber roof naked to the sky; or like the Bampfyldes, whose memorials fill the little church at Hardington, while a fragment of the mansion house, where they lived in pride for 300 years, survives as a row of farm cottages, and two proud stone pillars that guarded their drive stand forlornly by the side of the road on Buckland Down.

How are the seats of the mighty fallen! And yet it is the duty and the delight of the local historian to salvage such memories as he may from their ruins. In this respect there are two particular Mendip sites whose history I want to deal with at somewhat greater length than those so far described in this chapter, for the very adequate reason that they serve to illustrate some of the pitfalls and uncertainties that the curious inquirer into the past sooner or later finds himself involved in.

East Harptree

The first big house at East Harptree was Richmont Castle, a Norman building impressively sited on a steep brow overlooking the deep wooded combe. 'It stondithe in the rote of Mendype,' as Leland says. In 1138 Sir William de Harptree held it for Matilda until it was attacked by Stephen, who moved against it after laying siege to Bristol. By means of a ruse which drew the defenders out of what was a practically impregnable position, the King succeeded in capturing the castle, but he did not apparently attempt to destroy it. From the de Harptrees (who later came to be known as de Gournay) the castle descended to the Newtons, and in the time of Henry VIII it was pulled down by Sir John Newton, whose tomb stands in the porch of East Harptree church, where he lies beneath a stone canopy, attended prayerfully by his eight sons and twelve daughters.

'Gurney used to ly muche at Richemonte Castle,' says Leland.

'Yt is now defacid to the hard ground, and Syr John Newton now lorde of it hath made his house harde by the ruines thereof yn the very place wher the graunge of Richemonte castle was yn Gurney's time.' The new house was called Eastwood, adds Leland, who must have visited Harptree about 1540, observing that 'there standith yet a pece of the dungeon' of the castle.[14] Lewis's *Topographical Dictionary* of 1842 says that there was then still a small circular tower remaining, which was supposed to have been the keep; but today there is nothing to be seen above ground, though fragments of foundation and stonework can be traced in the uneven terrain.

The difficulty starts with the reference to Sir John Newton's new house at Eastwood, for Eastwood lies a mile to the east of the village, and the writers of guide-books invariably assume that the present Eastwood Manor is in fact Newton's house—'a fine house which is still standing', says *Highways and Byways in Somerset*; 'Tudor Eastwood', says the *Little Guide*. But Eastwood 'Manor' was built in 1874 from stone quarried in the field just below the house, and there was no earlier house on the site. There is, however, a very much older house, now known as Eastwood Farm, in the little valley still farther east, where the Whelly (or Welly) brook strikes down to join the Chew at Coley. The odd thing is that Lewis's *Topographical Dictionary* says that the mansion at Eastwood was no longer in existence in 1842. Perhaps this is an indication that, like so many old houses, it had lost its status and become merely a farmhouse, for although it appears on the 1817 O.S. map as Eastwood *House*, it occurs as Eastwood *Farm* in surveys of East Harptree made by the Scropes, to whom the Newton property had descended by the end of the eighteenth century. It was certainly not used as a residence by the Scropes, for in 1791 it was occupied by John Burleton, whose family continued there as tenants of the Waldegraves as late as 1839.

On a Waldegrave estate map of *c.* 1810 (and again on the tithe map of 1839) the house appears as an L-shaped block, with ranges of farm buildings out behind: in front, the little brook has been dammed up to form a chain of seven ornamental pools, described grandiosely on the tithe schedule as 'the waterworks'. It is a layout that seems altogether too impressive for a mere farmhouse. The 'waterworks' still survive, somewhat silted and overgrown. Most of the old farm buildings must have disappeared by 1860, when the spectacular model farm which we now see was erected by the Taylors, who had acquired the Harptree estate from the Walde-graves when they moved to Chewton Mendip.* At the cost of £15,000, an acre and a quarter of ground was roofed over with glass and galvanized iron to provide a complete farm under cover. The name of the architect of such a fine building should find a place in any local study: he was Robert Smith of Emmets Grange, South Molton, and his design was copied on a smaller scale on the Sandringham estate. Beside this magnificent pile the old house hardly catches the eye; but it is undubitably an old house, a solid squarish structure with casement windows (no longer mullioned) and some dormers in the roof, built of a mottled texture of stone: its age is difficult to assess. Is it, one wonders, all that remains of Sir John Newton's sixteenth-century mansion? or is it a later house rebuilt in part with the old material? A geologist could, I suppose, decide how much, if any, of the stone came from the Richmont site a mile away.

A strong tradition, however, maintains that Newton's house was not at Eastwood at all, but at Proud Cross, at the southern edge of the village, where the road climbs steeply up Smitham Hill towards the old lead mines and the Castle of Comfort. Here in a field were the ruins of a considerable house and a magnificent lime avenue: these were clearly visible when the Kettlewell family came to Harptree Court in 1873; I have talked with various people who remember the walls; and the lime avenue was not felled until after the First World War, some of the tree stumps still being visible today.

I am myself firmly convinced that these were not the remains of Sir John Newton's house: the house is remembered locally as Richmond House, and although it was 'hard by' the ruins of the Castle, Leland does specifically say that Newton's new mansion was erected at Eastwood, and Eastwood is a place-name for which there is documentary evidence as far back as the reign of Henry III (1216–1272). Leland also says that the new house was built where 'the graunge of Richmonte Castle was in Gurney's time', and this was not likely to be on the very doorstep of the castle

_____
* William Taylor, whose monogram appears on some of the cottages at East-wood, had married Miss Gurney of Harptree Court; their ownership of the Harptree estate lasted little more than ten years, after which it was split up, Charles Kemble acquiring Eastwood, where he built the 'Manor' in 1874, and his cousin W. W. Kettlewell acquiring Harptree Court.

itself, but on an outlying part of the estate. Furthermore, the field containing the ruins is called 'Maddoxes' on the tithe map of 1839; it is marked as lately belonging to Miss Walker on the Waldegrave estate map of *c.* 1810; and in the Enclosure Award of 1796 relating to the parish of East Harptree, a 47-acre plot of Mendip common is allocated to Ann Walker in respect of property in East Harptree which includes 'Maddocks's'. Richmond House, therefore, did not belong to the Scropes at this time; Eastwood did; and the Scropes were now the inheritors of the Newton estate.

For one glorious day I thought I knew what Richmond House looked like. I heard rumours of a splendid blue antique meat-dish, preserved in the village and alleged to represent the vanished house. Was it possible that a priceless relic of the old mansion had been preserved as an heirloom, by the descendant, perhaps, of a devoted servant? The plate was produced for me, in pieces but complete; it was a pale blue and edged with trellis work; it showed a castellated building, and in front of it was a lawn on which sat a man playing a musical instrument, to the strains of which two couples danced. This, I was told, was Richmond House, and one of the ladies was Madam Walters [*sic*.]. There was something suspicious about the Gothic turreted castle, when what I was looking for was a Tudor mansion, but it was worth a journey to the Bristol Museum. The verdict of the experts was even worse than I had feared, and there could be no appeal: it was a common design, dating from about 1840–50 and almost certainly represented Glamis Castle. And so one is no nearer to a glimpse of Richmond House; one can only assume that the Scropes let the house fall to ruin when they acquired the property called 'Maddocks's', and anyhow, by 1797, as we shall see, they had built themselves another mansion called Richmond Place or Richmond Hall.

The legend of 'Madam Walters' died hard: some of the superstitions relating to her are recounted in a delightful little collection of Harptree memories, *Trinkum-trinkums of Fifty Years* by Mrs F. B. Kettlewell, who came to live at Harptree Court in 1875.[15] 'Madam Walters' was a plain girl, and was supposed to have starved her beautiful sister to death in a cellar, out of jealousy, when a young officer paid her too much attention; after her death, untold wealth was alleged to have been taken up to London; and her ghost was said to haunt the lime avenue. This was the romantic figure that was identified with the dancer on the blue meat-dish; but as we have seen, her real name was Walker, and in the Litton parish register Mrs Ann Walker from East Harptree is recorded as having been buried on 20 October 1802—and that, I suppose, was the end of Richmond House.

My search for this lost house led most unexpectedly and gratify-ingly to the discovery of the early history of Harptree Court. W. J. Robinson in his *West Country Manors* states that there had been a house on the site from *c.* 1745, but it had generally been accepted that the present house was built for the Scropes in 1802 by an unknown architect, and by them sold to the Waldegraves in 1804. The Supplement to Collinson's *History*, based on Locke's survey, 1795–1806, referred mysteriously to 'Richmond Hall newly built with 1,100 acres lately offered for sale and sold to Lord Waldegrave for £35,000'. This was clearly not 'Madam Walters's' old mansion.

A few years ago a puzzling letter arrived in East Harptree from New Zealand, addressed to the 'Owner of Richmond Hall'. The letter was delivered to Mrs M. A. Hill who had previously lived at Harptree Court, but had recently moved to a new house, built on a site midway between the remains of Richmont Castle and the remains of the old Richmond House, and most appropriately (and luckily) called Richemont Lodge. The letter came from a Mr R. P. Wynniatt who was anxious to learn more about Richmond Hall: he possessed an engraving of 'A plan of the Lawn and Pleasure Ground before the North Front of Richmond Hall, East Harptree, one of the Seats of J. Scrope Esq.'.

It was an extraordinary coincidence that this quite gratuitous piece of information should arrive when I was already researching into the history of the houses at East Harptree. The letter was shown to me, and I at once entered into correspondence with Mr Wynniatt who, it transpired, was himself a descendant of the Scropes. He readily consented to have the plan photographed, and copies have now been deposited with the National Building Record, the Bath Public Library and the Somerset Record Office. The plan, which measures 16 in. × 32 in., shows quite unmistak-ably the ground-plan of the house which we know as Harptree Court, together with a recognizable picture of the park, with its lakes and pasture-land. The lay-out of the park, however, differs considerably from that of today, the plan of the house omits the Doric porch on the south front, which Bryan Little had already conjectured to be a later addition, and, most important of all, it records the name of the designer, C. Harcourt Masters of Bath. This architect is known as the architect of the Sydney Gardens Hotel in Bath (1795-7), now the Holburne of Menstrie Museum, as well as of several other buildings mentioned in Ison's *Georgian Buildings of Bath*. This gives the right date for his work at Harptree, and although the plan only states him to have designed the pleasure grounds, there is a strong case for claiming him as the architect of the house as well. We can now also date the house accurately: the series of Scrope surveys of the Harptree estate, included among the Waldegrave papers in the Somerset Record Office, show that where in 1795 there had been a property called Pools with 20 acres of land let to Arthur Franks, in 1797 there stood 'the Mansion House newly built called Richmond Place', on the site of the 'farmhouse, orchard and garden' which stood there before, while the new lawn, i.e. the park, had absorbed 30 acres of land covering 16 separate fields or closes.[16]

It was strange indeed that a letter from the other side of the world, addressed to a house whose name had not been in current use for 150 years, should have led to the solution of some of the vexed questions about this strangely baffling group of houses.

Hill Grove

Whereas the history of the inter-related group of houses at East Harptree takes us back to Norman times, the last Mendip house whose history I shall attempt to relate in this chapter has no real claim to antiquity, though once again it has been difficult to rescue its history from the 'Mendip mists' that so often descend the very moment one reaches out beyond living memory. Only a series of lucky strikes have given me a glimpse of the past splendours of Hill Grove. The lodge gates of the house front the main Bristol–Wells road near Green Ore. After the steep climb from Chewton Mendip on to the plateau at Nedge, the road runs dead straight for nearly two miles as far as the flank of Pen Hill, where it suddenly dips over the southern escarpment of Mendip and so down to Wells. All through Green Ore the land has lain tossed and tumbled since lead-mining days: Romano-British relics have on various occasions been turned up by the plough, and in 1956 D. A. Thompson of Rookery Farm unearthed four pigs of lead, made at the Roman lead-mines at Charterhouse, and stamped with a date from the reign of Vespasian (A.D. 69–79).[17] In fact the old name Hillesgruff—Hill's gruff or groove—clearly links Hill Grove with the Mendip groovers who were responsible for the 'gruffy ground' that we see today.

I first remember Hill Grove as a sanatorium, established, as the *Directory* says, for the open-air treatment of pulmonary tuberculosis, and presided over by what the local inhabitants unhappily referred to as 'the black doctor' (who was an Indian) and 'the white doctor' (who was not). Between the wars the institution was closed, and today it is a huge sprawling mass of building, partly gutted, partly still inhabited, though in a depressing state of decrepitude, and surrounded by a vast amorphous agglomeration of out-buildings and yards.

Nearby stands a farmhouse, well sheltered by a wood from the south-westerly winds—indeed the whole property lies snugly in a fold of the land, screened by trees except from the east. This, one would say at first glance, was the original house on the site, replaced at a later date by a 'gentleman's residence': there was even a tradition that this was monkish property, connected by an underground passage with Rookery Farm more than a mile away, where again there are religious traditions, pinpointed in the name Monks' Burial Ground given to a plot near the house. A second glance, however, reveals the house as Gothick, not Gothic. Even so, the back parts of the mansion itself are very much humbler than the quite imposing remains of the main front. Once again one is inclined to guess at the familiar pattern of an older farmhouse incorporated in a later mansion; and this is probably nearer the truth.

There is a puzzling reference to the house in an essay by Abbot Horne. The passage occurs during the description of a bicycle ride to Cheddar: 'the lodge gates of Hill Grove are reached—Hill Grove, where Mass was said for so many years, and which one way and another took a not unimportant part in the Downside life of the day'.[18] At first I assumed that this was a reference to the Hicks family, one of whom was to become Abbot of Downside (1933–8), but it soon emerged that the Hickses of Hill Grove were Anglicans, and anyhow Abbot Hicks was only born in 1878, whereas the article in *The Downside Review* must refer to a much earlier period. The Hicks family in fact came to Hill Grove about 1867 and before that there were various owners: the tithe schedule of 1839 gives the owner as Richard Thomas Bateman: one of the lodges is sometimes remembered as Bateman's Lodge, built in the Gothick style which appears again in the cottage at the top of the hill up from Wells, a well-known landmark often mistaken for a turnpike house. Diocesan records of the Roman Catholic Diocese of Clifton show that there was a Mass Centre at Hill Grove, which was served from Downside, between 1842 and 1852. I think that the Batemans must have been the Downside link referred to by Abbot Horne: there was a William Joseph Bateman in the school at Downside 1855–60.

By 1840 at any rate one can assume that Hill Grove was established as a fair-sized country house at the centre of a small estate. The land had originally formed part of the allotment in the Enclosure Award of St. Cuthbert Out parish in 1795, and was sold for £780 to Edward Tuson, a Wells attorney who was Bishop's Steward. A few years later Skinner was discussing the line of the Roman road at Green Ore with a Mr Tuson of Green Ore Farm.[19] This is now known as Rookery Farm, a pleasant stone-built house which still bears the date 1655. The allotment at Hill Grove was obviously made to Tuson by reason of his property at Green Ore. As this land was Mendip common, there cannot have been any house there before about 1800, unless there were the remains of a much earlier mining settlement. On old maps the house appears variously as Pen Hill House or Hillgrove Farm, but the main façade, whose ruins we now contemplate, must date from the declining years of the Regency tradition. A photograph taken by Lady Hobhouse of Oakhill about 60 years ago—the garden huts for the exposure of the tubercular patients to the rigours of the Mendip winter can be seen in the process of erection—gives a last glimpse of the house as it was in its days as a country mansion. It was a two-storeyed house, with a plastered façade of seven bays and a semicircular feature with a French window protruding at each end: it looked out across a sweep of lawn and a little ha-ha to the grey Mendip plateau rolling away towards Maesbury. The gardens and shrubberies have long since reverted to jungle, the neat drives are rutted and scarred farm tracks, and many of the outbuildings have crumbled into ruin or stand in a state of pathetic desolation.

Among them can be identified the coach-house. For Squire Hicks did things in style, and local memories still recall his long

Sabbath drive to church at East Horrington in his phaeton, attended by his dwarf servant, Jack White. Lady Hobhouse remembers driving over from Oakhill for dances and hunt breakfasts with the younger generation of Hickses. Accustomed as we are to drive from one end of Mendip to the other, for a meeting or a meal, in less time than it would have taken our grandfathers to have the horses harnessed to the carriage or the trap, we are inclined to forget the tedious hours of travel involved in any sort of social engagement a hundred years ago. (A hundred years before that, Edward Gibbon dreaded the period of the full moon which was usually reserved for more distant excursions to fulfil the social obligations of dinners and visits to his idle Hampshire neighbours.) To beguile the weary miles, leaving cards or returning calls, Julia Hodgkinson of Wookey Hole would play her bassoon, to the amazement of bystanders in villages where she was not known. If her love of music followed her from this world to the next, the memorial window in Wookey Hole church gives us a glimpse of her, crowned with immortality, blowing an accompaniment to the harmony of the chorus of angels.

Abbot Hicks's unpublished autobiography, preserved in the Downside archives, refers to his uncle's way of life at Hill Grove. He often drove over to Downside in a coach-and-four, and would take some of the monks out for drives on Mendip, frequently driving his friend Dom Anselm Barnewall to meets of the foxhounds; for Squire Hicks loved horses, and horse-racing, and gambling in general, and Hill Grove actually had to be shut down for a time after his losses over the Tichborne case.

Now Hill Grove is shut down for ever, until it crumbles into the Mendip landscape or is properly demolished: the roof has gone, the cellars are gaping craters, the staircases and the window-frames have been ripped out so that the house stares blindly out across the desolate parterre. Hill Grove and Hazel Manor, six miles apart, were the only mansions to be built on the plateau of Mendip: each alike had a brief heyday of social splendour and gaiety at the centre of its estate in the late Victorian and the Edwardian periods; each alike has collapsed into ruin, maintaining only a marginal existence by reason of the farm buildings in the background; and yet one cannot revisit such sites without a pang of regret for the days that they have seen—for they too have heard the chimes at midnight.

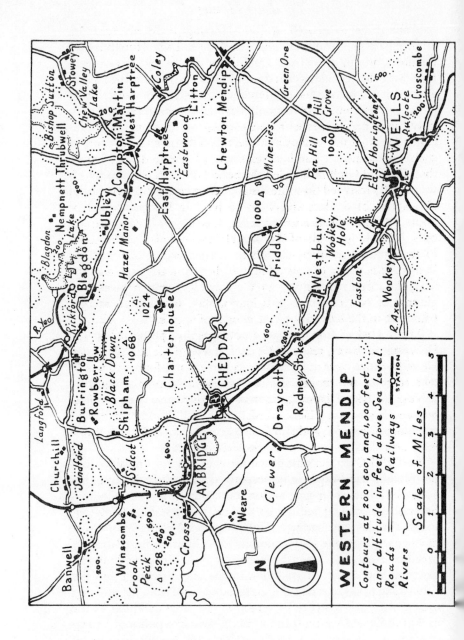

WESTERN MENDIP

Contours at 200, 600, and 1,000 feet
and altitude in Feet above Sea Level.
Roads ———— Railways ——o—— STATION
Rivers

Scale of Miles

0   1   2   3   4   5

CHAPTER FOUR

John Billingsley

A boast, benefit and ornament to his neighbourhood.

Bath Journal, 30 September 1811

Ashwick Grove was sold for demolition in October 1955, and when I saw it again a few months later, the demolition was well under way: only the shell remained, standing like a bomb-damaged ruin, with broken walls and gaping windows, and piles of rubble littering what had once been immaculate lawns. Today the scene has hardly changed, save that the desolation of the garden has become even more desolate, and the ruins even more ruinous, and that shrubs are already growing inside the house—a stark and tragic skeleton such as John Piper would delight to paint.

From an architectural point of view Ashwick Grove was disappointing. The plain Georgian façade was diversified only by a rather curious apsidal porch—so that one appeared to enter the house at a corner—and by a large bay window on the ground floor, outside which was added an uncompromising pillared portico. This south front was continued at a slightly reflex angle, with a much less formal façade concealing what was clearly a much earlier piece of building. Inside, neither the rooms nor their fittings were noteworthy, and apart from the 'state rooms' there was an absolute rabbit-warren of small rooms, and a series of bewildering passage ways and changes of level which gave the lie to the formal symmetry of the exterior.

The situation of the house was partly to blame, for it lay along, rather than across, a narrow steep-sided valley, with the result that though the house stood high up on the gradual northern slope of Mendip, the only view from the front windows was a grass bank twenty yards away, while at the back there was just room for a cobbled way which rambled along past a sudden classical doorway and under archways which linked the house with outbuildings abutting on the limestone cliff. The heavily wooded sides of the valley seemed to close in and stifle the house: for some years its empty windows had stared out across rank lawns; shrubs and climbing roses had strangled the portico; the sunken garden and the winding walks that led down the valley into the woods were hardly discernible; only the foundations could be traced of the old summer-house, described by Collinson, 'in which Dr James Foster, having embraced the obnoxious tenets of the dissentient dissenters, and retired here out of the way of clamour and confusion, studied and penned many of his works'.[1]

On my last visit to Ashwick Grove before the auction, 'deep in the shady sadness of the vale', I discovered a stone nymph, standing beside the pedestal from which she had fallen, in what must once have been a clearing in the wood. The fall had chipped her forehead and the hand with which she modestly clasped her breast; she was to be unromantically knocked down again as Lot 534, but as a shaft of autumn sunlight struck through the trees on to the forlorn grey figure, it was just possible to recapture for a moment the atmosphere of what had once been a gracious pleasance, 'in a very romantic situation,' as Collinson wrote, 'patched with immense rocks which project through the foliage from the lofty brow of the cliff.' On the bank in front of the house a lady artist was sketching the 'romantic' scene—a chance that might not come again. I wondered whether she was a local inhabitant who remembered how the estate was maintained before the war. That was under the Stracheys, who lived at Ashwick for more than a century: they were there by 1830, for the Rev. John Skinner of Camerton wrote in his *Journal* that a January visit to Ashwick, to dine with Mr Strachey and to stay the night, had to be put off because the lanes were impassable with snow; and it was their crest that was to be seen in the glass of the main staircase window, and carved on the central panel of the balustrade on the south front, which I found lying among the rubble on the lawn.

Many who attended the sale would have heard tell of the old Squire: few, if any, would have heard of John Billingsley. Collinson, writing in 1791, described the house as newly-built, but parts of it were palpably very much older, and anyhow the Billingsleys had been at Ashwick throughout the eighteenth century. They were a well-known dissenting family who came originally from

John Billingsley

Kent. Nicholas Billingsley the elder, of Eton and Merton College, Oxford, was deprived of his living at Weobley in Herefordshire in 1662, ministered among dissenters in Gloucestershire, and died at Bristol in 1709. Nicholas Billingsley the younger, his second son, was Presbyterian minister at Ashwick from 1699 to 1729, and was in turn succeeded by his nephew, Samuel, who ministered there for 18 years, which he described as the most useful, though the most fatiguing, part of his life. It was during Nicholas Billingsley's ministry that the egregious Dr James Foster found refuge at Ashwick in the 'humble and retired mansion' where he spent several years, 'secluded from the fury of bigots and the cares of the busy world', and in the famous summer-house composed many of the discourses that were to make his reputation. His sermons were indeed immortalized in a couplet by Pope:

> Let modest Foster, if he will, excel
> Ten Metropolitans in preaching well.

In the neighbourhood of Ashwick there was a flourishing Presbyterian community which 'long remained numerous and reputable', numbering at one time nearly 200, chiefly colliers and hosiers, but 'not without a fair proportion of well-cultivated minds'.[2] Nicholas Billingsley seems to have settled at Ashwick soon after the passing of the Toleration Act of 1689: before that date, Nonconformist meetings for worship were held, under considerable difficulties for fear of informers, in retired houses, or even in nearby woods, when the weather permitted. Their first meeting house was built at Downside between Ashwick and Shepton Mallet; but in 1696 they separated from the Shepton congregation, and in 1703 another meeting house was built nearer Ashwick, and yet another, in a still more central position, in 1758. This is now incorporated in the fabric of a nineteenth-century dwelling, formerly called Lancet House. This name suggests that it once had Gothick windows, but the doctor who lived there must have found the name embarrassing, for he turned the gateposts round to conceal the ominous legend, and rechristened the house. The Ashwick congregation eventually moved on from Presbyterianism to Unitarianism, as did the Shepton Mallet congregation: at Shepton, however, the original building of 1696 is still standing, though its appearance was altered by rebuilding in 1785, and it is now disused. It stands high above Cowl Street and is an interesting

47

example of an early Nonconformist chapel; it has a notable carved pulpit and tester with curving balustrades, set centrally in the wall which faces the congregation.

As far as Somerset is concerned, and Mendip in particular, the most famous member of the Billingsley family was John Billingsley (1747–1811), though unlike his great-grandfather, Nicholas Billingsley the elder (1633–1709), he has found no niche in the D.N.B. He was born and died at Ashwick Grove, and was the last member of his family to live there. Although described as a leading member of the Presbyterian congregation, it is clear that he was at some stage reconciled with the Church of England. His father's tomb stands in the churchyard at Ashwick, where John Billingsley himself was buried on 3 October 1811, with a magnificently eulogistic memorial tablet in the nave of the church. He almost certainly deserved every word of the eulogy, for he was one of the outstanding local personalities of his day, and above all a famous agricultural pioneer. Little is known about his early life, but he describes himself as 'a speculative man who turned farmer'. It has been conjectured that he was concerned with the woollen trade, but he was certainly a remarkable man with a finger in many pies: by 1790 he was the owner of the famous Oakhill Brewery; he was a member of local Turnpike Trusts; he was actively engaged in the promotion of the Kennet & Avon Canal, the Somersetshire Coal Canal, and the Dorset & Somerset (which, as originally planned, would have reached out to serve the Mendip collieries within a mile of Ashwick Grove), and even more actively concerned in the promotion of the Bath and West Society. Although he was not present at the inaugural meeting on 8 September 1777 at York House, Bath, he was considered to be one of the Founders of the Society, and his name appears on page after page of the first Minute Books, inscribed in the exquisite calligraphy of the Founder and Secretary, Edmund Rack; and for 32 years he was Vice-President.

'He drained Sedgmoor! He inclosed Mendip! He wrote the agricultural Survey of Somerset!' declared Sir Benjamin Hobhouse in a Presidential eulogy delivered to the Society after Billingsley's death. The *Survey* indeed is his great memorial.[3] It was drawn up for the consideration of the recently formed Board of Agriculture in 1794, further editions being published in 1797 and 1798. The Board of Agriculture and the Bath and West Society

JOHN BILLINGSLEY *ESQ*

9. John Billingsley of Ashwick (1747–1811), from the portrait by
Joseph Hutchissoon

10. (*above*) Ashwick Grove shortly before it was sold for demolition in 1955.
11. (*below*) The shell of Stoke House in 1925

were alike concerned with popularizing new methods of farming, pressing for the adoption of new agricultural machinery, and in every way possible increasing the productivity of the land, and the narrow margin of safety in British food supplies, in view of the outbreak of war with France in 1793. Billingsley's *Survey*, while primarily concerned with agriculture, includes chapters on Political Oeconomy, and in fact outlines the economic resources of the county at the end of the eighteenth century. The date is significant, because the Somerset scene is described in a period of transition under the double impact of the industrial and agrarian revolutions. Billingsley was an eager champion of the new order of things, and a keen observer of the developments going on all round him. He noted with pleasure the improved turnpike roads in the Wells and Bridgwater areas. Canals were also being cut to serve the rapidly expanding coalfield of north Somerset, where steam-engines were now being introduced to raise coal from hitherto impossible depths. On the other hand, he observed the reluctant and belated introduction of machinery by the woollen manufacturers, and assessed the inevitable repercussions on the economy of the neighbourhood. He himself proposed to perforate the main Mendip ridge by driving a five-mile level from Compton Martin to Wookey Hole, at a depth of 450 feet below the surface, thus conveying off all the water which was encumbering the working of the moribund Mendip lead mines.

'For the sake of perspicuity', Billingsley divides the county into three districts—north-east, middle, and south-west. The south-west district is briefly disposed of, for Billingsley probably had small personal knowledge of the area. His recommendations for the enclosure of Exmoor, and the building of a village near the solitary Simonsbath house, foreshadowed the work of John and Frederick Knight on the moor in the nineteenth century. In the middle district Billingsley's main concern is with the draining and reclamation of vast areas of turf-bog and flooded land—Brent-Marsh, lying between the Mendips and the Poldens, and South-Marsh or Sedgmoor—involving the straightening of sections of the rivers Axe, Brue and Parrett. In every region Billingsley's keen observation notes down vivid and interesting details of the local economy: the peat is cut and piled in pyramidal heaps; in the Somerton area the gardens grow cucumbers by cart-loads—'these they raise on hillocks, under which is placed about two bushels of horse-dung, collected in King's-Sedgmoor by children, and brought to their gardens on the backs of, or drawn in carts by, asses'. The Somerset oxen (akin to the red Devon breed) are driven to the London market—nine days travelling a distance of 130 miles—where they 'appear to bear the belle [*sic*], both in respect to fineness of grain and internal fatness'. Cyder-making is described in detail: the sorts of apple in best estimation are Royal Wilding, White-Styre, Court of Wick Pippin, Pounset or Cadbury, Flood-Hatch, Black-Pit Crab, Buckland, Mediate or Southam, Royal Jersey, Woodcock, Red-Hedge Pip, Old Jersey, and Redstreak. (How many of these old apples are still to be found in Somerset orchards, I wonder?) The result is 'a wholsome, vinous, heart-cheering beverage, nearly equal to the juice of the grape itself'. Wages, except during harvest, were one shilling a day, with cyder. Between Wincanton and Crewkerne, flax and hemp were cultivated in great abundance; in the north of the county, teasels and woad were important crops related to the local woollen industry, large quantities of teasels being even sent by water from Bristol to Yorkshire. There was also the native Mendip breed of sheep, 'a sort that will thrive on the poorest soil, and fatten on such land as will scarcely keep other sorts alive'.

It was the enclosure and improvement of this Mendip terrain that was Billingsley's greatest achievement. The first Mendip commons to be enclosed were those in the parishes of East and West Cranmore in 1769; by 1794 Billingsley estimated that 13,600 acres had been enclosed, leaving 11,550 acres still unenclosed. The familiar landscape of the main Mendip plateau with its wide straight roads, grass-bound and grey-walled, its scattered farmhouses each with a sheltering wind-break of trees, is a landscape that Billingsley did much to create. He argues cogently against the objections to the enclosures, details the relative cost of dry stone wall and quickset hedge, and suggests suitable lay-outs for farmhouses and outbuildings—to cost about £250. They were stone-built and thatched, for the tax on tiles had not as yet been repealed; but Billingsley deplores the inconvenience of thatch in a moist and windy climate: 'a roof will require coating every eight or ten years; it is a harbour for vermin; is more dangerous in respect of fire, and, every thing considered, is more expensive than tiles'. After enclosure, cultivation: here Billingsley is able to offer a wealth of advice about ploughing, manuring, and rotation of

GENERAL VIEW

OF THE

AGRICULTURE

OF THE

COUNTY of SOMERSET,

WITH

OBSERVATIONS

ON.

THE MEANS OF ITS IMPROVEMENT.

DRAWN UP IN THE YEAR 1795,

FOR THE CONSIDERATION OF THE BOARD OF AGRICUL-
TURE AND INTERNAL IMPROVEMENT.

BY

JOHN BILLINGSLEY, Efq;

Of ASHWICK-GROVE, near SHEPTON-MALLET.

AND NOW RE-PRINTED

With confiderable ADDITIONS and AMENDMENTS,
Accompanied with the REMARKS of some refpectable GENTLEMEN
and FARMERS in the COUNTY.

※

SECOND EDITION.

※

In urbe luxuria creatur: Ex luxuria exiftat avaritia neceffe eft:· Ex avaritia erumpit
audacia; Inde omnia scelera ac maleficia gignuntur. Vita autem hæc rustica quam
tu *agrestim* vocas, parsimoniæ, diligentiæ, justitiæ, magistra est.
                                        Tullii Orat. pro Sext. Roscio.

The City creates luxury; from luxury necessarily proceeds rapaciousness; and from
rapaciousness breaks forth insolence: Thence are engendered all villainy and wicked
deeds: But this country life, which you call clownish, is the regulator of æconomy,
industry, and justice.

BATH,

PRINTED BY R. CRUTTWELL, FOR THE AUTHOR;

AND SOLD BY

C. DILLY, POULTRY, LONDON.

MDCCXCVIII.

The title page of John Billingsley's *Survey of the Agriculture*
of the County of Somerset

crops including short-period leys, based on years of carefully recorded experiments on his own lands, the results of which are often to be found in the published Papers of the Bath and West Society.

Several beautiful silver trophies, which he won for raising potatoes, for instance, and for various livestock, including oxen, now belong to his great-granddaughter Mrs. W. Moger of Bath, who has on several occasions lent them for exhibition at Bath and West Shows.

The greatest single contribution which Billingsley made to the improvement of Somerset agriculture, and, incidentally, the occasion of his greatest personal triumph, was the introduction of the double-furrow plough. For ten years, he says, he had used the plough, preaching its virtues both in season and out, to neighbours who disregarded and despised him. ('They are much bigoted to old customs,' he says elsewhere of the farmers of his own district.) Finally a trial of the different sorts of plough was organized by the Bath and West Society, and this, the first ploughing competition ever held in this country, took place on 27 March 1787, at Barracks Farm, near Bath, in a field of strong old ley-ground. There were six entrants, of whom five were from north Somerset and the sixth was Lord Weymouth from Longleat, each entering with a different type of plough, drawn by various yokings of horses and oxen. Billingsley himself was a champion of oxen in preference to horses, and his plough was drawn by six oxen with yokes and bows. Six parallel pieces of ground were marked out, near one acre each, and all the ploughs were to begin at the same time, and to plough their respective lots at pleasure, but as nearly as possible 3 in. deep and 8 in. wide. Two of the entrants withdrew, their ploughs being found unequal to the contest, and a point of rock just under the surface broke Lord Weymouth's plough and put it out, leaving only three contestants. The result was a complete vindication of Billingsley's views; for his plough finished its lot in 3 hours and 4 minutes, Farmer Sully of Midford (with a single plough drawn by three horses) finished in 5 hours and 5 minutes, and Mr Thomas of Keynsham (with a light swing plough drawn by four small Welsh oxen) in 5½ hours. The committee of judges, which consisted of five practical farmers, judged that the double-coulter plough layed the furrow flatter than the others, 'consequently exposing more new surface to the influence of the elements, and preventing more completely the growth of grass and weeds between the furrows'. Billingsley was thereupon awarded a premium of six guineas, with a gratuity of one guinea to his servants. To prove the economy of his technique, he published a statement of the cost of using his plough.

	s.	d.
Six oxen at sixpence each per day for food	3	0
Ploughman and driver	1	8
Wear and tear of plough, yokes, etc.	0	4
	5	0

Extent ploughed per day—ley, $1\frac{1}{2}$ acres at 3s. 4d. per acre, fallow land, $2\frac{1}{4}$ acres, at 2s. per acre.[4]

The whole episode is typical of Billingsley's thoroughness, which is the most noticeable characteristic of his *Survey*. Apart from his apostolic zeal in the cause of the improvement of the agriculture of his county, one relishes the occasional touches of ironic humour in his writing: of the Mendip rabbit warrens, he observes that 'could coneys be preserved from the depredation of two-legged and four-legged vermin, the occupation would be very profitable'.

From long personal experience Billingsley was convinced of the advantages of contract labour over daily labour, for 'no practical man will deny that where daily labour prevails, a considerable portion of the day is wasted in sauntering, holding tales, and in a sluggish use of those limbs which are capable of more lively motion'.

Soon after Billingsley's death, which occurred at Ashwick Grove on 26 September 1811, the Bath and West Society approached his widow for permission to copy in oils a crayon portrait of her husband. The Secretary's letter expressed the general wish of the Society 'that such a Representation of the Person of our thus highly valued associate might be hung up in our room as may bring ever before our eyes the image of him who can never be dismissed from our memories but must live ever in our hearts'. Samuel Woodforde, R.A., himself a Somerset man—he was Parson Woodforde's nephew—was commissioned to execute the new portrait, which was to be hung 'in a conspicuous part of the great room' of the Society. It was exhibited at a General Meeting in the summer of 1812 and 'afforded great satisfaction'. Unfortunately, it is no longer in the 'great room' or indeed in the Society's possession, and all my efforts to trace it have so far failed. There is, however, another portrait now in the Victoria Art Gallery in Bath: this portrait, by Joseph Hutchissoon, the Irish painter who settled in Bath at the end of the eighteenth century, previously belonged to Billingsley's descendant, Mrs W. Moger, by whom it was presented to the Gallery. It shows an elderly man with a remarkably young face, calm, dignified and resolute, yet with signs of gentleness and humour about the mouth and eyes. In the background is the double-coulter plough, an appropriate symbol for the man whom his obituary notice in the *Bath Chronicle and Herald* described as 'a most intelligent and truly useful member of society'.

CHAPTER FIVE

Mendip Paper-Makers

I shewed the young people the paper mills, each
being permitted to make his own sheet by way of
memorial of his visit to the spot.

JOHN SKINNER: 10 August 1832

There are two curious omissions in Billingsley's survey of
the Political Oeconomy of North Somerset: he makes no
mention either of the paper or of the iron industries, both
of which were dependent upon the geology of Mendip, and
flourished widely in the area during his lifetime—in fact, at
different periods, both industries were carried on in Stoke Bottom,
little more than a mile from his home at Ashwick.

Stoke Bottom lies on what was once called the river Frome,
between the coalmining areas of Nettlebridge and Coleford, where
the river separates the parishes of Stoke St. Michael and Stratton-
on-the-Fosse 'a country pleasingly divided with hills and valleys.
Some of the valleys are deep, gloomy and picturesque; the accli-
vities clothed with hanging woods, intermixed with romantic
rocks'. Such was Collinson's impression of the place in 1791: he
noted a logwood mill and a paper mill, in the middle of a hamlet
of about 40 houses, which included a Georgian mansion—and
about 200 inhabitants, according to his estimate.[1] The 1841 census
returns show 145 inhabitants living in 38 houses in the same area,
even though neither of the mills was then working. The logwood
mill had been advertised for sale in 1784 and is a link with the
woollen industry in the district.[2] The blocks of logwood were
imported from central America: Dampier's *Voyages* describes the
logwood industry, for he himself worked among the lawless log-
wood-cutters of the Bay of Campeachy in the Gulf of Mexico
from 1676 to 1678. The blocks of wood were split into chips
and laid in water to ferment until they formed the glossy green

crystals that made part of the black dye used in the local cloth trade.

Stoke Bottom today presents a very different appearance: the only houses are a modern farmhouse and a small country house built out of a row of Georgian cottages. The mansion and the labourers' cottages have disappeared; only the truncated outer walls of the mills remain. The one thing that has not changed is the water, pouring clear and copious from St. Dunstan's Well under the rock in the hillside, and tumbling down to join the river in the valley bottom—the same water that was the very reason for the place having once been a busy industrial site.

'Quick streams and clear water,' was what the paper-makers required, in the words of the spokesman of the English white paper-makers in 1696, and this was something that the pervious Mendip limestone offered in abundance. This need governed the location of the paper mills, which were nearly always built as close as possible to the spot where 'quick streams' emerged from the flank of the hill. The Wookey Hole mill is a perfect example of this, situated astride the river Axe, a few hundred yards below its emergence from Wookey Hole caves, with a private canal leading the pure water straight from the very mouth of the cave to the mill. The need for absolute purity in the water was emphasized by the lawsuit brought by Hodgkinsons against the proprietors of the St. Cuthbert's leadworks at Priddy, to which reference was made in Chapter One. Farther down the Axe there were three more mills within four miles, and Dulcote mill, a mile east of Wells, was nowhere near the head of the valley; but all the other mills were right up against the hill: Cheddar, Banwell, Rickford, Compton Martin and Sherborne near Litton.

There was another group of mills to the north of Mendip: at North Wick near Chew Magna (marked on Greenwood's 1822 map), at Pensford, and farther down the Chew towards Keynsham; and yet another group in the far north-east of the county: at St. Catherine, at Batheaston, at Bathford (which still operates, and specializes in making paper for the printing of Bibles), and near Monkton Combe. This last mill, which is shown on the 1817 O.S. map, was also known as the Combe Down or de Montalt mill. Baron de Montalt—later Viscount Hawarden (1729–1803)—had married Ralph Allen's niece and thus inherited Prior Park in 1796. His son, the second Baron, took a great interest in founding the paper mill, which was built in 1805 of stone from the Combe Down quarries and took its name from the de Montalt family. It was worked by Messrs. Bally, Ellen and Steart, but by 1834 it had been taken over for the manufacture of gutta-percha, and later still was used as a cabinet works. It is a dignified stone building situated, surprisingly, high up on the southern flank of Combe Down, almost directly over the mouth of the noisome tunnel from which the Somerset & Dorset line emerged to run down to Midford. Only a very small stream now ripples down the hillside at that point, but the spring water was originally collected in a stone-built basin to provide power for the mill wheel.

Most of these mills were at work in Billingsley's day, and it is therefore all the more surprising that he makes no reference to the paper-making industry. The excise duty on home-made paper, imposed in 1712, was not repealed until 1860. The tax was collected from the mills by areas, and details of output and ownership, dating mostly from about 1800, are preserved at the Public Record Office and at the Library of H.M. Customs and Excise. Many very interesting details are to be found in a survey by Dr Alfred H. Shorter of Exeter University.[3] One immediately noticeable feature is the widespread recurrence of the same family names among the paper-makers and proprietors. There was Joseph Coles, paper-maker, of Wookey Hole in 1788; James Coles of Lower Wookey, i.e. Henley mill, in 1816; and later there was a Henry Coles, whose name is also found in connection with Stoke Bottom. There were Gillings at Cheddar, and at Sherborne, and at Stoke Bottom; and most famous of all, the Fussells—Henry Fussell, paper-maker of Stoke Bottom, who is recorded as taking an apprentice in 1802;[4] Jacob Fussell, paper-maker of Stoke Lane, who was declared bankrupt in 1826; and Walton Fussell, paper-maker of Stoke Lane, whose child was baptized in 1815, and who later appears at Sherborne. It is the same today at Wookey Hole, where many local families have worked in the mill for several generations—the Lunnons, and the Roses, and the Richards (who migrated from Cheddar), and the Lees, three of whom in succession have held the post of manager.

The Wookey Hole mill, which was in existence as a paper mill before 1610, may well have been one of the first to be established in England. The invention of printing in the fifteenth century had stimulated the European paper-making industry. Caxton, whose first books were printed about 1475, used paper imported from the Continent, and this was the case with most books printed in England in the sixteenth century. Caxton's successor, Wynkyn de Worde, used paper made in the first English mill which was established in 1495 near Hertford, but the mill failed. The real foundation of the industry dates from about 1588, when John Spilman established a paper mill at Dartford in Kent. Dr Shorter has noted the existence of 38 English paper mills during the first half of the seventeenth century, and by 1712 there were probably about 200 in the whole country. Many of the early paper mills were converted from corn or fulling mills. At the end of this period of expansion, England was able to produce two-thirds of the paper consumed in the country instead of importing it as previously, first from France and the Netherlands, and later from Italy.

Impetus was given to the industry, after the revocation of the Edict of Nantes in 1685, by the influx of Huguenot refugees, among whom there were a number of Protestant French paper-makers who contributed capital and enterprise to the industry as well as their skill and techniques. (Many of the technical terms of the paper-making industry are French in origin: the terms 'coucher' and 'layer', for instance, deriving from the French *coucheur* and *leveur*, are still in use at Wookey Hole.) There were Huguenot colonies in Bristol and Glastonbury, and groups settled in various villages at the western end of Mendip—Shipham, Rowberrow and Axbridge, for instance, where the names Thierry and Lalonde are of Huguenot origin. The name Thierry also appears at Hinton Blewitt, and there is a Thierry House at Litton, attractively close to the Sherborne paper mill, but there is no direct evidence of Huguenot connection with the Somerset paper trade.

By 1800 about 400 mills were at work in England, and Somerset played an important part in the Westcountry paper industry. But it must be realized that most of the mills were very small concerns, consisting of only one or two vats, employing one or two paper-makers, and seldom more than a dozen workers altogether. One must not visualize anything approaching the scale of the modern Wookey Hole mills. To judge by the names mentioned earlier, the industry was often very much of a family business, and many of the mills were simple buildings, situated in remote villages and depending on the vagaries of water power.

Mendip Paper-Makers

By soon after 1800, however, the effects of the Industrial Revolution were beginning to make themselves felt. Steam power was being introduced, but only slowly, and only for driving the Hollander or rag-beating machinery; for there was the danger of producing more material than could be handled by small mills with only a few vats, especially as these were not likely to be situated in places where the transport of coal was easy or economic. The de Montalt mill, however, installed a steam-engine in 1808—part of the slender tapering chimney still stands detached from the main building—but not the new-fangled paper-making machinery. This was the Fourdrinier machine, named after the firm of London wholesale stationers who introduced it into England about 1802–6: its basic principle was the manufacture of paper on an endless belt of woven wire instead of on separate moulds, man-handled by the traditional method for the making of each single sheet of paper. Together, steam power and the Fourdrinier machine eventually insured the production of the vastly increased quantity of paper now required in the country; but this meant the spread of the industry to places where transport and coal were readily available, and where new and larger mills could be built, and this spelt the inevitable decline and extinction of the small local mills, which could not be adapted to the new machine age: often remote from coal and from the new forms of transport, they could not compete economically with the newer and larger units. Where possible, the hand-made mills managed to survive for a time by concentrating on the highest grades of paper for which a demand persisted, but during the 1820s and 1830s the output of hand-made paper fell steeply, until in 1850 it accounted for only 4 per cent of the paper produced in the country.

Between 1800 and 1860 most of the small Somerset mills went under: this was the case at Compton Martin, where the Churchwardens' Accounts for 1821 contain a reference to 'paper-makers in distress'; at Stoke Lane in 1826 Jacob Fussell, paper-maker, was declared bankrupt, and in the following year the parish Rate Book shows that he was allowed relief from rates to the sum of £2 17s. 9d. 'for the two paper mills which are out of employ'. Both these mills finally left off work in 1839.

At Banwell (which worked until 1850) Rutter says that good quality writing-paper and banknote paper were produced;[5] and surviving watermarks show that writing or letter paper of a fine quality was manufactured all over the district. Hodgkinsons still produce a Wookey Hole notepaper as a commercial side-line with a certain prestige value: their main products are high-grade papers for ledgers or for legal requirements, as well as banknote paper for the Bank of Scotland and various foreign banks. *The Story of Our Village*, compiled by the Wookey Hole Women's Institute in 1953, was printed on hand-made paper made in the village: a touch of local pride echoed at Stoke St. Michael more than a century earlier, when a number of parish Account Books and Vestry Books were made of local paper, watermarked *FUSSELL* and *COLES*.

Wookey Hole is the lone survivor of all these mills, and even there only a few vats maintain the old tradition, for most of the mill is now mechanized and produces machine-made paper for the Inveresk Paper Co., the proprietors of St. Cuthbert's Mill, half a mile down the valley. From 1848 to 1951 the mill at Wookey Hole was owned by the Hodgkinson family, who, like the great John Dickinson in another part of the country, spared no pains for the welfare of their employees and their families. Wookey Hole as we see it today is almost entirely a nineteenth-century industrial village, the creation of an enlightened employer whose relation to the local inhabitants was very much that of the father of his family. His own house, Glencot, built in the neo-Tudor style, the village school, the church, the club, and many of the cottages, were all built under the Hodgkinson régime out of the local stone: the mill itself, a fine dignified building with a splendid façade facing down the village street and spanning the narrow defile down which the Axe winds its way from the mouth of the caves, is built of the same stone, quarried from the field known as Hole Ground.

In the mill one can still watch the traditional process of paper-making in operation, almost exactly as it was watched by John Evelyn when he visited the mill at Byfleet in 1678, and described what he saw in his *Diary* for 24 August:

> I found them making a coarse white paper. They cull the rags which are linen for white paper, woollen for brown; then they stamp them in troughs to a pap, with pestles, or hammers, like the powder-mills, then put it into a vessel of water, in which they dip a frame closely wired with wire as small as a hair and as close as a weaver's reed; on this they take up the pap, the superfluous water draining through the wire; this they dexterously turning, shake out

like a pancake on a smooth board between two pieces of flannel, then press it between a great press, the flannel sucking out the moisture, then, taking it out, they ply and dry it on string, as they dry linen in the laundry; then dip it in alum water, lastly, polish and make it up in quires. They put some gum in the water in which they macerate the rags. The mark we find in sheets is formed in the wire.[6]

I salute the village people whom I have watched at work there, my friends over a period of thirty years: in particular the paper-makers themselves, kings of the craft, stooping to dip their moulds into the vats of 'stuff', with those horny and delicate hands giving that simple yet bafflingly dexterous movement that alone suffices to make a flawless sheet: Dick Beveridge, Ted Sheldon, Tom Jones, Nant McEwan—proudly I set your names upon my page.

But the other mills are silent: sometimes their very site has been forgotten; on other occasions my search has been met with blank incredulity, though I may actually have been standing against the walls of a derelict mill or of one that has long since been adapted to some other use. The earliest reference to a paper mill at Dulcote is in 1752, and paper was made there throughout the nineteenth century; about 1898 the mill was turned over to the production of leather board—fibre board used for stiffeners in the boot and shoe industry—but was destroyed by fire, 23 September 1904.[7] The ruined buildings and the chimney still stand, upstream from the main road, behind the Georgian mill house.

At Bleadney, on the Axe, the paper mill has disappeared except for a few pieces of wall. This was not the Lower Mill—now beautifully converted into a dwelling house—which was a corn mill, though also at one time used as a paper mill, but a building a few yards upstream beside the Piccadilly Inn. It had been bought in 1784 by one of the Band family, who are also recorded as paper-makers at Wookey Hole, but was later the special concern of the Horsingtons, William Horsington, of the firm of Clark and Horsington, being recorded there on the Wookey tithe schedule of 1841. Paper-making at Bleadney ceased about 1850, but the Day Book which records the sales between 1840 and 1850 has survived: the names and addresses of the purchasers show that 80 per cent of the output went to London; the railway had reached Bristol in 1841 and Taunton in 1842, but most merchandise must still have gone by road. There were also regular customers at Bath, Wells and Bridgwater. On an average 2,600 reams a year were sold at this time, supplies being built up during a slack period to meet the demand of the London trade.

At Cheddar there were three paper mills in Collinson's time: the last of these, belonging to the Wansbrough Paper Company of Watchet, continued at work until May 1900, when Louis Evans, then a young clerk at the mill, remembers writing out the dismissal notices for the 120 employees. The buildings later became a pottery, and are now incorporated in a large concrete works not far from the Market Cross: portions of the older building are easily identifiable, as is the site of the waterwheel where the stream flows through the middle of the building. Across this stream, on a new bridge built by the company, John Wookey, the local haulier, used to drive his famous horse, Black Prince, to and from Cheddar station—the railway had arrived in 1869—bringing rags and coal to the mill and taking away the paper. I possess one sheet of this paper, given to me by W. M. Hill, whose family have served as parish clerks at Cheddar for more than 100 years. It is a strong blue hand-made paper, 20 in. × 16 in., watermarked with a crest and the legend CHEDDAR MILLS 1867 T & B. This was the trademark of Messrs. Tanner and Budgett, the name Tanner appearing in connection with the Cheddar mills as early as 1833. The other two mills are shown on the tithe map of 1839, farther upstream towards the mouth of the Gorge.

At the western end of Mendip there was a mill at Banwell working as early as 1710. The tithe schedule of 1837 records the mill as still belonging to the Emerys, as in 1710, but occupied by Robert Alford and Company who were also the lessees of one of the Cheddar mills; in 1850 it was converted to a flour mill and a brewery, and then became a grist mill, until the site was finally acquired by Weston-super-Mare Waterworks. Some of the buildings survive as cottages, but the site of the pond which was filled by the spring and which was such a pleasant feature of the village scene, has now been laid out as a bowling-green contained within the old circular boundary wall: the overflow of sparkling clear water flows away to the north-west as the River Banwell, to reach the Bristol Channel in Woodspring Bay.

Both at Cheddar and at Banwell the acquisition of the spring water by waterworks companies serves to underline the value of the 'quick streams and clear water' to which the paper industry had been tied. It was the same at Rickford and at Sherborne* on the northern side of Mendip, where powerful springs have been harnessed to supply Bristol water.

At Rickford the original mill-pond has been developed into an ornamental lake beside the road at the foot of Blagdon Combe, the leat that conducted the water to the mill being still visible behind the mill house. The mill itself was later used as a printing works. There are various references to the family of Hall, paper-makers, in the first half of the nineteenth century. Giles Hall owned the mill in 1832 when it was broken into (for the third time) and fifteen reams of writing-paper stolen. The thieves were apprehended by a constable as 'suspicious characters' on their return to Bristol, six reams of paper being found in their possession, and five more reams being afterwards found in Barrow Wood.[8]

Moving eastwards along the flank of Mendip, we come next to Compton Martin, where ruined walls of the mill survive to the north of the picturesque village pond, beside the main road from Bath to Weston-super-Mare. The pond itself is the source of the River Yeo, the main supply of Blagdon lake, which is augmented by water from springs at Rickford and Langford. The Compton Martin mill seems to have ceased work by 1830, as does Herriotts mill near West Harptree, the site of which is now drowned by the waters of the Chew valley lake. Sherborne mill, some parts of it at any rate, still stands derelict in its tiny secret valley close to the Litton reservoirs. These were constructed about 1850 to provide compensation water in the Chew valley when the head springs at Chewton Mendip were tapped for Bristol's water, the Sherborne spring itself being piped direct to Bristol in 1885.[9] The Litton tithe map of 1839 shows two mills at Sherborne within a few yards of each other, the lower mill being specified as a grist mill. The ruins of the upper mill, which one assumes to have been the paper mill, have charm even in decay, with a façade centred upon a surprising little classical doorway with a delicately moulded architrave. Local tradition says that the mill was later used as a button factory, Elihu Tucker being recorded as a button dealer in the Litton census returns of 1851. Only three houses survive in what was once a thriving and prosperous hamlet. A network of lanes led to the mill from almost every direction, some now used merely for farming purposes, others abandoned and long since

* The place-name Sherborne derives from O.E. *scir burne*, clear stream.

choked with undergrowth, serving no useful purpose in the local economy: only the double hedges and the deeply trodden trackways between high red banks show how much traffic the lanes once carried.

And so, eastwards again, to Stoke Bottom, where we find the same sad features of a vanished community and an abandoned industrial site: the fast-flowing waters, the roots of the thick walls of a once prosperous factory, and the ruined sites of more than a score of humble cottage homes. What was unique about this particular industrial site was that it formed a cluster round a mansion house which had no concern with it at all. In fact there almost seems to have been a conspiracy of silence about Stoke House. I have found no reference to it in any early topographical work— not even in Collinson's description of the hamlet of Stoke Bottom. I had been told vaguely of a ruined mansion, with a splendid staircase and Adam fireplaces, standing astride the little river at the bottom of the valley: it was into this river that the daughter of the house, the victim of an unhappy love-affair, had long ago thrown herself from her bedroom window, and her ghost was still said to haunt the ruins.

The house was described by Abbot Horne in 1905 as 'now fast becoming a ruin'.[10] His guess was that it was probably built by a former owner of the paper mill, but I do not think this was so. The original owners of Stoke Bottom were the Bisses (whose name has survived in Biss's Hill nearby); by 1500 the land was owned by the Normans who were clothiers in Shepton Mallet. When William Norman died in 1778, the property came to Henry Chichester of Northover who had married Mary Norman: by 1778 she was already dead, but the Chichesters moved to Stoke, and three generations lived in Stoke House, though they are all buried at Northover where their memorials may be read upon the church wall. It was the third generation, John Hody William Chichester, who was living at Stoke House in 1841, the year in which the tithe map and the census returns enable us to get some sort of picture of the hamlet. His two elder brothers had both died in infancy, and he was the third to be christened John Hody William, to carry on the family names. A detail in one of the parish Account Books brings him alive for us, for in March 1831 he was fined 'for coursing a hare in the snow', and the fine was expended on a suit of clothes made by the village tailor for one, Joseph Wilson, pre-

12. Wookey Hole mill in 1794, from an old drawing

THE MILL (OLD FRONT)

13. (*above*) Wookey Hole mill about 1890. 14. (*below*) The mill house at
Sherborne, near Litton

sumably a pauper. But in 1831 he was still the Squire's son; by 1841 he was the Squire, a bachelor Squire, living with his sister Frances, and three indoor servants. The house with its stables and outbuildings, lawns and pleasure gardens, occupied 5 acres with another 10 acres of pasture and woodland adjoining, and three different drives leading down to the house; the waters from St. Dunstan's Well, emerging from below the paper mill, were led 'through the garden, over falls, under arches, and between walls of stone, cut with care and set in cement, that must have cost a little fortune in their day'. Thus far Abbot Horne: but what he did not mention, in the walled garden across the river, is the keystone of an arched gateway in the wall; and carved on the crumbling stone one can just detect an emblem—a heron with a snake in its beak. One day a Downside boy, climbing about the overgrown ruins, found himself to his amazement face to face with his own family crest—for his name too was Chichester.

By a sheer stroke of luck I have been able to discover exactly what the house looked like, for though many of the villagers could talk about Stoke House, no photograph or print seemed to have survived. Seldom indeed is one lucky enough to come across so detailed and reliable a source of information as the late Herbert Parfitt of Stoke St. Michael. Not only did he demolish most of the mansion with his own hands, but his memory stretched back to 1887 when, as a small boy of four, he sat on a wall and watched the sale at which the contents of the house were disposed of. After John Chichester's death, Stoke House came to his niece and her husband J. L. Burnard; after Burnard's death there were several short-time occupants, until the Spencers of Oakhill bought the land through the Bottom for the fishing rights. Some of the house they dismantled; the main fabric was left to crumble and rot away. The mantelpieces and some of the windows with their stone dressing went to Hillylands, the house which Maitland Spencer was building for himself at Oakhill: the flagstones from the cellars went to floor the dairy at Hillylands Farm about 1897—Herbert Parfitt worked on that job as an apprentice; a fine triple window, and a carved and moulded classical doorway, are now incorporated in the Church Room at Oakhill. By 1928 the ruin had become dangerous, and Squire Strachey, who had acquired the site, invited Herbert Parfitt to demolish it. Little did he know that his own house at Ashwick would suffer the same ignominious fate at

the housebreaker's hands a generation later. But with a difference
—for much of the material from Stoke House was used in the
village as occasion arose: the entrance gateposts stand outside
Moon's Hill Farm; two houses are largely constructed of stone
from the mansion; the front doorstep of a modern bungalow is a
Portland stone slab from the Chichesters' staircase. Contrary to
popular belief, the modern house that now looks across the site of
Stoke House was not built from its ruins, but incorporates a row
of cottages that stood there in the nineteenth century beside John
Chichester's garden. This is the only survivor of the hamlet of
Fernhill in Stratton parish, where in 1841 there were 16 inhabited
houses containing 53 persons, including miners, a tailor, a cattle
dealer, a shoemaker, a shopkeeper and a publican, as well as a
number of agricultural labourers.

Such were the neighbours of the Georgian mansion, thronging
closely on one side: on the other side were the derelict mill, and
among a number of ruined cottages, two inhabited houses, one
still occupied by a Fussell. It can never have been a good site for a
country house, secluded though it was in one of Collinson's picturesque valleys with their 'hanging woods' and 'romantic rocks'.
It would be truer to say that it is hemmed in by the hills that shut
out much of the sunshine, and inevitably damp from the waters
that flow past it in the narrow valley. The house itself, as sketched
for me by Herbert Parfitt with delicate draughtsman's lines, had a
certain dignity. It was a three-storey house built over cellars,
which is surprising, seeing that they must have been below the
level of the river. Three steps led up to the front door, above which
was a fanlight framed in a semi-circular moulding with a promi-
nent keystone; on either side of the front door were two bays,
making five in all; above the windows of the top storey ran a
moulded parapet of Doulting stone, hardly concealing the easy
slope of the roof and a pair of symmetrical chimneys rising firmly
from the ridge.

The remarkable accuracy of Herbert Parfitt's memory—it was
more than 35 years since he had demolished the house—was
vindicated by a photograph which was brought to my notice
several years later. This was taken by Godfrey Halford of Holcombe, who with other boys used to ramble all over the house in
its final period of dereliction. Except for the exact position of the
chimneys, every proportion and detail of the facade was exactly as

Herbert Parfitt had sketched it for me. What was perhaps most interesting of all was that the stone dressings surrounding a number of the gaping windows had been removed: these were presumably the stonework incorporated in the fabric of Hillylands (now Oakhill Manor).

For a glimpse of the interior in the days of its decay we turn again to Abbot Horne:

> It has a fine entrance hall, and there is panelled wood and moulded plaster in the fashion of its age. The rooms are high, chilly and damp, and the old stairway was once imposing. Now emptiness, cobwebs and decay make the house look a fit meeting-place for all the ghosts in the countryside. The water too, which used to run by the back-door between strongly built containing walls, has broken its bounds and fills the cellars and adds to the damp and destruction.[10]

Today the destruction is complete: a few ruined walls where the stables and outbuildings stood, and for the rest, some mounds of rubble where one plunges through the brambles and brushwood in what were once cellars. Only Herbert Parfitt standing beside me could tell me where the front door once stood, and how far the façade stretched in each direction; only the snowdrops in the early spring hinted that here were once the lawns and pleasure grounds of yet another of the lost houses of Mendip.

CHAPTER SIX

Mendip Ironmasters—Fussells of Mells

(1) *The Rise to Fame*

> Out of those *Mineral-mountains* arises the river
> *Frome*, which hastens eastwards by these pits of coal,
> made use of by smiths as most proper to soften iron.
>
> CAMDEN'S *Britannia* (1695)

The other Mendip industry of which Billingsley makes no mention is the iron industry. This is all the more surprising because Mells, where the Fussells were already well established, is only a few miles from Ashwick, and Billingsley was himself a promoter and proprietor of the Dorset & Somerset Canal, a project in which the Fussells were particularly interested. On the other hand, practically no information about the iron industry is forthcoming at all, though it has left many traces at the eastern end of the Mendip range: iron ore was worked in small quantities at various places from Emborough to Nunney; near Witham, Iron Mill Wood and Iron Mill Farm appear on the 1817 map, and quite apart from Fussells, there were mills which produced edge-tools at Stoke Lane, Doulting and Chilcompton, while at Gurney Slade a primitive water-powered hammer survived in a small ironworks long enough to be photographed and described by Dr R. D. Reid.[1] This was destroyed when the Downside waterworks were rebuilt about that time, but a picturesque account of the old forge, and of Arthur Steeds, the last occupant, can be found in Dom Hubert van Zeller's *Willingly to School*.[2]

The only published source of information about the Fussells is an article by Edward Tylee which appeared in *The Somerset Year-Book* for 1934. Tylee gives some interesting pictures of the edge-tool industry based on local reminiscences, but many of his historical statements are inaccurate and give a misleading picture of the Fussell family and of the development of the industry. Only by laborious delving into parish registers, by following up the most unlikely clues, and by the fortunate discovery of private papers to which I have generously been allowed access, have I been able to piece together the story of the Fussells. Even so, I am well aware that there are still numerous gaps, especially as no Fussell papers relating to the business appear to have survived.

Tylee, for instance, states that the ironworks were established at Mells, early in the nineteenth century, by a member of the family who had been working in some ironworks in the north of England. This may possibly refer to a reorganization of the business or to the introduction of new machinery, but Collinson shows that the industry was already well established at Mells by 1791.

> It is worthy of remark that in this sequestered vale there are two iron forges which at this period are carrying on a trade, little inferior, in point of extension, to those in the northern part of this Kingdom. All the Western counties are supplied at these manufactories with every iron implement of husbandry, and their connexions extend to the European and American continents.[3]

In fact, the business was already half a century old, for among the Horner papers preserved at Mells Manor is a document dated 25 December 1744, by which John Horner leased a plot of ground to James Fussell of Stoke Lane, edge-tool maker, for 99 years, with liberty to erect 'a good, firme and substantiall Mill or Mills for Grinding Edge Tools and forging Iron plates'.[4]

The parish register of Stoke Lane dates from 1644, and the name Fussell appears on the very first page. Here, as indeed wherever they settled, the Fussells proliferated alarmingly—the Mells register records the desperate appellation of one, Final Fussell—and it is no easy matter to settle the genealogy of the family.* Fussells continued to live at Stoke Lane, where we have found them owning a paper mill in Stoke Bottom at the beginning of the nineteenth century, and as late as 1871 there was another firm of edge-tool makers, Messrs. Fussell and Wise of Stoke Lane Iron Works, who were quite independent of Fussells of Mells. One of the descendants of the James Fussell who migrated to Mells, Rev. William James Fussell Edwards, returned to Stoke

---

* See the skeleton family tree on page 94.

Lane as vicar from 1834 to 1885. One branch of the family established itself at Frome, another at Rode, from whom the present family of brewers is descended, and they crossed the county border into Wiltshire. Apart from their prime interest in iron, they are to be found as doctors and lawyers and clergymen. The ramifications of such a large family are further complicated by the fact that a genealogical tree, belonging to descendants of the Mells Fussells, contains details which are at complete variance with entries in the registers, and which sometimes conflict with other well-established facts.

James Fussell I, son of Thomas Fussell, was born at Stoke Lane in 1646; his son, James Fussell II, was born in 1677, and a generation later, in 1710, came James Fussell III, to whom the lease at Mells was granted in 1744. The last-named must have established himself very quickly in Mells, for he was elected churchwarden in 1753 and 1754, and again from 1763 to 1767: his last signature in the parish records is dated 1769, and he died 7 December 1775. He may be regarded as the founder not only of the business, but also of the Mells branch of the family: his eldest son, Austin Fussell (1737–1794) of Woodlands End, followed his father as churchwarden at Mells from 1773 to 1781, and is commemorated by a tablet at the west end of the south aisle of Mells church, which describes him as an 'eminent edge-tool maker'. Austin's son, John Fussell II, and grandson, John Fussell IV, stayed in Mells and carried on the family business there. John Fussell II (1766–1810) lived at Woodlands End, and married Mary Hounsell of Bridport. The family name Hounsell is only one of the many names adopted by later Fussells as Christian names, just as their own name appears in families into which they married. John Fussell IV (1799–1869) is variously described as living at Tents Hill, Bilboa and Rock House. He was a figure of considerable importance in Mells, and his name appears frequently in parish records as chairman of the vestry, overseer, guardian and haywarden, right up to the time of his death. '

Of Austin Fussell's brother, John Fussell I, nothing is known except that he broke away from Mells and lived at Nunney, where he started the ironworks which later bore the name of his nephew, Isaac Fussell (1778–1831), who succeeded him there. But it was the next brother, James Fussell IV, and his descendants, who were the most important and interesting members of the family.

James Fussell IV was born in 1748, and like his brother was churchwarden, from 1791 to 1800. By this time he must have been the proprietor of the ironworks which his father had founded and which were described by Collinson. He was also an active promoter and proprietor of the Dorset & Somerset Canal, several of the early meetings concerned with this venture being held at the Talbot Inn, Mells. A branch of the canal was planned to run from Frome to the Mendip coalfield, passing close to Mells, and for this section James Fussell designed a patent balance lock or canal lift which was successfully demonstrated in 1800–1802 (see Chapter Fourteen). By 1803, however, capital had run out, and, in the words of a contemporary pamphlet, 'public attention was diverted by the military preparations and repeated alarms of the day'. Work on the canal was suspended, and the whole project abandoned. There is nothing to record the disappointment that James Fussell must have felt at the collapse of his hopes, though the pamphlet mentioned above, which was written about 1825 in an attempt to revive the scheme for the canal, points out that 'the extensive Iron-works at Mells and Nunney, which have justly acquired so high a reputation, would find a Canal or Rail-road invaluable to their purposes, both in receiving the raw materials and conveying their manufactured goods'.

The abandonment of the Canal could at least be regarded as a patriotic gesture, for this was the moment of anxiety so well depicted by Hardy in *The Dynasts* and *The Trumpet Major*, and preparations against invasion by Napoleon were not confined to the Dorset coast. Three companies of voluntary cavalry and two companies of infantry were formed in Frome; and Mr J. D. Middleton and Mr Edward Newport, who were Frome carriers, each offered the government five waggons and forty horses against any emergency. These details are recorded in a paragraph from Bonner and Middleton's *Bristol Journal* 6 August 1803, which was shown to me by W. B. Fussell, a great-great-grandson of Austin Fussell.

The paragraph continues:

At this eventful and momentous crisis, when the heart of every Briton beats high with true loyalty and patriotism, we feel pleasure in recording the spirited offers made to Goverment [*sic*] for the defence of the country. Mr. James Fussell, of the Mells Iron Factory, near Frome, has offered to prepare (gratis) 1,000 pikes, and afterwards to supply Government with 2,000 weekly as long as they may be wanted.

The editorial comment one hundred years later shows a proper sense of local pride in this generous offer, and is also a tribute to the esteem in which Fussell tools were held.

> Good old patriotic James Fussell! When I was a lad, your name was still a household word in the district for bill-hooks, reaping-hooks etc., and my grandfather had tools of your make he set great store by. It may be so still, or that of your successors, so far as I know, if the cheaper but not better Sheffield tools have not overrun the market. I will warrant your Somerset pikes would have rendered good service in the hands of Somerset men had it come to the push, and the West Country men had not been bungled between rhines, where they could not come at their foes, as they were at Sedgemoor.[5]

James Fussell IV lived to the fine old age of 84 at a house 'on the Island' at Mells, where he died in February 1832. He left eight children, of whom five were sons who all play a part in the history of the family business. The eldest was James Fussell V (1774–1845) whose lifetime marks a definite stage in the social advance of the Fussells: previous generations can have been little more than craftsmen who had developed a successful local industry, but James Fussell V built himself a mansion, and the next generation was to include public school and university men who could claim to be included in the ranks of the local squirearchy. There is a significant moment in the Mells register which records the baptisms of the children of Thomas Fussell, brother of James Fussell V; the earliest entries describe the father as 'Edge Tool Maker' or 'Proprietor in the Iron Works', but in 1832 he is styled 'Gentleman'.

Somewhere about this time the memorial tablet in Mells church already referred to must have been erected. The bronze plate, inset in stone and inscribed by Gingell of Bath, commemorates James Fussell III who died in 1775, Austin Fussell (d. 1794), his two wives and his surgeon son (of Temple Cloud), the last-named dying in 1826. Was this the moment when the Fussells considered themselves to have been socially established to the extent that they could erect a family memorial among the Horner monuments at Mells?

By now 'The Chantry' had been built. This was the mansion of

James Fussell V, situated about a mile from Mells near the hamlet of Little Elm. Here another branch of the industry was established, certainly by 1828, when it was referred to by Rev. John Skinner in his *Journal*. There is no means of knowing whether the works or the house was built first. The name of the house seems to indicate that it stood on lands appropriated to the chantry chapel founded by Sir Oliver de Servington (or Cervyngton) about 1350 in the neighbouring church at Whatley. Perhaps too there was a touch of the romantic affectation which was sprinkling the countryside with bogus 'Abbeys' and 'Castles' in a period of architectual 'revivals'.

'The Chantry', however, is a classical house, built probably about 1825. It is unusual-looking, solid rather than graceful, aloof and not entirely at ease, on the skyline where the parkland falls away to the valley. What strikes one at once about the south façade is the apsidal central feature, for there is no door on this front, the main rooms being on the first floor, supported by a basement storey where the ground slopes away. The central feature is carried up through the balustraded roofline to form a squat upper storey where the chimneys are all clustered. This must have been part of the original design, but the symmetry of the building is spoiled by a one-storeyed wing which formerly contained the Catholic chapel added by Edward Tylee—in ironic juxtaposition to the parish church of which he was the patron, and which stood 100 yards from his front door. In all, it is an original but uncompromising house: there are too many vertical lines and it does not blend comfortably with its surrounding landscape. Is it fanciful to criticize it as the gesture of a self-made man who was not quite sure of his place in society?[6]

From the house one looks down at a lake, formed by damming one of the fast-flowing Mendip streams in its narrow valley, and designed to serve a double purpose—as a landscape ornament and as a source of power for the ironworks. In the hillside a little way back from the shore of the lake are a series of grottoes, presumably built at the same time as the house as part of the fashionable layout of a gentleman's grounds. Grottoes are today an outmoded fashion: no guide-book deigns to mention the Chantry grottoes, and even Miss Barbara Jones ignores them in her delightful *Follies and Grottoes*. But one can still aspire to recapture the romantic thrill that these strange structures were intended to excite, as one gropes through dark winding passages to emerge into vaulted chambers of irregular shapes and sizes. One of these contains the broken pieces of a large grindstone which was obviously salvaged from the ironworks to serve as a picnic table on mid-Victorian afternoons. Another period fixture is an ice-house, a deep stone-lined pit on a northward-facing hillside, whose only occupant on my last visit was a dead goose, its white wings full-stretched as if in crucifixion, shining faintly from the darkness far below.

Such then was the house of James Fussell V, which he must have occupied for about twenty years until his death in 1845. He did not marry: his heir was to be his brother Thomas's eldest son, James Fussell VI, and he seems to have planned for him an education appropriate to the son of a 'Gentleman'. The boy was at Shrewsbury from 1830 to 1832, and in Dr Butler's MS. Register there he is entered on 27 January 1830 as the son of James Fussell, Esq., Mells near Frome. This may only be a slip of the pen; on the other hand it may indicate that James, and not Thomas, Fussell was the man with whom the headmaster had corresponded about the boy's entry.

The boy was admitted to Trinity College, Cambridge, as a pensioner in 1832, but there is a curious interval of nine years, for which a reason will be suggested later, between his admission in 1832 and his readmission and matriculation in 1841 at the age of 28: thereafter he had a distinguished academic career, took his B.A. in 1845 and was ordained priest in 1846. The end in view was that he should be installed in the newly-founded family living—perhaps the last stage necessary in the establishment of the Fussells among the squirearchy. The Horners had been Lords of the Manor at Mells for nearly 300 years, with the gift of the living, which was at the moment held by a member of the family: the Fussells would do the same at Chantry.

The development of the ironworks—by this time there were six different centres of production—had led to a considerable increase of population in the surrounding villages. A deed in the Diocesan Registry at Wells records how 'for the spiritual advantage of certain of the inhabitants of the several parishes of Whatley, Mells and Elm who reside at an inconvenient distance from their respective parish church and for whom there is not accommodation to attend divine service thereat', James Fussell had decided to build and endow a church at Chantry. The parish of Chantry was

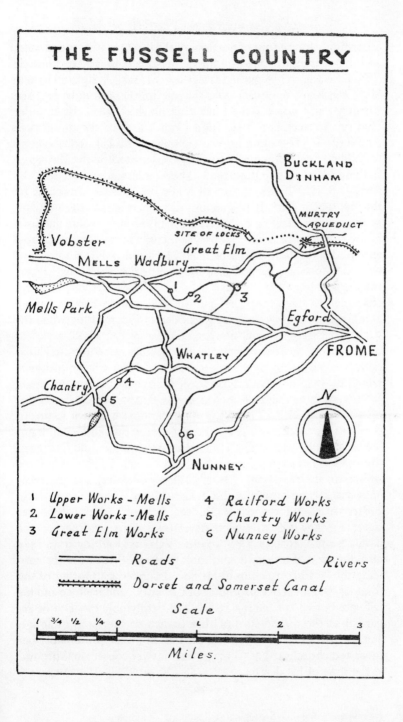

THE FUSSELL COUNTRY

BUCKLAND DINHAM

MURTRY AQUEDUCT

SITE OF LOCKS

Vobster

MELLS Wadbury

Great Elm

Mells Park

Egford

FROME

WHATLEY

Chantry

NUNNEY

1 Upper Works - Mells   4 Railford Works
2 Lower Works - Mells   5 Chantry Works
3 Great Elm Works   6 Nunney Works

━━━━━━ Roads   ⌇⌇⌇ Rivers

┅┅┅┅ Dorset and Somerset Canal

Scale

1 ¾ ½ ¼ 0   1   2   3

Miles.

accordingly formed out of portions of the three parishes mentioned; and the church, designed by Sir Gilbert Scott in the Gothic style ('What his admirers regarded as a little gem,' says A. K. Wickham in his *Churches of Somerset*), was begun in the grounds of 'The Chantry', and was for the most part finished when the founder died on 7 December 1845. (For a note on Chantry church, see Appendix I.) The building was completed by his nephew, who was already a deacon, and was duly consecrated by the Bishop of Bath and Wells on 4 June 1846. The first lesson was read by the Rev. J. S. H. Horner, Rector of Mells, and the second lesson by the incumbent elect. It was an almost Gilbertian situation: the installation of a vicar in a church built in the grounds of his own house, partly at his own expense, as incumbent of a living created specifically for him, and which he had been duly educated and trained to occupy. Careful examination of the church will reveal the Fussells' trademark, just like the rebuses left on medieval churches by their founders, but in this case perhaps a unique combination of pious motive and business acumen: between the gargoyles there are angel-figures, holding in their hands a variety of sacred and profane objects, among which, quite unmistakably, there are specimens of the edge-tools and other iron implements which by 1846 had made Fussells of Mells a world-famous name.

There will be much to record in due course of the later career of the Rev. J. G. C. Fussell: in the meantime we must return to consider the careers of the brothers of James Fussell V, builder of 'The Chantry'. Isaac (1778–1831) moved to Nunney and took over the works there from his uncle, John Fussell I. The works are shown on the 1817 map (Fussells Edge Tool Mill), and the business was carried on under the name of Isaac Fussell & Co. Isaac Fussell, married but without children, built, or more probably rebuilt, Nunney Court, which hereafter became another of the family 'seats'. Jacob (1788–1867) was Vicar of Doulting from 1823 until the time of his death, and took the part of Reader at the consecration of Chantry church. He was described as 'brother of the founder, and an active promoter of the work', and both he and his wife are buried at Chantry, which had clearly now come to be regarded as the mausoleum of that branch of the family, though James Fussell V 'slept with his fathers' at Mells, presumably because the churchyard at Chantry was not yet consecrated ground at the time of his death.

Mendip Ironmasters—Fussells of Mells

Two more brothers, John Fussell III (b. 1783) and Thomas Fussell (b. 1785), remained in Mells, though John later moved to Nunney. They were the protagonists in what we may call 'the Horner affair', acting on behalf of their father and of their elder brother, who must have moved away to Chantry about this time. It was a crucial moment for both families. The Horners had ruled Mells since the time of the Reformation; they were gentry who had intermarried with most of the leading Somerset families. By comparison, the Fussells were newcomers to Mells; they were engaged in trade, and were clearly considered as social inferiors by the Horners. By about 1800, rapid expansion of the Fussells' business threatened to inflict Mells with the horrors of the Industrial Revolution, and this was what the Horners were determined to prevent; for the Fussells, it was a question of expand or burst—hence the establishment of their branches in a ring of neighbouring villages. It was a situation reminiscent of Galsworthy's play *The Skin Game*: the old order was being challenged at its own front door.

A bundle of Horner papers preserved at Mells Manor enables us to follow much of the long-drawn-out struggle, and though many details are not clear, it is not the details that are important in this affair. The papers cover nearly 30 years in all, for the Fussells must have begun to feel anxiety about their future as soon as the conclusion of the 99-year lease granted to them in 1744 came slowly and ruthlessly into sight: the bulk of the correspondence, however, dates from between about 1829 and 1841 when a settlement was at last reached. Many of the papers are memoranda made by members of the Horner family, copies of letters addressed to John or Thomas Fussell, or letters of the Horners to each other; there are also a number of lawyers' letters, dealing with the interminable negotiations or detailing the opinions of Counsel; and, most interesting of all, there are a few original letters from John and Thomas Fussell, and from a cousin, one of Austin Fussell's sons from Corsley, just across the Wiltshire border, who was clearly called in as a mediator. The general tone of the letters exchanged is resolute, but dignified and courteous: there were even tender inquiries when Thomas Fussell was laid up with an injured leg. Each party was clearly mistrustful of the other's intentions, both were inordinately stubborn in negotiation, and beneath the veneer of fair words the Horners' real opinions of the Fussells emerges only in their letters between themselves.

77

Quite apart from social jealousy, a further motive for the bitterness between the families is suggested in the autobiography of Richard White (1828–1905). John White farmed at Mells, and his son Richard, in his old age, wrote an account of his early life in the village. Richard White's mother had strong sympathies with Methodism—her grandfather had been a friend of Wesley's—and she and her son used to attend meetings in Mells on Sunday evenings, when there were no services at the parish church. These meetings took place in a chapel at Woodlands End built by Thomas Fussell. Many of the ironworkers had been converted to Methodism, and Thomas Fussell had joined the Movement, later driving from Wadbury every Sunday morning and evening to attend meetings. Such activity was hardly likely to propitiate the reigning Squire, Colonel T. S. Horner (1762–1844), who was head of the family throughout the period of the dispute the with Fussells, especially when (according to White) Thomas Fussell had often made himself disagreeable to the Colonel at Vestry Meetings. When the Fussells made application for a renewal of their lease, it is not surprising that they met with a direct refusal.

The issue is put fairly and squarely in an undated memorandum by Colonel Horner:

> The Fussells have been for many years endeavouring to persuade me to let them have the Mills but I always refused & said I could never part with them at last they endeavoured to frighten me into letting them have them by beginning works in a field called Huntleys, adjoining my park—these works were for a mansion house for Mr. T. Fussell & a Forge, Steam Engin, Shops &c &c. Still I refused parting with the Mills—tho an old Copper was taken up there & hammered upon, for the purpose I presume of letting me know the sort of noise I had to expect. Still I held out & about this time my son came home & he appeared a good deal annoyed at the idea of these buildings taking place (for the proposed house was to be so situated as to command a view of my house, park & pleasure ground). I then relaxed a little and offered an exchange of leases.

It was particularly galling to the Horners that Huntleys was the only piece of land in the parish of Mells which they did not own. Quite probably Thomas Fussell did not really want a house there, but the Fussells were prepared to hold this pistol to the Horners' head, confident that they could ultimately obtain possession of the Mills which they so desperately wanted; those were situated in the deep wooded Wadbury valley, downstream from Mells, and out of sight and earshot of the Horners' park.

The Fussells' viewpoint is firmly put in a letter from John Fussell to Col. Horner on 4 December 1829:

> I have just had an opportunity of conferring with my father and brothers upon the subject of your proposal to purchase a portion of the land belonging to my father in Mells, and granting a lease of the Mills; after mature deliberation we are decidedly of opinion that such a Tenure may to us prove extremely unsatisfactory and you will certainly see the reasonableness of our position; whilst . . . two or three hundred pounds would suffice for a boundary wall to Huntleys being *land*, we must of *necessity* expend as many thousands at the mills being *leasehold*, for the improvements made to machinery by our competitors in the North have of late been so rapid and important, that unless we keep pace with them we may as well take the Articles of our Manufacture at once out of the Market, we mention this merely to convey to you how prejudicial it will be to us to remain any longer in a state of inactivity upon a point which involves so extensively our commercial interests. In the discussion of a subject like this it would be frivolous to attempt to impose upon your better understanding a desire to oblige and serve you to our own hurt; but this we venture to say without hesitation, our whole family have ever entertained *considerable* respect towards you, and we should regret any circumstance which may transpire to cause the slightest deviation from it.

The Fussells held the whip hand in the negotiations, and the Horners were inclined to vacillate: at one time they were prepared to endure the worst that the Fussells could do on Huntleys, in the belief that they would eventually be able to get rid of the industry altogether from the parish; at other times they were prepared to offer almost anything, but when agreement was apparently reached, the Fussells would present increased demands which Col. Horner would inevitably reject. There were endless proposals and counter-proposals for the exchange of lands. One is reminded of Galsworthy's *Strife* when, after ten years or so of intervening wrangling, practically identical terms are put forward again. At one stage the Fussell brothers are anxious to get the matter settled so that their father 'may have the opportunity of affording us his advice whilst he has spared to him the capability of doing so'—for James Fussell IV was 81 years old. But the old man had been dead for some years, and his property on 'The Island' had become one of the many bones of contention, before the cease-fire was sounded.

Various minor issues were fought out over the years: from the very beginning, the Fussells' title to Huntleys had been challenged on the grounds that James Fussell had purchased it while holding it as a Trustee for Sale. A long Chancery suit had been instituted, the costs of which each party was anxious to avoid. Control of the water in the river, the fishing liberties, the exact demarcation of the lands in Wadbury which were to be included in the exchange and where Thomas Fussell was to build his mansion, the reservation of use of Col. Horner's favourite plantations, rights of way and approaches to the disputed territory—all these points must have helped to enrich the lawyers, if nothing else. There must have been a whispering campaign as well, for there are several drafts of a letter which Col. Horner wrote in May 1839 to the Messrs. Fussell:

> It having been recently mentioned to me that you are impressed with the idea that I entertain a feeling of hostility towards you & a wish to put you out of the Parish & that the late disputes in Mells respecting the poor Rates originated with me from ill-will towards yourselves & those rumours being *contrary* to the *fact*, I think it right to express to you my assurance to that effect—indeed the terms conceded by me in the first instance ... show that such a statement was without foundation, & as to the second statement, as to the Mells disputes, I can *most truly* say I *knew nothing of the matter*.

The letter continues with a reference to a meeting between the parties at Wells, which was brought to an abrupt close by John Fussell walking out of the room. By December 1840, however, the end was clearly in sight, and Col. Horner wrote to Thomas Fussell:

> I am happy to find that our tedious negotiations are now fast drawing to a friendly termination & to the satisfaction of both parties—& I trust that the trifling mistakes which now, I apprehend, appear in the deed, will be easily put to rights ... & that shortly after that, we may all meet round my table to sign seal & deliver & drink success to both parties.

Final agreement was reached on 1 March 1841. The steam hammer on Huntleys was to be stopped immediately, and other work within a fortnight: the Fussells were allowed three months

15. (*above*) Fussell's ironworks at Mells in 1880, from a photograph by James Long, the village bootmaker. 16. (*below*) A view of the same building in 1961

17. (*above*) Edge-tool angel—detail from the church at Chantry built by the Fussells in 1846. 18. (*inset*) William Austin Fussell of Mells (1830–1911), manufacturer of spade-trees and garden furniture, from a palinotype taken by himself

to remove their buildings, and they were also to surrender their property on 'The Island'. In return they were to obtain possession of lands at Wadbury and of the lower Mill, with a renewed lease of the upper Mill; and Hunt's *Directory* for 1848 duly records Thomas Fussell residing at Wadbury House.

Tylee's account of the whole affair is inaccurate and inadequate. He simply states that the ironworks began in the early years of the nineteenth century on a piece of land called 'Studday', belonging to Colonel Horner, who did not like the idea of chimneys arising within sight of his windows, and so allowed the Fussells to have some land in the valley by the river where they established themselves.

Yet even this misstatement contained a hint which enabled me to solve a minor mystery; for nobody in Mells today had ever heard the name Huntleys or could tell me where the piece of land lay. Clearly it must have been between Mells Green and Finger Lodge. Studday is a field close to Clavey's Farm, but the tithe map of 1841 shows that part of the field was at that time a separate enclosure called Huntleys, a flat terrace just outside the park wall, and a perfect site for the Fussells' attack against the Horner demesne.

(2) *Decline and Fall*

Squeeze into the works through broken windows, or
  through damp-sprung doors;
See the rotted shafting, see holes gaping in the upper
  floors.

W. H. AUDEN: *Poems* 1930

It is difficult to give any detailed account of the industry in its earlier stages. By 1791, according to Collinson, Fussells were supplying the western counties with agricultural implements, and exporting to Europe and America. On 15 July 1828 the Rev. John Skinner of Camerton (who was staying with the Hoares at Southfield House, Whatley) walked over to Nunney 'to purchase a scythe for mowing the garden, as the best in the county, perhaps in the Kingdom, are made by the Fussells, who have mills at Mells, Nunney and Little Elm, and have realized an immense property among the fraternity by their superior skill in hardening edged tools'. He saw two men grinding scythes, 'with their noses literally at the grindstone', and launched out into a tirade against the

soi-disant philanthropists who strain at the gnat of West Indian
slavery and swallow the camel of industrial bondage.[7] Fussells
were clearly a firm of some reputation by now, for in 1813 the
name of James Fussell & Sons appears in a list of firms, engaged
primarily in mining or metallurgy, who were issuing their own
notes and apparently did their own banking business.[8]

By the middle of the nineteenth century, when the future of the
firm appeared secure as a result of the settlement with the Horners,
we are on somewhat firmer ground, though the absence of any
original documents leaves an enormous gap in our knowledge.
The 'and Sons' of James Fussell and Sons must refer to the sons
of James Fussell IV and provides a clue to the organization of the
business. It is difficult to know how far the branches run by the
sons, and in turn by the grandsons, of James Fussell IV, were
independent of each other. Tylee says that the branches did
different classes of work and so did not injure each other's business, but his account is confused to say the least. Morris's *Directory* for 1871 lists:

    (I) James Fussell Sons & Co.—Mells Ironworks
       (Scythes, bagging and reaping hooks, hay and chaff
       knives.)
   (II) John Fussell & Co.—Upper Ironworks
       (Spade, shovel & edge tool manufacturers.)
  (III) William A. Fussell—Rock House
       (Spade & shovel tree manufacturer.)
  (IV) Isaac Fussell & Co. of Nunney
       (Spade, shovel, draining & edge tool manufacturers.)

This list needs some clarification. 'James Fussell Sons & Co.'
worked the Lower works, situated just below Thomas Fussell's
new house on Wadbury; they also had works at Great Elm, a mile
farther down the river, and at Railford and Chantry, and after
Thomas Fussell's death the controlling partners were his two
eldest sons, Rev. J. G. C. Fussell of Chantry and Rev. J. T. R.
Fussell. 'John Fussell & Co.' refers to the direct descendants of
Austin Fussell, represented throughout the first half of the nineteenth century by John Fussell IV (1799–1868) whom we have
already noticed as a leading figure in parish affairs at Mells, where
he appears in the register as 'Edge Tool Maker'. He had no fewer
than 10 children, born between 1828 and 1841. His eldest son was
John Hounsell Fussell V (1828–1910) who was eventually to take

over the Nunney business from his cousins; the next son was William Austin Fussell who seems to have had quite a separate business at Mells, which included making the wooden handles for the tools made by other members of the family. There must, however, have been considerable fluidity in the organization of the businesses: a catalogue published at the very end of the firm's history carries the imprint of James, Isaac & John Fussell Ltd., Mells and Nunney Works, which indicates the fusion of several branches of the family.

When this catalogue was printed at Stourbridge about 1890, Fussells had ceased to be an independent firm. The reasons for the failure of such a well-established and obviously successful business—they had exhibited agricultural implements at the Great Exhibition of 1851, and they had even been awarded Gold Medals for reaphooks and scythes at an Exhibition at Vienna in about 1860—are not very obvious. Tylee says that, at the Lower Works, rolling-mills were built at great expense with the object of improving on the old-fashioned system of hand-forging, but that the new system was not perfected for a long time, and by then things had begun to go wrong, and the business was declining. We have seen John Fussell's anxiety, as early as 1829, about the rapid and important improvements made in machinery by their competitors in the north, and the need to keep pace with them. It may have been a case of too little and too late among the hard facts of nineteenth-century industrialism—just as the West-country woollen industry had succumbed, through failure to introduce machinery or to use the new sources of power available for driving the machines. Fussells depended largely on water power, though latterly they used steam, and in 1850 actually owned collieries at Vobster Marsh and at Coal Barton near Coleford, only a few miles from Mells.

The sudden disastrous collapse of English agriculture in the seventies must also have affected a firm that was largely concerned with making agricultural implements. At any rate, about 1880, according to Tylee, a Northcountry firm took over the business of James Fussell and that of John Fussell, formed a company and carried on the business for a while, until finally the whole concern was moved to Sheffield. This again is a very garbled version of what actually happened. The firm in question was Isaac Nash of Belbroughton, Worcestershire, which is now an associate company of Brades Skelton & Tyzack Industries of Oldbury near Birmingham.

The Fussell catalogue referred to above must have been printed about 1890, for manuscript notes in the copy preserved at Oldbury are dated 1891, and refer to the prices of one of Nash's competitors. The catalogue must have been produced by Nash during the period when Fussells' business was still being carried on under the old name at Mells and Nunney. By 1895 all production had stopped, and the Nunney works at any rate were described as 'simply ruins'.

Some light is thrown on this final period—though with particular reference only to the Nunney works—by papers belonging to the Daniel family of Frome who bought Nunney Court from John Hounsell Fussell in 1883. In 1882 a company had been formed to run the works (James, Isaac and John Fussell Limited), and 'on declining business and selling his whole plant and goodwill', John Hounsell Fussell had assigned to the company the lease of the half-share of the works which he had acquired from his cousin James Fussell VI. The company had already bought the other half-share of the business, and when it was adjudged bankrupt and liquidated in 1894, J. H. Fussell after various legal complications, had to buy back the half-share which he had previously rented, and finally conveyed it to the Daniels in 1898. The goodwill of the business was presumably acquired by Isaac Nash on the bankruptcy of the company in 1894.

From the catalogue we get a comprehensive view of the range of Fussell products. The index lists 111 different types of tool: there are 36 plates of engravings and the prices of 433 different models are quoted. Pride of place is given to the Patent Self-Adjustable Lawn Scythe, followed by pages of Hay-Knives, Slashing-Hooks, Hoes, Forks, Spades and Shovels. There are 46 different patterns of Bagging* and Reaping Hooks, 42 different Bill Hooks and 43 different Axe Heads. The vast number of patterns, often with minimal differences, is very interesting, as the names are given, showing how each district demanded its own special pattern tool: for instance, there are Sherborne Bean Hooks, Epsom Bills, Kent Rips and Banbury Turnip Hoes. The fact that none of the patterns bears a Somerset name, and seldom even a

* O.E.D. Bag (badge): to cut corn, pease or beans with a bagging or badging hook.

LAWN AND GARDEN CHAIRS

In all the newest and most comfortable designs, with Pitch Pine
Seats, either varnished or painted.

THE NEW LAWN TENNIS OR CROQUET CHAIR,

So much in request during the past season.

MELON & CUCUMBER FRAMES.

Garden Hand Lights, from 12 to 24 inches square, or 24 inches
wide to 6 feet long.

IMPROVED PORTABLE STEPS.

Somersetshire Hay Collectors, &c.

ALSO

FUSSELL'S NEW MINIATURE

Hothouse, or Propagating Stove

The simplest, cheapest, and best ever introduced for raising seeds
and striking cuttings.

This handy little apparatus is designed expressly to meet a want long
felt by possessors of gardens not containing the expensive appliances of
Stoves, Hothouses, &c., for raising all kinds of half-hardy and tender
annuals, biennials, cucumbers, vegetable marrows, melons, ornamental
gourd; striking cuttings of choice plants; and in fact for any purpose
requiring a steady heat.

Full particulars, with directions; also Illustrated Catalogue of Garden
Chairs to be obtained on application to

WILLIAM A. FUSSELL,

MELLS, FROME.

A Fussell advertisement from Harvey's *Frome Almanack* for 1881

Westcountry name, implies that the catalogue was not designed for local circulation. It even includes South American Draining Tools, American Spades and Canadian Wedge Axes, an interesting reminiscence of Fussells' transatlantic connections referred to by Collinson in 1791. The catalogue was obviously a trade list, giving quotations per dozen: Bill Hooks are quoted from 21s. to 32s. per dozen, while a set of Garden Tools consisting of a Border Fork, a Ladies' Spade, a Rake, Hoe and Trowel, is priced at 10s. 6d.

Three Fussell pattern books, dating from 1844 to 1874, have been presented to the Curtis Museum at Alton, in Hampshire. They contain full-size outline drawings of tools such as chaff-cutter blades and various types of hooks and knives. The patterns are named according to the place to which they were supplied, such as 'Chard, Hewing Vincent's Pattern 1845', and one volume shows the marks of the steelers, scythers, temperers, platers and grinders for 1844. The Curtis Museum also contains articles made by Fussell.

One or two of the articles described in the catalogue have a period ring about them, such as the London Mud Scoop, or the Road Scraper, or even the Yorkshire Slash or Sir Tatton Pattern, called after the famous Sir Tatton Sykes of Sledmere. Even more of a period piece is William Austin Fussell's advertisement published in Harvey's *Frome Almanack* for 1881. William Fussell is usually described as a spade-tree manufacturer, but this advertisement, set in eight varieties of type, ranges from Lawn and Garden Chairs 'in all the newest and most comfortable designs, with Pitch Pine Seats, either varnished or painted' (including the 'New Lawn Tennis or Croquet Chair, so much in request during the past season'), to Melon and Cucumber frames and Somersetshire Hay Collectors. The high light, in Gothic type, is Fussell's New Miniature Hothouse or Propagating Stove.

During recent excavations on the Wadbury site, various pieces of ironwork were unearthed, including what was clearly a left-handed scythe blade. Several tools were exhibited at an Historical Exhibition held in Frome in the summer of 1956, and there must be a number of jealously-preserved tools in private hands in neighbouring villages. I have been shown several of these tools, though with the passing of years they have often been ground down so far as to obliterate the trademark. I have even seen one of Isaac Fussell's spades, in mint condition, with which Mrs Taylor (who came to Nunney as a girl in 1880) planted a Coronation tree in the village in 1953 as well as a Golden Jubilee tree in 1887. It is still possible to buy Fussell grass and hedging tools from iron-mongers today, but these are of course Nash products, for Nash continued to use the Fussell trademarks, though the only two in current use are FUSSELL MELLS and JF.

It is now time to return to the story of the family who con-trolled the business. Thomas Fussell, who had previously lived at Selwood House, New St., Mells, settled at Wadbury House, which was presumably built as soon as the agreement with the Horners was reached. It is a ponderous Victorian mansion, but there is a splendid view eastwards down a grass terrace between trees, bounded by the Westbury White Horse and the long line of the Wiltshire Downs. From the cellars, which are cut out of the live rock, a brick-arched tunnel leads under the lawn to emerge high up on the wooded cliff-face of the Wadbury Valley above the Lower works. One wonders if this was merely a convenient sub-way for use in wet weather, or a secret route by which the iron-master could suddenly descend upon his workmen. The Fussells had a reputation for being hard taskmasters, and Skinner's out-burst about industrial slave-drivers may not have been so far from the mark. (There is also a story of rioting at Chantry against the Fussells, over the question of the eviction of some cottagers from houses that were required for their workers.) Tylee's article is illustrated with some interesting photographs taken at Mells works about 1880 by James Long, the village bootmaker: these show various ranges of long low buildings in the narrow wooded valley, with large workshops and several chimneys. The Horners had long ago considered the ironworks as a nuisance which was very prejudicial to the parish, and a beautiful valley had been spoiled, but it must be admitted that they were very well hidden away as far as the countryside at large was concerned.

None of Thomas Fussell's sons succeeded him at Wadbury after his death: James Fussell VI (Rev. J. G. C. Fussell) had inherited 'The Chantry' in 1845, and his brother, Rev. J. T. R. Fussell, held various livings in the Westcountry, and finally settled in Pem-brokeshire. It is rather odd that both these men went up to Trinity College, Cambridge, at the age of 27 or 28—unusually late. We have noticed the gap of nine years between James Fus-sell's admission to Trinity from Shrewsbury and his readmission and matriculation. One possible reason for this delay is that the Fussells may have been waiting for the Horner affair to be settled, and when it was finally settled in their favour in 1841, the elder son immediately proceeded to Cambridge, and plans were then made for the creation of a parish at Chantry. But this is merely hypothesis.

James Fussell VI was nothing if not versatile: another possible reason for the decline of the business may be that the two brothers were absentee proprietors, engaged primarily in other careers, unlike the earlier generations who lived right on the spot and gave themselves up whole-heartedly to the business. James Fussell VI was Vicar of Chantry from 1846 to 1852 (and again from 1877 to 1879); he owned the business of James Fussell Sons & Co at the Lower works, Mells, with its several branches, as well as a half-share in the Nunney works; and from 1852 to 1883 he was H.M. Inspector of Schools in the London area, and was often away from Chantry. This side of his life led to the foundation of Chantry school. Here, under the same roof as the National school, and an infant school, was an industrial school, as well as a boarding school for girls. The school was erected in 1857, and the report of the inspection by the Board of Education in 1860 gives us an interesting picture of this early Comprehensive school.

'The Industrial School contains 14 girls, who (for a certain payment) are clothed, fed and boarded by the school managers. These girls are engaged (according to a time-table) in the household work of the school, such as cleaning the premises, waiting at table, assisting in the bakehouse, where about 160 lbs of bread is baked weekly (being about one-half of the weekly consumption), and attending under a laundress to the entire washing for the institution and for the family at the Chantry.' This would account for the comparatively small accommodation at 'The Chantry' for domestic servants, considering the period of the house. Obviously the school was assumed to be an institution which would last for ever, supplying all sorts of domestic help as required. 'These 14 girls are supervised by one of the certificated teachers, and by her taught for a given time every evening in such matters as are deemed essential, e.g. geography, reading, writing and arithmetic.' This at any rate showed a greater sense of social conscience than the Gradgrind educational establishments of the period. The report concludes: 'It is impossible to visit the institution without feeling that no care and expense are spared in making the school efficient and the young persons happy.'[9]

The boarding school consisted of girls training for governesses and teachers. Its object, according to Kelly's *Directory* for 1875, was 'to bring within the reach of persons of limited income the benefits of a good education, including French, German, music, drawing, and such other accomplishments as are usually imparted in Schools of superior character'.

There is an amusing picture of Chantry school in that once popular, and now almost forgotten, novel *Comin' Thro' the Rye*, which was published in 1875. The author, Helen Mathers, was a pupil at the school, which is disguised as 'Charteris'. James Fussell VI appears as Mr Russell, 'tall, erect, a little grey, his dress showing but little of the clergyman about it (he is one of the committee, and owns "The Charteris", the only big house in the place. He is married, and has olive branches).' Mr Russell had instituted cricket at Charteris, 'and many a pretty young mother makes an excellent long-stop or field to her sons, thanks to the training she received at this school', and he is praised for having, for a time at least, emancipated the girls from the slavish thraldom of their petticoats; for cricket is played in 'bloomers', and the breathlessly excitable and romantically-minded heroine, Helen Adair, who has lost her head about Mr Russell at first sight—'how my heart leaps when I look at him'—takes part in a game of cricket which should be a classic piece of description in every sporting anthology. Mr Russell is playing amongst his protégées, bowling fast round-arm and batting with a determination and vigour that strike consternation into feminine souls, but after a glorious week he is gone—calling in at the ironworks, we must suppose, on his way back to the Ministry.

The 'olive branches' numbered three. James Fussell VII (1848–1927) remained a bachelor, was called to the Bar, and presumably took little part in the business; Mary Fussell, who died in 1921, was for many years headmistress of Chantry school; Sarah married the manager of the ironworks, a Welshman called Morgans, and died in childbirth in April 1887: she is buried with her infant son, Hamish Hwfa, by the south door of the chancel of Chantry church. During recent repairs to the church a number of deep pits were revealed beneath the chancel floor, clearly intended as a family vault for generations of Fussells yet to come—a vain hope, for by 1880 it must have been clear to James Fussell VI that there would be no more ironmasters.

At Nunney, meanwhile, another branch of the family was now established. The name of Fussell is not found in the Nunney registers before 1800, and the occupation of shear-grinder or shear-maker is not recorded before 1815. John Fussell I had set up business there by 1791, when his name appears as edge-tool maker of Nunney in the *Universal British Directory of Trade and Commerce*. He died in 1821 and was succeeded by his nephew Isaac Fussell (1778–1831). It was Isaac Fussell's business which was visited by Skinner in 1828, and on his death he was succeeded there by his brother John Fussell III, who is referred to in one of the Horner papers as 'having built at Nunney'. (This must refer to further alterations at the Court, which had already been rebuilt by Isaac.) He was settled at Nunney by 1833, when the baptism of his first child is recorded in the register. He had five children between 1833 and 1842, but all his three sons died in childhood. By then he was 59, and his wife, who was French, was 21 years younger than he was. Perhaps this series of bereavements drove them from Nunney, for when John Fussell died in 1853 at the age of 70, he is described in the Nunney register as 'of London, Mayfair, in the County of Middlesex'. One of his daughters, Maria Mary (1834–1881), is commemorated by a tablet in the crypt of St. Paul's Cathedral. She left £110,000 to the London Diocesan Home Mission, who between 1883 and 1903 created 32 new parishes. The tablet was erected by her lifelong friend, Sophia Crosland, and by supporters of the Mission.

In itself there is nothing very significant in this, but it shows that the Fussells' sphere of influence was moving away from Somerset, it gives some idea of the wealth of the family, and it underlines their devotion to the Church, which is apparent again and again throughout their story.

Because he had no son to succeed him, John Fussell III took into Nunney works a young cousin, with the intention of his having a share in the business; this was S. J. C. Skurray, his sister Elizabeth's grandson, who lived at Rosemount, Great Elm. Nothing, however, seems to have come of this introduction of new blood, and no mention of Skurray is to be found in the Daniel papers that cover the closing stages of the Nunney business.

Nunney Court was inherited by John Fussell III's nephews,

Rev. J. G. C. Fussell and Rev. J. T. R. Fussell, but shortly after-
wards it was sold to John Hounsell Fussell V, who lived there
until 1883. As we have seen, he was the eldest son of John Fussell
IV of Mells, and thus descended from the senior branch of the
Mells family. His only son died in infancy, and in 1883 he sold
Nunney Court to the Daniels of Frome, and retired to Beaminster
in Dorset. He died there in 1910 and is buried there with his wife.
Yet another branch of the family was extinct.

The oldest parts of Nunney Court date from the time of Queen
Anne, and some of the interior features, such as the recessed cup-
boards and the door handles, are from the same period, but the
house as a whole did not benefit from the additions by the Fussells
in the 1830s, nor by further additions in the 1930s. It is situated
high above the little river, which here flows through a narrow
combe, and to which a terraced garden and walks lead down. A
few hundred yards upstream are the romantic ruins of the Castle,
which actually belong to the Lord of the Manor, and below the
Court the stream was dammed to provide power for the ironworks. There is an almost undecipherable jumble of ruined buildings lying along the river; at what was once the manager's house
or office, one can still see the pay-hatch taking the place of one of
the windows, and everywhere in the gardens the walls are topped
with the remains of Fussells' worn-out grindstones, cut across
like Dutch cheeses or petrified half-moons.

The ruins of all the other works, like those at Nunney, lie at the
bottom of valleys, grouped about the streams on which they originally depended for their power; the Mendip streams, flowing
north and east into the river Frome, cut themselves deep gorges
which are generally wooded and picturesque, and one comes
across the ruined ironworks with some surprise. Chantry village
stands on a ridge, astride the old main road from Frome to Wells,
where it begins its long climb to the Beacon. On one side of the
road stands Chantry school, a large gaunt stone building, not
without dignity, yet strangely silent. It is used as a furniture store,
for inevitably, in as small a village as Chantry, the children are
now whisked away elsewhere to school. One wonders if Mary
Fussell's ghost revisits the empty schoolrooms. The low stone
wall which encloses the weed-grown playground is topped with
old grindstones, as at Nunney. Across the main road stand the
church and 'The Chantry', looking down on to the placid lake,

which one would assume to be a conventional landscape feature in the grounds of a late Georgian house, but a dried-up canal shows how the water supply was taken to the ironworks. Here, according to Tylee, grinding and plating were done, and there was a blast-furnace for casting their own iron tools, as well as a steel furnace. It seems almost incredible, as one stumbles about amongst undergrowth and brambles, amid fragments of masonry and large pits which are gradually being filled up with rubbish by the people who live in cottages on the site.

A little lower down the valley, Railford pond is marked on the map, a long narrow strip of blue water; but the dam gave way a few years ago, and the site is now a reedy swamp. Deep in the wood are the crumbling walls of the Railford works.

It is the same story in the valley below Mells: three times the little river is dammed up; and almost buried under the trees, especially in the summer, are the Upper and Lower works and the Great Elm works, where Tylee says 'they beat out the iron and split it, and put steel in the centre'. The most spectacular feature of all the ruins is the amazing amount of masonry which was erected: there are hundreds and hundreds of yards of solid stone-walling, controlling the flow of the streams and containing the sites of the workshops. The recent excavations at the Lower works revealed a complicated series of underground channels (like a complex London Tube junction) leading the water to the different levels required for various operations. Except for one range of buildings more or less complete, it is difficult to identify any of the buildings shown in the 1880 photographs, though some of the shells are impressive ruins still.

For the rest, there are derelict cottages crammed against the side of the valley on the way to Elm; there are the houses where the Fussells themselves lived in the villages round about; but there are no ironmasters today, except in the village churchyards. It is, indeed, amazing how completely the family has disappeared, though there are still Fussells in the neighbourhood who must derive from the same stock: how quickly, too, their work was obliterated, and their history forgotten, except where it survives in stone or iron.

Arthur Raistrick in his *Dynasty of Ironfounders*, which tells the story of the Darbys of Coalbrookdale, says that the first Abraham Darby 'is one of those tantalizing persons who from time to time emerge from an obscure background, and by their life and actions attain a position which commands the interest of succeeding generations'.[10] The same might be written of James Fussell III, though it would be idle to pretend that the significance of the Fussells was in any way comparable to that of the Darbys. Yet each, from humble beginnings, established a famous industry. In contrast to the social conscience of the Darbys, whose personal control and interest in their business never weakened, and who ploughed back into the business such profits as they made in good times and in bad, Raistrick describes another type of ironmaster. These 'had amassed fortunes and many of them built palatial mansions, gathered estates and dissipated their wealth in sport and high living, leaving behind them, in the place where the wealth was made, little but the ruins of a derelict industry'.[11] He is writing of the Midlands and south Wales in particular, but yet again the words might be written of the Fussells.

The story of the Fussells is one tiny facet of the Industrial Revolution, typical perhaps of the story of many small firms in many parts of England. A century ago Fussells of Mells was a household name both at home and abroad, and the trade name must have been a valuable asset to Isaac Nash. Yet few people today can be aware of the long history attached to the name, stretching back 200 years and more. The absence of records, and the unreliability of the only published material, have made it very hard to piece together the story; for even in their own villages the Fussells have become almost mythical figures. In parish registers, on page after page, one may read their names, generation after generation, in faded ink on yellowing paper: their graves are levelled out in the graveyards beside the churches where they worshipped; the houses which they built for themselves and their heirs have passed into alien hands; and the Mendip streams wash against the crumbling walls of their once noisy and prosperous factories.

In the summer, the beautiful gardens of Nunney Court are sometimes opened to the public. Among the advertised attractions on such occasions are 'Nunney Castle: fourteenth century' and 'Ruins of Fussells' ironworks'. Colonel Horner might well be surprised to find that the nuisance which he had fought for so long to extirpate should so comparatively soon have come to be regarded as a romantic attraction. The Fussells would already seem to have been absorbed into the pattern of English history.

THE FUSSELL FAMILY TREE

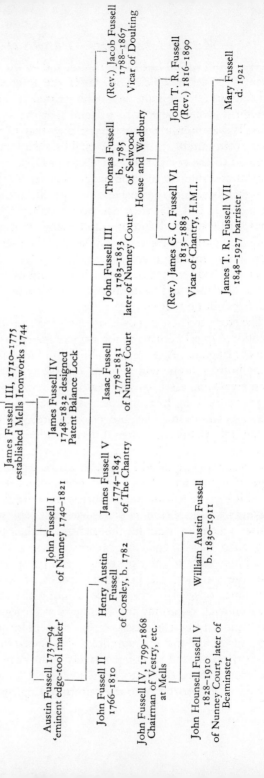

Thomas Fussell of Stoke Lane

James Fussell I, b. 1646

James Fussell II, b. 1677

James Fussell III, 1710–1775
established Mells Ironworks 1744

James Fussell IV
1748–1832 designed
Patent Balance Lock

John Fussell I 1740–1821
of Nunney

Austin Fussell 1737–94
'eminent edge-tool maker'

Henry Austin
Fussell
of Corsley, b. 1782

John Fussell II
1766–1810

John Fussell IV, 1799–1868
Chairman of Vestry, etc.
at Mells

William Austin Fussell
b. 1830–1911

John Hounsell Fussell V
1828–1910
of Nunney Court, later of
Beaminster

James Fussell V
1774–1845
of The Chantry

Isaac Fussell
1778–1831
of Nunney Court

John Fussell III
1783–1853
later of Nunney Court

Thomas Fussell
b. 1785
of Selwood
House and Wadbury

(Rev.) Jacob Fussell
1788–1867
Vicar of Doulting

(Rev.) James G. C. Fussell VI
1813–1883,
Vicar of Chantry, H.M.I.

John T. R. Fussell
(Rev.) 1816–1890

James T. R. Fussell VII
1848–1927 barrister

Mary Fussell
d. 1921

CHAPTER SEVEN

From the Beacon to Soho

(1)

All over the countryside
Moon-dazzled men are peering out for invaders.

C. DAY LEWIS: *Watching Post*

When James Fussell IV made his offer to supply the Government with 2,000 iron pikes weekly for as long as they might be wanted, his patriotic gesture epitomized the state of preparedness throughout the Westcountry against the threatened French invasion. The military preparations in the Mells area included the formation of the Frome and East Mendip Regiment of Volunteer Cavalry (founded as the Frome Selwood Volunteers in 1797, and from 1814 known as the North Somerset Yeomanry Cavalry). Colonel T. S. Horner was the first Colonel Commandant of the Regiment, two of whose troops were based on Mells.

The spirit of the local Volunteers is recalled by many of Hardy's pages, based on the traditions and memories of the French wars which were still current, forty years later, during his Wessex childhood: troops are concentrated, the local Volunteers drill, Buonaparte for a while supplants the reddleman as the formulated threat of Wessex mothers, and hope and fear and quiet courage walk abroad—the perennial emotions felt in the face of imminent invasion, whether it is to be launched by Philip of Spain, Napoleon or Hitler. The same emotions reappear in two of C. Day Lewis's poems written in the summer of 1940: *Watching Post* and *The Stand-to*.

> Among the stubble a farmer and I keep watch
> For whatever may come to injure our countryside—

95

Light-signals, parachutes, bombs, or sea-invaders.
The moon looks over the hill's shoulder, and hope
Mans the old ramparts of an English night.

Just so, for centuries it seems, on lonely Westcountry hill-tops,
'The dawn wind blew, the stars winked out on the posts' where
the watchers lay. It was certainly so at the Beacon, a few miles
west of the ironworks at Mells, on the edge of the parish of Stoke
Lane from which the Fussells had migrated two generations before Napoleon encamped on the cliffs at Boulogne.

From my desk, unless Mendip is shrouded in mist, I look straight
across to the Beacon on the skyline; for Beacon Hill is one of
the most conspicuous points on the long Mendip ridge. Its summit, 950 ft. above sea-level, now crowned with a clump of magnificent beeches, is a landmark, visible far away to north and south,
which has guided travellers since prehistoric times; for here the
ridge road running from Old Sarum to the Bristol Channel
crossed the Foss Way—indeed, looking south from the Beacon,
one can still see The Foss, beside a green lane, undulating down
off Mendip towards Ilchester, far out on the plain.

Collinson, writing in 1791, describes 'a very large stone which
serves as a sea-mark, being seen from a vast distance by mariners
navigating the coast'.[1] This is hardly credible, as it is 20 miles and
more to the nearest point on the coast in Bridgwater Bay, and the
landmarks listed in the Admiralty's *Sailing Directions for the West
Coast of England* are all within a mile or two of the shore: a conspicuous clump of trees on Bleadon Hill, for instance, Brent
Knoll, or the leaning tower of Burnham church; in fact Crook
Peak is the most inland point mentioned. Phelps, however, writing in 1836, notes that a clump of fir-trees [*sic*] now obscured
what was previously 'a point distinctly marked in the outline of
the hill'.[2] There was also a tumulus 12 ft. high, on which stood an
upright stone, a further 5 ft. high, of which only the stump now
remains. Barrows and earthworks in the immediate vicinity em-
phasize the prehistoric importance of the site, though recent
plantings of conifers by the Forestry Commission have obscured
the configuration of the ground, and in time even the eminence of
the beech clump may be challenged.

As a watching-post, the site was superior to most, Phelps observed: 'signals made on the coast of the Bristol or English
Channels could be repeated instantly and communicated into the

19. The Beacon from the Shepton Mallet–Bristol road

ABANDONED TURNPIKE ROADS
20. (*above*) The original Bristol–Bridgwater road near Churchill. 21. (*below*) A disused section of the Bristol–Wells road above Stoberry Gate, Wells

interior of the country'.[2] The old mining maps of Mendip which
date from the sixteenth and seventeenth centuries mark the beacon
site clearly. On the Chewton map the name Rybury occurs between Marsbury (Maesbury) and Asham. This name has now disappeared, but 'the topp of Ryebury' is referred to in the 1571 survey of the parish of Kilmersdon: 'Rye beacon uppon Mendip ys the
next beacon to this lordship three myles distant'.[3] The affirmation
that 'this lordshipps tenants did never any watch, nor to any other
beacon, nor Doe paye nor do anye things to ye mayntenaunce of
any beacon', reminds us of the defence measures that were in
operation throughout the reign of Elizabeth I until after the defeat of the Armada. At Crook Peak, for instance, the authorities of
the parish of Banwell maintained the beacon there in readiness for
many years before the Armada actually sailed. In 1580 the Churchwardens' accounts include the following item: 'Pd. the firste daye
of July for one load of Wood for the Beaken and for carrynge the
same to Croke peke 0–5–0.'[4]

In *The Trumpet Major*, and later in *The Dynasts*, Hardy gives a
vivid picture of the manning of the Dorset beacons against the
expected invasion by the French, 200 years later. Beacons were
erected on Badbury Rings and Rainbarrow, on Bulbarrow and
Dogbury, on Nettlecombe Tout and Blackdown—where the
monument to Nelson's Hardy now stands. The beacon-keepers
made themselves as comfortable as was possible on their lonely
hill-tops in huts of clods and turf, with brick chimneys for cook-
ing, and waited for Buonaparte. Hardy records that in 1903, when
he was writing *The Dynasts*, the remains of the hut on Rainbarrow
were still visible, consisting of some half-buried brickbats and a
little mound of peat overgrown with moss. At Dundry, in north
Somerset, looking across the Severn into Wales, on the western
summit of the hill in 'a most bleak, dreary and solitary situation',
Collinson saw 'one poor forsaken building' erected as a beacon-
house. Actually it was hardly more than a very primitive form of
shelter, constructed of two stones put slantwise for a covering,
with an arched doorway 3 ft. high, and a 'room' within, 5½ ft.
long and 5 ft. wide.[5]

At the time of the Armada, orders were issued that the Somerset
beacons were to be closely watched and warded, and that none
should be fired except by direct order of a Justice of the Peace.
There was a prescribed code of signals. When a beacon was fired

in a maritime county, the military force of the next inland county was to march towards a prearranged place. When the Bubb Down beacon to the south of Yeovil, for instance, was fired, the Somerset force was to proceed at once to Dorchester and wait for orders there. The firing of the beacons, in fact, was far more than merely a general alarm: it was the signal for a preconcerted series of troop movements. There was to be no disordered rush to the coast as had happened in previous false alarms. But when the Armada actually approached, its course was too far out at sea to be seen from the Dorset coast, and no beacons were fired there. The Hampshire beacons, however, were fired from the Isle of Wight, and a force of 3,000 Dorset men moved in to protect Portsmouth, being replaced by a similar number sent from Somerset.

The beacon-keepers in *The Dynasts* have similarly precise instructions. The old man, John Whiting, scolds young Jems Purchess for 'glowering and staring' at the wrong point: 'The words of my Lord-Lieutenant was, whenever you see Kingsbere-Hill Beacon fired to the eastward, or Black'on to the westward, light up; and keep your second fire burning for two hours. Was that our documents or was it not?'

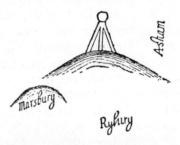

Rybury Beacon—detail from a
seventeenth-century map of Mendip

The 'second fire' is a reference to the two great ricks of fuel that stood on the beacon site ready for firing: one of heather and furze for a quick flame, the other of turf and wood for a long slow radiance. When the long-awaited signal came, it was only a moment's work to strike a flint and steel, ignite a wisp of dry furze and set the first stack of fuel in a blaze. On Dunkery, Collinson even noticed the ruins of several large fire-hearths, 8 ft. square, built of rough unwrought stones.[6]

From the Beacon to Soho

At Rybury, the Mendip mining maps represent the beacon itself by a tripod supporting a circular brazier; the same symbol appears for Westbury Beacon a few miles to the west, on the southern escarpment of Mendip.[7] It was probably the brazier or basket containing the signal fire that gave their name to many of the Galley or Gallows Hills in the southern and western counties. It is hard to believe that all these hills, many of them far away from any village or proper road, were really the sites of gallows or gibbets. It seems much more likely that the name derives from the Old English *a-gaelwan*, to alarm. With this connotation, the verb 'to gallow' was still current in 1600; in Kent's description of the storm (*King Lear*, III, ii, 42),

> the wrathful skies
> Gallow the very wanderers of the dark
> And make them keep their caves.

The word lingered in Hardy's Wessex, as when Jonathan Kail, describing to Tess and Angel Clare how 'poor little Retty Priddle hev tried to drown herself', tells how they have all 'been gallied at the dairy at what might ha' been a most terrible affliction'. Less obvious, but no less significant, are the widespread Westcountry dialect names for a scarecrow: 'gallibagger' and 'gallicrow'— whose function is to sound the alarm as surely as the signal fires that blazed from the beacons.

One wonders how far the beacon fires were visible, even in the best of weather conditions. From the top of Rybury on Mendip one looks out across broken hills and low-lying moors towards a ring of other beacon sites: Melbury and Lamyatt, Corton Denham and Bubb Down, Lewesdon and Cothelstone, and far to the west, where Dunkery rises from the great mass of Exmoor. At a glance one sees Rybury as a single link in a vast chain of communication, designed, as Collinson puts it, 'to alarm the country in times of civil discord or foreign invasion'. From Dunkery Collinson estimated that 15 counties could be seen, and that the horizon span was 500 miles, while the eye ranged from Plymouth to Malvern Beacon, a distance of more than 150 miles. But there could be no possibility of a signal carrying more than a fraction of such a distance; indeed, one remembers with some disappointment 'those twinkling points of light' emitted by the beacons lit on such occasions as V-E Day or Coronation Day: from an empty hill-top, on a dark night, there was no way of judging distances and picking up landmarks, and what one assumed to be a glowing beacon on a distant ridge turned out to be a bonfire on a neighbouring village green.

Macaulay's poem *The Spanish Armada* gives a dramatic description of how 'the ghostly war-flame spread' from the firing of the beacons 'along each southern shire', though with a good deal of poetic licence, for the Dorset beacons, as we have seen, were never actually fired at all. Even so, it is a splendid picture of how:

> O'er Longleat's towers, o'er Cranborne's oaks, the fiery
> herald flew;
> He roused the shepherds of Stonehenge, the rangers of
> Beaulieu . . .
> Till like volcanoes flared to heaven the stormy hills of
> Wales . . .
> Till twelve fair counties saw the blaze on Malvern's
> lonely height.

One gets a vivid impression of the whole of the English countryside ablaze with light, and if in actual fact 'the rugged miners poured to war from Mendip's sunless caves', they must surely have been roused from Rybury, where the beacon stood ready for firing, as Phelps says, on 'any occasion of alarm endangering the tranquillity and safety of the inhabitants'.

(2)

One night
Monmouth marched to his ruin out of that valley.

C. DAY LEWIS: *Watching Post*

Half-way between the Beacon and Mells lies the hamlet of Soho, in the parish of Leigh-on-Mendip—a mere handful of houses on the edge of a ridge that falls away to the north with a fine view of the broken foothills of the range. It was almost certainly this view which was responsible for the name of the hamlet, outlandish enough in the green Somerset countryside; for Soho was the Duke of Monmouth's password during his rebellion in the summer of 1685.

After the successful battle at Norton St. Philip on 27 June,

Monmouth marched to Frome. But instead of the expected rein-
forcements, bad news met him here; Feversham, commanding the
royal army, had already moved across his intended line of advance;
and on 30 June Monmouth turned west towards Shepton Mallet.
The retreat had begun, and in a week's time the campaign was to
reach its tragic climax on Sedgemoor.

During Monmouth's two days' stay at Frome, tradition relates
that parties of his men were stationed on Roddenbury Hill and
Marston Hill outside the town. It is possible that Soho may mark
the site of another of the chain of outposts, strung out along the
high ground to discover Feversham's intentions. Soho, standing
600 ft. up, where the ground falls away steeply to the valley of
what was then called the river Frome, affords a wide prospect to
the north and east. On the other hand, the name may simply mark
the flank of Monmouth's line of withdrawal, lying only about a
mile off the old ridge road from Frome to the Beacon.

Nearby, at Downhead, stood Monmouth's Oak, where the men
of Mendip joined him on his march to Bridgwater. These would
have been the lead-miners, of whom Evelyn wrote in his *Diary* on
8 July, when news reached London of Monmouth's utter defeat
on Sedgemoor: 'The slain were most of them *Mendip-miners* who
did great execution with their tools, and sold their lives very
dearly.' It was among the miners, too, that memories of Monmouth lingered. More than a century later Hannah and Martha
More found among the rough miners at the western end of Mendip a wild legend that King Monmouth was at hand who would
set right all wrongs.

Memories lingered, especially at places like Norton St. Philip,
where Monmouth's supporters paid the price of their treason.
There was the Norton song:

> The Duke of Monmouth is at Norton Town
> All a-fighting for the Crown—
> Soho! boys, Soho!

which survived until early in the last century. Macaulay had heard
of old Sedgemoor peasants who related that in their childhood
they were accustomed to play on the moor at the fight between
King James's men and King Monmouth's men, and that King
Monmouth's men always raised the cry of 'Soho'. In the years
that immediately followed the rebellion it is reasonable to assume

that the children's battle game was played as much on east Mendip as down on the moor.

The exact site of the Mendip rallying point is forgotten, though I have come across vague traditions of a very large tree that was cut down not so very long ago, within living memory. The 1817 map marks Downhead Tree, which suggests that it was a famous landmark 130 years after the Monmouth episode. Close by, on what was formerly Downhead Common, there is now a plantation significantly called Battlefields Wood. This in turn is less than a quarter of a mile from Cranmore Tower, the lofty Folly built in 1862 to command the wide rolling panorama to the south, from a viewpoint as commanding as Soho on the northern side of the ridge.

There are two more tangible relics in Wells. Built into the fabric of the new Blue School in Milton Lane are two free-stone slabs inscribed 'Soho'. These were removed from above a doorway which led from Chamberlain Street into the old Blue School and from the wall of the school building itself—the latter stone having originally been built into the old headmaster's house, which stood on roughly the same site, until its demolition in 1911. The house itself, which was purchased for the Blue School about 1820, was called 'Soho', perhaps commemorating Monmouth's lodging in the city or the encampment of part of his army, though evidence and tradition are both lacking on this point.

Monmouth took his password from the London property granted to him by his father. In 1681 he built himself a house on the south side of Soho Square (formerly King's Square); but he can have lived there only a comparatively short time before his banishment in December 1683 for complicity in the Rye-house plot.[8]

At that time, Soho—now redolent of Chinese restaurants and chop-houses in the little network of crowded streets at the heart of the West End—was a centre of fashionable life: was not Sir Roger de Coverley's town house in Soho Square? Long before Soho Square or the Duke of Monmouth were heard of, the locality was known as Soho Fields. Where Soho Square now stands, the Mayor and Corporation of London once hunted the hare, and 'soho' was the cry of the Berners or huntsmen. The area known as Soho in Birmingham likewise stands on what used to be Birmingham Heath, once frequented by sportsmen whose hunting cry is commemorated in the name. For 'soho' is a far older cry than 'tally-ho', which is not found in any of the sporting writers until the eighteenth century. Edward Allde wrote in *The Book of Hawking, Huntyng, etc.* (1586):

> All maner of beastes whatsoever chased be,
> Have one maner of woord soho I tell thee.
> To fulfill or unfill all maner of chase,
> The hunter in his mouth that word hase.

But it was used specifically as a term of encouragement when picking up a line. Greswell, in *The Forests and Deer Parks of the County of Somerset*, describes how a west Somerset rustic catching sight of a hare would walk straight ahead, intimating the fact to his companions by saying, 'See-ho!'

At Soho on Mendip there is only one house old enough to have witnessed the events of Monmouth's rebellion. It is a long low farmhouse, and until a few years ago it boasted a hooded doorway and mullioned windows, similar in style to several of the houses in the neighbouring village of Leigh-on-Mendip which bear dates from the latter part of the seventeenth century. Recently, however, the main part of the house was completely rebuilt, except for a small section at one end which still retains one of the mullioned windows. From this window watchers may have looked out anxiously at the marches and countermarches of those stormy days of June 1685, or at sentinels whose password gave the little hamlet its name.

CHAPTER EIGHT

The Mendip Turnpike Roads

Nothing so much contributes to the improvement of a
county as good roads; before the establishment of turnpikes, many parts of this county were scarcely accessible.

JOHN BILLINGSLEY:
Agricultural Survey of Somerset 1798

One of the half a dozen houses at Soho is a turnpike cottage. The road through Soho to Coleford was taken in
hand by the Frome Turnpike Trust in 1796–7. In the
Somerset Record Office there is a map of the roads belonging to
the Trust about 1815, and near Soho there is a pencilled note:
'Here is the bar (i.e. the toll-bar) thrown down by river.' This
suggests that the original turnpike gate at the bottom of the hill
had not been able to survive the attentions of the Coleford miners
and for safety's sake had been re-sited at Soho. The miners were
the section of the community most resentful of the tolls imposed
upon the users of the new system of roads, though the appalling
state of many of them in the Mendip area was directly due to
traffic to and from the coal-pits, and the miners stood to gain most
by the improvements. Billingsley put the situation clearly enough:
'Before the turnpike-roads were established, coal was carried on
horses' backs to the distance of fifteen or twenty miles from the
collieries; each horse carried about two hundred and a half weight.
Now one horse, with a light cart, will draw ten hundred weight,
or four times more than the horse could carry: Can an insignificant
toll be put in competition with this saving?'

By 1800 the main network of Mendip turnpike roads was complete, though there were still a number of extensions and improvements to be made: in fact a close examination of the 1817 map reveals many deviations from the line of the roads which we use today, and a search for the old line is often an absorbing pastime. A

slight dip in a field, visible only in certain lights or when the field
is freshly ploughed, an apparently meaningless stretch of double
hedge, or a bank in the middle of a field, containing the stumps of
what were once hedgerow trees—any of these may mark the line
of what was formerly an arterial road. It is important to realize
that ours is not the only age to tackle the problem of the roads: the
turnpike trusts and their surveyors were just as eager to make the
crooked straight and the steep places plain. It was they who
planned the first by-passes or who drove a new road across virgin
fields. The magnificently engineered A.36 from Warminster to
Bath simply does not exist, north of Woolverton, on the 1817
map: it was planned in 1833 by the Black Dog (Warminster and
Frome) Trust, to avoid the breakneck gradients of the climb over
Claverton Down past the Brass Knocker, or over Odd Down and
down the Holloway to the Old Bridge: instead, the new road
sweeps along the Avon valley past Limpley Stoke and Bathamp-
ton, beside the Kennet & Avon Canal, as far as the corner of
Sydney Gardens. In the same year 1833, a group of Bristol citizens
held a meeting 'to take into consideration the expediency of pro-
moting the formation of a rail road from Bristol to London'. The
birthday of the GWR, which saw the arrival of what John
Loudon McAdam called 'the calamity of railways', was also the
beginning of the end for the turnpike roads of the Westcountry.

The first Turnpike Trust in England was established by an Act
of 1663 at Ware in Hertfordshire. Between 1700 and 1750, four
hundred road Acts were passed; between 1751 and 1800, no fewer
than sixteen hundred. Throughout the country, bodies of Trustees were busily erecting gates and toll-bars, and collecting the
tolls from the actual users of the roads in return for repairing and
maintaining the specific stretches of highway under their jurisdiction. By 1840 there were 22,000 miles of good turnpike roads in
England with nearly 8,000 toll gates and side bars.[1] The by-roads
remained in the care of the parish until 1835, but at the beginning
of the nineteenth century England was criss-crossed by a network
of main roads at last comparable to those which the Romans had
left behind them 1,400 years before.

The first Trust to be established in north Somerset was the
Bath Trust in 1707-8; Bristol followed suit with Acts in 1727 and
1731, amended in 1747-9, the earlier Acts having achieved nothing in the face of the determined opposition of colliers and

farmers. In mid-century a further group of Trusts was established: Shepton Mallet and Wells in 1753, Bruton in 1756 and Frome in 1757. The Buckland Dinham Trust (later known as the Radstock Trust) was established in 1768, and the West Harptree Trust in 1793. There were four others which impinged upon the periphery of the Mendip turnpike system: the Warminster and Frome Trust (1752)—later known as the Black Dog Trust from the coaching inn on the Warminster–Bath road where the meetings were held— the Langport, Somerton, Castle Cary Trust (1753), the Wedmore Trust (1827), and the Wells and Highbridge Trust (1841). Most of these continued to operate until the 1870s, except for Bristol, which was wound up in 1867, and Wells, which lasted until 1883.

In the widest terms we are therefore concerned with the Mendip roads from 1707 to 1883, but for practical purposes the limits can be narrowed to the period between the 1750s, when the three main Mendip Trusts were set up, and the 1850s, when the railway began to reach the area. Thereafter there would be no further additions to the system of roads; in fact it was inevitably a period of retrenchment, while the Trusts faced decline and ultimate dissolution. The peak years were 1820–30, the last decade before the impact of the railway began to make itself felt in the Westcountry, and the figures for the mileage controlled and for the income and expenditure are quoted from the returns made in this period (see the table on p. 119). It is necessary to consider each Trust in turn, in so far as it impinged upon Mendip, and to give some idea of what still remains to be seen by the curious traveller.

(1) BRISTOL

By 1799 the Bristol Trust was the most extensive road authority in England, maintaining 148 m. of road in Somerset and Gloucestershire: this had increased by 1825 to 172 m. of which 69 m. were in Somerset, and brought in an annual income of £21,766 in 1831. Three Bristol roads reached south to Mendip. The most important, then as now, was the Bridgwater road (A.38), emerging from Bristol through Bedminster Gate, across Bedminster Down and Broadfield Down, still unenclosed, and over Red Hill into the Yeo valley. Churchill Gate guarded the approach to the gap in the hills through which the road to the west finds its way. The original gate was sited farther west, towards the village of

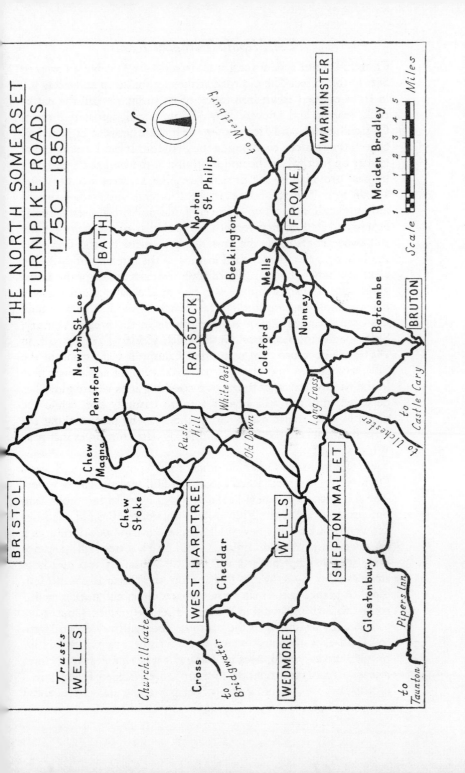

THE NORTH SOMERSET
TURNPIKE ROADS
1750 - 1850

N

Trusts
WELLS

BRISTOL

BATH

WARMINSTER

FROME

BRUTON

RADSTOCK

WEST HARPTREE

WELLS

WEDMORE

SHEPTON MALLET

to Westbury

Norton St. Philip

Beckington

Mells

Nunney

Batcombe

Maiden Bradley

Coleford

White Post

Long Cross

to Castle Cary

to Ilchester

Newton St. Loe

Pensford

Chew Magna

Chew Stoke

Rush Hill

Old Down

Cheddar

Glastonbury

Pipers Inn

Churchill Gate

Cross

to Bridgwater

to Taunton

Scale
1 0 1 2 3 4 5
Miles

Churchill, until a new road was driven past Dolebury Camp to Star in the 1820s. The old road strikes up the steep and stony hill in front of the Crown Inn: much of its surface is still the native rock, scarred and uneven; it winds, unfenced, across the top of Churchill Batch, and drops down the hillside between high hedges to join the modern road beside the Star Inn. It can be explored at leisure on foot, while the holiday traffic to the west roars past on a by-pass provided by the Bristol Turnpike Trustees a century and a half ago. The toll-house at the Churchill cross-roads was a famous landmark, a two-storeyed building with its semicircular façade and its Regency veranda, very similar to the Ashton Gate toll-house controlling the entrance to Bristol on the Clevedon road. It was, alas, demolished in 1961 in the interests of visibility, at a point where two streams of traffic intersect. One of the actual gates with its original posts survives as the gate of a drive to a private house at Langford. In fact much of the Bridgwater road has been changed out of all recognition in the present century: Sidcot Gate and Compton Gate (which yielded £788 13s. 4d. in 1831), are no more than memories. Compton Gate stood in the village of Cross where the old road makes a right-angle turn: here in the narrow street, with the two coaching inns whose glory has departed, one can still savour a more leisurely age, while the north-to-west traffic passes along the 1927 by-pass, making for East Brent, where the Bristol and Bridgwater turnpikes met near White Cross.

On Bedminster Down another road split off, soared over Dundry and dropped down Limeburn Hill into the Chew valley. The toll cottage at Chew Stoke survives close to the Stoke Inn, but on the way to the Blue Bowl a section of the old road lies drowned under the Chew Valley lake, emerging forlornly as a causeway in years of drought. And so up Harptree Hill—and nobody who has not pushed a bicycle up it has any real idea how steep a hill it is—to Wells Way Inn on 'the North Brow of Mendipp'. A glance at the map shows what a direct and untrammelled route this is from Bristol to Wells, and yet the gradients must have told heavily against it in the turnpike age: half-way down Harptree Hill is a milepost which says 'Bristol 11', which always puzzled me as a child, because I knew it was 14 miles from Harptree to Bristol, and nobody in their senses tackled Dundry in a motor-car in 1918. Now the wheel has come full circle, and I deliberately choose this approach to Bristol. Perhaps the Bristol Trustees expected a certain amount of traffic from the lead mines on Mendip, but in 1831 Chew Stoke Gate took only £134 4s. 3d. The road strides on past the Castle of Comfort, the Miners' Arms and the Hunters' Lodge, and drops down Rookham to enter Wells as the old Bristol Road—but it was never turnpiked by the Wells Trust.

The third southbound Bristol road is the orthodox route to Wells (A.37): the gates at Knowle and Whitchurch have disappeared, but the toll-house near Chelwood bridge survives, and the road met the Wells Trust at the top of Rush Hill. (Later in 1778–9 the Bristol Trust's jurisdiction came to an end at White Cross, Hallatrow, where the Bath Trust took over; a short-lived turnpike gate was established at White Cross from 1818 to 1839, and the toll-house is still standing.) Some interesting deviations from the present road can be seen at several points—noticeably at Hursley Hill, south of Whitchurch, and at Pensford, where the old road cuts the new at right angles and climbs steeply past the old village lock-up, presenting to the motorist's view the backs of the houses on what was once the main street.

(2) BATH

The Bath Trust maintained 51 lucrative miles of road, from which their income in 1820 was £11,870. These are shown in a series of very beautiful large-scale folding maps, now in the Somerset Record Office, drawn by C. Harcourt Masters, the Bath architect and surveyor in 1787, and showing every detail of the roads, and every building and enclosure abutting on them, with minuscule representations of the gates included for good value.

There were two routes to Wells. The Lower Wells Road (A.39), with gates at Newbridge (where the toll-house was recently demolished) and near Marksbury, met the Bristol Trust at White Post, Hallatrow, and the Wells Trust at the top of Rush Hill. The Upper Wells Road (A.367) climbed over Odd Down and through Radstock to meet the Wells Trust at the White Post, a mile north of Stratton-on-the-Fosse. The toll-house at Peasedown Red Post still stands. This road follows the line of the Foss Way, and, with its continuation to Wells, is of such historic interest, and contains so many interesting features, that it deserves fuller treatment on

its own (see Chapter Ten). The inhabitants of Wells never seem to
have been quite sure which was the best way to Bath. In 1719
Claver Morris went by Paulton, and was five hours on his
journey;[2]* the map in the 1798 edition of Billingsley only marks
the road by Chewton Mendip and Marksbury, but the mail
coaches came through Radstock; even today the motorist leaving
Wells is confronted, at the bottom of New Street, with road-
signs directing him to Bath or, alternatively, to Bath via Radstock.

(3) WELLS

The Wells Trust maintained 44 m. of road in 1820: their original
jurisdiction extended about 10 m. north and south, meeting the
Bristol and Bath Trusts at Rush Hill and at White Post, and ex-
tending through Glastonbury and Street to Piper's Inn, where the
Bridgwater and Taunton roads divide. Later, the road to Shepton
Mallet was taken over: this was not the modern road through
Croscombe and up the beautiful valley full of sewage works, for
there was no road up this valley until the 1850s. Instead the turnpike climbed steeply up Church Hill (Critchill) near Dinder and
joined the Glastonbury road just outside Shepton. Another road
taken over was that from Dulcote through North Wootton to
Steanbow, between Shepton Mallet and Glastonbury. The importance of this road is not obvious at first glance: its antiquity is
suggested by the wayside cross at Worminster and by the position
of the Queen's Head Inn at North Wootton. Its continuation
southward from Steanbow is also significant, climbing straight
over the ridge of Pennard Hill, and dropping down through
Parbrook on to the Foss Way near Lydford. The section over Pennard Hill is uncoloured on the sixth series Ordnance Survey one-
inch; but, duly coloured on the seventh series, it catches the eye
as obviously as it does on the first edition of 1817, as a through
road to Wells from the south-east of the county, and it must have
carried a fair amount of traffic, bearing in mind that Wells was an
Assize town as well as a Cathedral city. The London road was also
turnpiked past Masbury 'to the Beacon on the Forest of Mendip
where the Frome road ends'.

Five of the Wells toll-houses survive, and beautifully lettered

* Ogilby's *Britannia* (1675), Moll's Map of Somerset (1724), and Bowen's Map of
Somerset (1756), all show this as the main route from Bath to Wells.

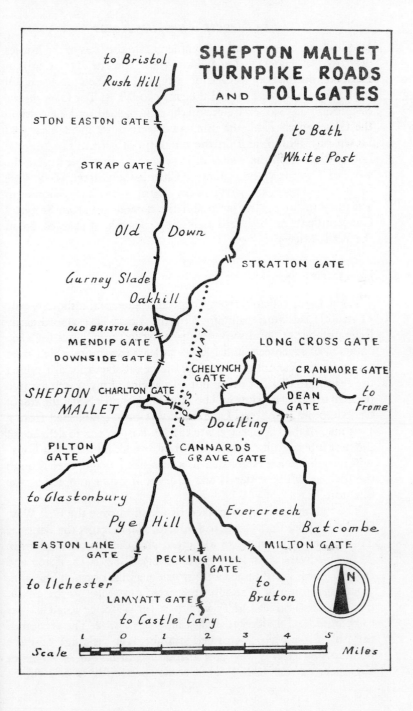

plaques have been erected to commemorate the sites of the houses destroyed at Hawkers Lane, East Wells (on the Bath road), at Hartlake, on the way to Glastonbury, and on Chewton Plain. Of the survivors, three guarded the entry to Wells: Tor Gate on the Shepton Road, Stoberry Gate on the Bristol road, and Keward on the Glastonbury road; the other two were outer gates, near Old Down on Mendip, and on the outskirts of Street. The original houses erected on these sites in 1753 cost £30 each, and were the work of Thomas Parfitt, joiner, of Chamberlain Street, Wells. One of the actual gates still survives on a farm at Bleadney, another in a factory in Street; the lamp and the nameboard from Stoberry Gate, and part of the board exhibiting the scale of charges, are in the Wells Museum.

(4) SHEPTON MALLET

Eight roads radiated from Shepton Mallet, and although only 51 m. of road were maintained by the Trust, an extraordinarily large number of gates were set up: a list in the minutes for 1800 enumerates seventeen, and I know at least two more which were set up later. I cannot pretend that I have satisfactorily discovered the exact sites of all of them, but an account of my search for two particularly elusive gates will be found in Chapter Nine; the site of Chilcompton *alias* Strap Lane Gate was only established from a 1775 map of the Hippisley estate at Ston Easton, and in defiance of the best informed local opinion; while at Oakhill there is a house which tradition has established as a turnpike cottage, even though the road on which it stands was never at any time adopted by the Shepton Trust.

The two main roads turnpiked by Shepton were the Foss Way, from the White Post nearly to Lydford, where it met the Ilchester Trust seven miles short of Ilchester; and the Bristol road from Rush Hill to the Ansford Inn near Castle Cary (A.37, A.367 and A.371). These roads joined at Downside, a mile north of Shepton, wound laboriously through the narrow streets of the town, through Cowl Street and Town Street, for Waterloo Road had yet to be built, and divided again at Cannard's Grave. The section of the Bristol road which stormed straight over the ridge near the Mendip golf course was later abandoned in favour of an easier alignment nearer Oakhill, while some spectacular reverse curves

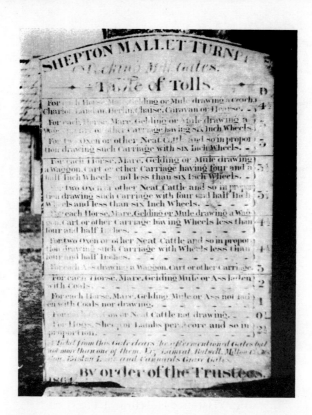

22. (*above*) Toll-board dated 1864, from Pecking Mill Gate near Evercreech. 23. (*below*) The gate from the Churchill turnpike, removed in 1866 and now restored to use at Langford

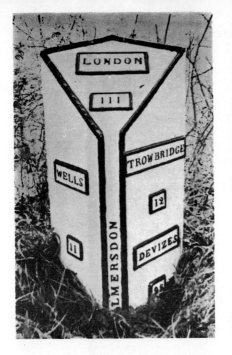

MILE-POSTS

24. (*above, left*) Kilmersdon (Radstock Trust). 25. (*above, right*) White Post (Bath Trust). 26. (*below, left*) Nettlebridge (Shepton Mallet Trust). 27. (*below, right*) Harptree Hill (Bristol Trust)

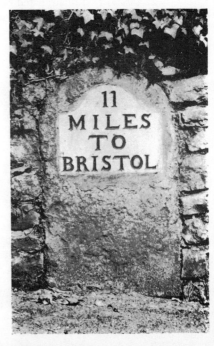

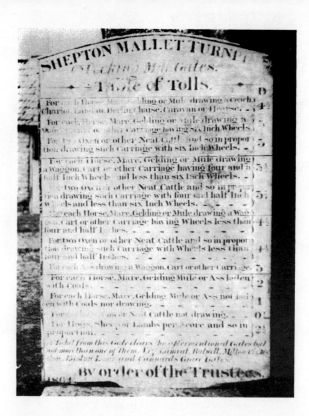

SHEPTON MALLET TURNPIKE

Pecking Mill Gates.

Table of Tolls.

For each Horse, Mare, Gelding or Mule drawing a Coach, Chariot, Landau, Berlin, Chaise, Caravan or Hearse.

For each Horse, Mare, Gelding or Mule drawing a Waggon, Cart or other Carriage having six Inch Wheels.

For two Oxen or other Neat Cattle, and so in proportion drawing such Carriage with six Inch Wheels.

For each Horse, Mare, Gelding or Mule drawing a Waggon, Cart or other Carriage having four and a half Inch Wheels and less than six Inch Wheels.

For two Oxen or other Neat Cattle and so in proportion drawing such Carriage with four and half Inch Wheels and less than six Inch Wheels.

For each Horse, Mare, Gelding or Mule drawing a Waggon, Cart or other Carriage having Wheels less than four and half Inches.

For two Oxen or other Neat Cattle and so in proportion drawing such Carriage with Wheels less than four and half Inches.

For each Ass drawing a Waggon, Cart or other Carriage.

For each Horse, Mare, Gelding Mule or Ass laden with Coals.

For each Horse, Mare, Gelding, Mule or Ass not laden with Coals nor drawing.

For each Ox, Cow or Neat Cattle not drawing.

For Hogs, Sheep or Lambs per Score and so in proportion.

A ticket from this Gate clears the aftermentioned Gates but not more than one of them viz., Cannard, Babwell, Milton &c. Ston, Bristol Lane and Cannards Grave Gates.

BY ORDER OF THE TRUSTEES.

1864

22. (*above*) Toll-board dated 1864, from Pecking Mill Gate near Evercreech. 23. (*below*) The gate from the Churchill turnpike, removed in 1866 and now restored to use at Langford

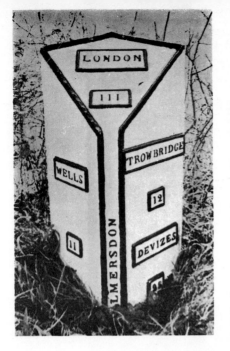

MILE-POSTS

24. (*above, left*) Kilmersdon (Radstock Trust). 25. (*above, right*) White Post (Bath Trust). 26. (*below, left*) Nettlebridge (Shepton Mallet Trust). 27. (*below, right*) Harptree Hill (Bristol Trust)

solved the problem of the deep Nettlebridge valley on the Foss Way. Here too, until 1962, was one of the two surviving Shepton toll-houses—apart from the group to be described in Chapter Nine: a little low building on the long hill up out of Nettlebridge, it stood empty and forlorn for some years until finally demolished in the interests of public safety. Better, perhaps, a neatly cleared site than another of the ruinous eyesores that pathetically litter the Mendip countryside; all the same it is sad that the bulldozer can sweep away in a morning a piece of history like a toll-house which had occupied its site, perhaps since 1780. I had never bothered to photograph it, *mea culpa*, and now a faded postcard dating from the 1920s, and retrieved for me by a friend in the village, is probably the only surviving record of the appearance of Stratton Gate. The other outlying Shepton toll-house is at the top of Pye Hill on the Foss Way, three miles to the south of the town. Towards Frome the Trust operated as far as Leighton (A.361), where it met the Bruton Trust; while from Doulting a road ran up on to the Mendip ridge at Long Cross to meet the road from Frome to the Beacon. From Long Cross another Shepton road struck south through West Cranmore to Batcombe—very much a by-road, but boasting a good set of mileposts.

Two interesting relics are the boundary stone of the Shepton and Ilchester Trusts, which stands by the side of the Foss Way near Lydford Park, replacing the Red Post mentioned in the original Act of 1753; and the recently discovered toll-board from Pecking Mill Gate.

(5) FROME

The Frome network of roads totalled 43 m., reaching out in every direction except towards Bath, where the Black Dog Trust maintained the road from Beckington. The roads to Westbury, Warminster and Maiden Bradley were turnpiked between 1756 and 1772, with various minor extensions, including one to the Horse and Jockey at East Woodlands, where the gate controlled traffic approaching from the direction of Longleat. In the Mendip direction the main road stretched westwards through Whatley and Little Elm, climbing slowly past 'the Public House on Mendip called Tattle House' (now Tadhill), and past Long Cross, to meet the Wells road at the Beacon. Although unclassified, this is a magnificent road for motoring, with wide views on both sides and very little traffic: the crumbling remains of the Tadhill toll-house can still be seen. Roads branched off to Mells and to Coleford through Soho; and there were also short stretches of turnpike road to Nunney and to Buckland Dinham, with a gate at Coal Lane near Murtry to intercept the traffic from the Radstock pits. The large map of the Frome roads in the Somerset Record Office, which dates from about 1815, shows no fewer than fourteen gates: the sites of all these, and of various others erected at different times, have been identified and recorded by the Frome Society.

There was clearly very heavy traffic in the district, for the woollen industry flourished until about 1820, and it must be remembered that Frome was still the second largest town in Somerset. Several of the toll-houses survive: at Soho and Coal Lane, for instance, at Cottle's Oak (now a shop) and at Critchill (on the Nunney road). Another group suggests that at one stage the Frome Trust may have had a standard design, for the toll-houses at East Woodlands and at West Woodlands (Bull's Bridge) are very similar to the now demolished house at Styles Hill, at the junction of the Warminster and Westbury roads just outside Frome: in each case a gabled porch juts out from a projecting wing of the house, as it were to survey the road and halt the traffic. Frome's unique relics of the turnpike era, however, are a pair of cast-iron plates marking the turnpike and parish boundaries: these are to be seen, one in Bridge Street, opposite the main entrance to the Market Yard, on what was the original main road out of Frome to the north, and the other in Christ Church Street East, at the foot of Stokes Croft, opposite the site of yet another vanished toll-house.

(6) BUCKLAND DINHAM (RADSTOCK from 1830)

The Buckland Trust was established in 1768, five years after the discovery of coal at Radstock: it is not easy to see why a small independent Trust—only 19 m. of road were maintained—should have been set up so close to Frome. Perhaps the Trustees were shrewd enough to realize the increased traffic that must flow from the mines to the Frome area. The project for the Dorset & Somerset Canal in the 1790s came to nothing, the railway did not reach

Radstock from Frome until 1854, so that all the coal must have been moved along the turnpike roads. In 1817 it was noted that the dilapidation of the fine old fifteenth-century bridge at Murtry was being accelerated by the passage of about forty coal waggons a day from the pits. The two main roads turnpiked were from Radstock to Buckland (A.362), meeting the Frome road at Murtry; and from the White Post through Kilmersdon to Norton St. Philip (B.3139 and A.366), forming a link in the route from Wells to Trowbridge, and giving an outlet through Devizes to the London road at Beckhampton.

Several other short stretches in the Radstock-Kilmersdon area were turnpiked, and attempts were made to extend in the Bristol direction as far as Timsbury and Hallatrow; these came to nothing, and as motorists know to their cost, there is still no good direct route to Bristol from the Radstock district. This is in marked contrast with the enterprise of the Black Dog Trust in driving their new road from Woolverton to Bath in 1833.

The toll cottage at Tucker's Grave on the road to Norton St. Philip is still to be seen; and a delightful little specimen stands at the western entrance to the village of Kilmersdon on the road from White Post. Originally at the top of the hill, it was moved when the new road was made here about 1830, the line of the old road still being visible as a narrow winding gash in the adjoining field; a number of deviations were also necessary to the east of the village, first when Ammerdown Park was enlarged in 1843, and again when the railway came. Some of this work may have been done under the aegis of the Jolliffes, but it does give a very clear idea of what the Trustees of a small Turnpike Trust could do to improve the roads of their immediate locality. In 1820 the income of the Buckland Trust was £1,265, about half the Wells Trust's income, and a third of Frome's.

(7) WEST HARPTREE

The hexagonal toll-house at Stanton Drew must be one of the best known and most photographed buildings in north Somerset. I passed it regularly for many years on the road to Bristol, and when I began to study the turnpike system, I naturally assumed that it was one of the outer Bristol toll-houses. I have known the Harptrees intimately for many years, and yet none of my friends there ever seem to have heard of the West Harptree Trust, which maintained 27 m. of road, linking up with the Bristol, Bath, and Wells Trusts at various points. Their main road ran from Fore Cross, more familiar to us as Churchill Gate on A.38, through Blagdon and West Harptree, crossing the Bristol–Wells road at Chelwood Bridge and joining the Bath Trust road at Marksbury (now A.368, which carries the holiday traffic from Bath to Weston-super-Mare). Off this, roads branched to reach Chew Magna and Pensford (hence the toll-house at Stanton Drew), and through Chewton Mendip to Emborough on the Bath–Wells road near Old Down (B.3114).

The last West Harptree road included under the Act of 1793 is something of a puzzle: it is the one-and-a-half-mile stretch from Nine Elms, North Widcombe, across Widcombe Common to Coley. It puzzles me because I lived beside this road for nine years, and anything less like a turnpike road it is hard to conceive. It threads three scattered hamlets, serves no villages, feeds no major road: it saves perhaps a mile, *if* one were cutting across country from, say, Chew Magna to Chewton Mendip. Today it is all that a country lane should be, undulating across a common with a duck-pond and a large farm on it, winding between elm-studded hedges with a wide grass verge, and finally meandering so sinuously that any speed above 20 m.p.h. seems desperately suicidal, until it humps over the infant Chew at the site of Coley Mill, and then climbs a long deep cutting in which two vehicles can barely pass, to join the Chewton Mendip road. Perhaps the Mill provides the answer: a Jolly Miller, or the Miller's Daughter? Or was there some forgotten traffic to be catered for? Or did one of the Trustees bring his influence to bear—for Skinner comments bitterly on some of the Bath Turnpike Commissioners who 'seem openly advocating their private interests, under the specious name of consulting for the public good'.[3]

I have produced and pondered this problem, because we have here an example of the work of a small unit in the overall picture of the Mendip road system. The 1820 returns show the Trust's average income over the previous three years to have been £401 8s. 5d. and their expenditure £180 16s. 5½d. Among the original Trustees were a surprising number of important land-owners—Bampfylde of Hardington, Hippisley Coxe, Hippisley, Horner, Jolliffe and Tooker of Chilcompton—some of them living

well outside the area of the Trust's operations. It is good to be
made aware of the public responsibilities shouldered by such
people for the benefit of the community, and also to realize that
there was probably a great deal of movement about the countryside, 150 years ago, by means of roads that have either fallen completely into disuse or lost their original function. Why was this
road ever made? and what is its real function today? are questions
we must frequently stop and ask ourselves, if we are to understand
the pattern of roads in any particular vicinity. Comparison between a modern map and the 1817 map shows that the West
Harptree Trust must have been responsible for tidying up a messy
network of lanes near Stowey: this may have resulted from the
development of coal-mining at Bishop Sutton and Bromley and
the consequent need for better roads. At any rate there was a
turnpike gate near Bromley Colliery, though the toll-house has
now disappeared: houses in West Harptree and Chew Magna have
been pointed out to me as turnpike cottages, but if the Trust built
any specific toll-houses I have so far found no clue as to their
whereabouts. None is marked on Greenwood or on the 1817
Ordnance Survey (Cp. Note on p. 130).

(8) OTHER TRUSTS

Several other Trusts linked up with the Mendip road system.
BRUTON, a large Trust with 66 m. of turnpike road, thrust up
from the south: it met the Shepton Trust at several points south
and east of Evercreech, and one of its roads actually reached
through the Frome Trust's territory by way of Nunney, Whatley
and Mells, to meet the Radstock Trust at Babington. The original
turnpike road from Bruton to Frome was not the present main
road through Wanstrow and Nunney (A.359), but an exciting
switchback road over steep hills to Batcombe, where it passed in
front of the Three Horse Shoes Inn and struck straight up Walter's
Hill, now merely a rutted farm track; from here a narrow lane
winds on to Leighton, where the toll cottage still survives at the
junction with the Shepton Trust's road (A.361); before Frome,
there were gates at Hartgill (near Holwell), Nunney Catch and
Marston. Except beyond Leighton, it could hardly look less like a
turnpike road, but it provides two notable relics: the fourth milestone from Bruton, buried in the undergrowth of the hedge on the

steep climb northwards out of Batcombe; and the toll-board from the old Batcombe Gate at Hedgestocks.

The BLACK DOG (Warminster and Frome) Trust operated mainly to the north and east of Frome: their great achievement, today's A.36, has been mentioned before. They maintained the Frome–Beckington Road (A.361), with a gate at the top of North Parade in Frome; a delightful little toll-house set up by them still stands near Shawford Bridge on the road to Bath, and there was another at Woolverton.

At the opposite end of Mendip, the WEDMORE Trust puts in a surprisingly late appearance. I had always assumed the beautiful little toll-house at Shipham to be a side-gate to the Bristol-Bridgwater road. But in 1827 the Wedmore Trust had turnpiked one single road, and a remarkable road at that, starting at Pedwell between Glastonbury and Taunton, climbing over the Poldens at Shapwick, crossing the Brue at Westhay, where the toll-house survives, and so to Wedmore: northwards again across the Axe and the Yeo at Clewer where the toll-house still stands and Hythe, once little ports on their sluggish moorland rivers, by-passing Cheddar on the west, and striking up through Callow Rocks to Shipham, to reach the Bridgwater road only a mile from Churchill Gate. A remarkable road, because it is quite independent of any other turnpike road, and must have served to open up an entirely new piece of countryside, supplying a direct route to Bristol instead of the circuitous road through Glastonbury and Wells with the wearisome climb over Mendip. It looks as if the central moorlands were being developed, as envisaged in the drainage schemes outlined in Billingsley's *Survey*. The flow of the Axe had been controlled by the building of the floodgates at Bleadon in 1802, the course of the river was straightened, everywhere on the moors new drains were being cut, and new possibilities were emerging for the waterlogged levels. The building of the Glastonbury Canal (1827–1833) suggests that real headway was being made, and a glance at the 1817 map shows what a vital artery the Wedmore turnpike road was to form, in a piece of country where hitherto there simply had not been any south-to-north road whatsoever.

The WELLS and HIGHBRIDGE Trust was a separate foundation from the Wells Trust: it was established in 1841, even later than the Wedmore Trust, but was very successful, winding

The Mendip Turnpike Roads

up free of debt in 1870. It maintained 21 m. of road, from Wells to Highbridge and from Wells to Cheddar, the two roads joining at Portway Elm, one mile west of Wells, still a well-known local landmark. The existence of this Trust is another indication of the prosperity that followed the draining and the development of the moors, while the main road from Wells must have been a profitable feeder connecting with the Bristol & Exeter Railway which reached Highbridge in 1841.

THE TURNPIKE TRUSTS OF NORTH SOMERSET

Trust	Date of the Original Act	Termination	Road maintained (miles)	Average annual income for 3 previous years (as given in returns made under the Act of 1820) £
Bath	1707/8	1878	51	£11,870
Bristol	1727	1867	172*	£21,766*
Black Dog (Warminster and Frome)	1752	1879	19**	£3,219**
Shepton Mallet	1753	1878	51	£3,489
Wells	1753	1883	44	£2,611
Bruton	1756	1876	66	£2,436
Frome	1757	1870	43	£3,913
Buckland Dinham (Radstock)	1768	1872	19	£1,265
West Harptree	1793	1876	27	£401
Wedmore	1827	1874	14	£348***
Wells and Highbridge	1841	1870	21	£416†

     * 1831 return; 69 miles of road in Somerset.
     ** Return made to the Clerk of the Peace of Wiltshire.
  *** Average for 1829–1832.
    † Income for 1847.

A return made to Parliament in 1839 gives the number of gates maintained by the various Trusts at that date:

Bath	17	Frome	11
Black Dog	8	Buckland Dinham (Radstock)	5
Shepton Mallet	16	West Harptree	10
Wells	9	Wedmore	4
Bruton	15		

CHAPTER NINE

Turnpike Travellers

> That it may please thee to preserve all that travel by
> land. . . .
>
> *The Book of Common Prayer*

As long ago as 1617 the inhabitants of Stoke St. Michael petitioned about the road over Mendip, as being 'founderous and bad for travelling' owing to constant traffic to and from the pits. In the middle of the eighteenth century the Somerset roads were still described as full of carriers, with strings of horses, sometimes as many as ten, passing and returning, laden with coals. In fact the preamble to the Bristol Turnpike Act of 1747 complains that the roads were still in as ruinous condition as they were before the passing of the 1727 and 1731 Acts, and that the Bridgwater road, which carried many heavy carriages daily, was impossible to maintain. If that was the case with the arterial roads, one shudders to think what the by-roads were like: in March 1724 Dr Claver Morris of Wells recorded in his *Diary* a journey in which his horses were so bemired, that one of them could not stand to draw, and he was forced to send to his cousin for his oxen to pull the calash out.[1] One is reminded of Cobbett's outbursts against some of the roads he found himself using on his rural rides a whole century later. This state of affairs was to continue as long as there was no competent highway authority. 'Whenever a farmer is called forth to perform statute-labour,' wrote Billingsley, 'he goes to it with reluctance, and considers it a legal burden from which he derives no benefit. His servant and his horses seem to partake of the torpor of the master. The utmost exertion of the surveyor cannot rouse them, and the labour performed is scarcely half what it ought to be.'[2]

The turnpikes were a very different story. John Byng, at the beginning of one of his tours, says that he was just old enough—

he was born in 1743—to remember turnpike roads few, and those bad; and when travelling was slow, difficult, and, in carriages, somewhat dangerous. By 1798, however, Billingsley could boast that the public roads in the northern parts of Somerset were pretty good, considering the traffic upon them, while, south of Mendip, the Wells and Bristol turnpike roads that led to Bridgwater were 'as smooth as a gravel-walk'. This he attributed to the great attention paid to the breaking of the stones, which was done by men with small sledges in a sitting posture, the stones being reduced to the size of a pigeon's egg, at the cost of sixpence per ton.[3]

In Billingsley's eyes nothing contributed so much to the improvement of a county as good roads, and this was even true of their appearance. The Mendip roads which were built at the time of the enclosures are extraordinarily in keeping with the landscape to whose pattern they contribute; and the great sweeping curves of some of the later turnpikes, like Hursley Hill, north of Pensford on the Bristol–Wells road, the beautifully-engineered stretches of Stoberry Hill coming down into Wells, or the spectacular crossing of the Nettlebridge valley—these have truly been absorbed into the landscape, like the railways and the canals and, as one hopes and prays, as the new motorways will eventually be absorbed.

The toll-houses too are often a delightful architectural feature. They are sometimes Gothick as at Chilcompton, or classical as at Kilmersdon, or even Regency as at Churchill. These, however, are touches of fancy: as a rule one need only describe their architecture as vernacular. They are built of local material, they are simple and functional and generally unmistakable, though sometimes their proportions have been spoiled by later additions to provide more spacious living quarters. Yet there is almost infinite variety in their design, sometimes one-storeyed, sometimes two-storeyed, sometimes flush with the road, sometimes oddly shaped to give a view of traffic approaching a road junction at an awkward angle, sometimes with sturdy little porches or deep overhanging eaves, to give some shelter to the gatekeepers.

Besides the gates there were boards announcing the scale of charges. The tolls to be taken at the Bristol turnpike gates, as laid down by the Act of 1727, may be taken as typical of the early years of the period: packhorse 1d., with coals ½d. (but under the 1749 Act coal carts were exempted, no doubt as a result of prolonged hostility by the colliers); waggons drawn by six horses or oxen

1s., by four horses or oxen 4d., by two horses 4d., and by one horse 2d.

There are fragments of the Stoberry Gate toll-board in the Wells Museum, and of that from Northover Gate (Ilchester Trust) in the Yeovil Museum. Two complete boards, however, have luckily survived, one belonging to the Bruton Trust, the other to Shepton Mallet. The story of their discovery only serves to show how precarious is the survival of such priceless pieces of local history. The Bruton board originally stood at Batcombe Gate, at the top of the long hill out of the village on the old Bruton–Frome road. It was recently discovered in the village, broken into three pieces and serving as the lid of a corn-bin. Miraculously, the three pieces fitted together perfectly, and after being displayed for a time in the Three Horse Shoes Inn, the board has now been presented to the Ward Library at Bruton, where it adorns the wall of the Reading Room. The owner's grandfather was a carpenter who had helped to demolish the toll-house when it was no longer required, and the board remained in the possession of the family thereafter. The history of the Shepton board is very similar. It stood at Pecking Mill Gate, near Evercreech, on the Castle Cary road, and was found complete in a loft on a farm near Bruton. The present owner's father bought the toll-house shortly after the Trust was wound up, and about 1887 demolished it to use the stone for building.

The Bruton notice is worth quoting in full, both for its intrinsic interest, and because it is a most tangible piece of evidence of the day-to-day working of the turnpike system in the Mendip area.

BRUTON TURNPIKE—BATCOMBE GATE

	Tolls
	D
For every Horse or Mule drawing any Coach, Barouche, Sociable, Chariot, Landau, Chaise, Phaeton, Curricle, Gig, Cart upon Springs, Hearse, Litter, or other like Carriage—	$4\frac{1}{2}$
For every such Carriage, on more than two wheels, being empty, drawn at the tail of any other Carriage—	3
For every such Carriage on two wheels only, empty, and so drawn—	$1\frac{1}{2}$

For every Horse or Mule drawing any Waggon, Cart, Caravan or other such Carriage—having the fellies of the wheels of less breadth than four and half inches—	6
Ditto of the breadth of four and half inches and less than six inches	5
Ditto of six inches and less than nine inches	4
Ditto nine inches and upward	3

The Toll of two Oxen or Neat Cattle drawing to be equal to that of one Horse.

For every Ass drawing any Waggon, Cart or other Carriage—	4
For every Horse or Mule not drawing—	1½
For every Ass not drawing—	1
For Oxen, Cows, or Neat Cattle, each	½
For Hogs, Calves, Sheep, or Lambs, each	¼

A Ticket taken at this gate clears the next gate passed through on the Bruton Trust

The Shepton notice, which is dated 1864, includes Berlins and Landaus among the vehicles catered for; charges ranged from 4½d. to ½d.; and there was the same scaling of tolls in relation to the breadth of wheel, the principle being that the narrower the wheel, the greater the damage to the surface of the road, whereas wider wheels served as miniature rollers.

Tolls were assessed in various ways by different Trusts at different times, taking into account such considerations as horse-power, number and breadth of wheels, and weight. Richard Wason (1864–1936), who was born on a farm at Inglesbatch near Bath, records in his *Memoirs* that their four-wheeled cart, being under 4 cwt., paid the same as a two-wheeled. Two of the Shepton Mallet gates (Cannard's Grave and Downside) had weighbridges, according to the list made in 1800. Bath had five in 1790, and they were a regular feature of any busy road.

Under each Trust there were likely to be concessions for particular classes of road-users. At Bath, for instance, the 1739 Act specified that any traffic returning the same day through any of the gates where toll had already been paid was exempt from paying a second time. Tourist traffic too was encouraged, even at this early date. 'All Persons Residing in Bath, who with Horses, Coaches, Chariots, Calashes and Chaises, shall pass through any or either of the said places where the Toll is Collected, for Taking the Air, or for Recreation, are, if they return the same Day into the City, to have the Money reimbursed them, by the Collectors, which they paid upon their going out of Town.'⁴

Exemption from double payment at the same gate on one day was normal. There was a steadily increasing list of general exemptions, finally codified in 1822 and 1823. The main classes of these were His Majesty's business (including the mail coaches), most of the operations of farming except taking produce and stock for sale, going to church or chapel, and going to county elections. In addition there were special exemptions in the local Acts.

Some Trusts imposed a 50 per cent surcharge for all traffic between 31 October and 1 May. In our tarmac days, we are apt to forget how susceptible the old roads were to variations of weather, changing from a dust-bowl to a glue-pot in a matter of hours. Wason describes how the parish roads in particular 'were mended with a soft stone which the first passing wagon ground to powder and the next rainstorm converted into about an inch of creamy mud which stuck to the boots like wax'. The surcharge discouraged winter travel, if discouragement were needed, but added considerably to the expense of any necessary journey. And journeys could be very expensive. Parson Woodforde often had to travel between Ansford and Oxford: riding alone on his own horse, the two-day journey cost him 17s. 9d. with meals, lodgings, tips to ostlers and maids, and turnpike charges; but when he travelled by coach from Oxford to Bath, and on by post-chaise, spending the night at Cirencester on the way, his journey cost him £3 7s. 6d. (31 January–1 February 1774). On another occasion he shared a post-chaise from Bath to Oxford with Coleridge's brother, which cost them £1 14s. 6d. apiece—at a time when a labourer's wage was a shilling a day, and a curate's pay was not much more than £30 a year. The tolls between Ansford and Bath when Woodforde travelled by chaise were 2s., and on a long journey they must have totalled a considerable sum. Wason reckons that they used to pay about every seven miles, each ticket indicating which gate it would clear.

And through the gates streamed the motley collection of vehicles, Barouche, Berlin, Chaise, Coach, Curricle and Phaeton, not forgetting the oxen on their nine days' journey to Smithfield, counted over and paid for every seven miles or so. A generation before the turnpikes, Dr Claver Morris describes a visitor to Wells arriving by the Exeter coach from Bath, but this is almost the only reference in his *Diary* to a regular service: most of his own travelling was done on horseback at an average speed of 4-4½ m.p.h., taking five hours for the ride to Bath, for instance, on 29 April 1724. His son was at school at Sherborne, and the journey from Wells would be made in the calash (which he had built in London at a cost of £42), taking a whole day—9.30 a.m. to 7 p.m., with 2½ hours at Ansford Inn for dinner: seven hours' travelling for 25 miles.

Not that the turnpike era immediately inaugurated any spectacular sort of speed: in 1774 Woodforde records the first occasion he ever travelled in one day from Oxford to Ansford. He came all the way by post-chaise, and took 14½ hours over the journey of 100 miles: average 7 m.p.h. By coach he might expect to take 15 hours for the 70 miles to Bath, an average of less than 5 m.p.h., though there were breaks for breakfast at Burford, dinner at Cirencester and tea at the Cross Hands. Before 1784, when John Palmer introduced the mail-coach, the stage-coaches were taking seventeen hours from London to Bristol, with an average speed of 7 m.p.h. over the 119 miles. Another generation was to elapse before even the mail-coaches could be timed to average 10 m.p.h.

Besides passengers, there was goods traffic, moving slowly along the turnpikes: very slowly by our standards, but incomparably faster and easier than in the bad old days when seven or eight horses were necessary to draw a two-ton load twenty miles in a day. Now, says Billingsley, 'the same number of horses will draw five tons, and travel thirty or forty miles'. No longer were strings of horses to be seen passing and returning, though there is a horrifying glimpse of Buckland Dinham, on the turnpike road between Radstock and Frome, about 1830: here coal was drawn through the turnpike gate, in trucks containing from two to twelve hundredweight, by men, women and even children under nine years of age. About twelve tons a day would be conveyed through the village by this form of agonizing sweated labour.[5] A pleasanter reminiscence (told me by Tom Payne of Chew Stoke) is of an old lady who, as a child, used to be sent down from Breach Hill with a donkey to fetch coal from Bishop Sutton pit: on the way down she would take the donkey round by footpaths to avoid the Chew Stoke toll-gate, and so save ½d.; but on the return journey the loaded donkey had to keep to the road, and pay the toll. But the halfpenny saved was a halfpenny gained, and that was something in those far-off days.

The toll-house and gate at Buckland Dinham, through which the human beasts of burden dragged their loads of coal, are only a memory today: the little low building, hardly more than a small shed, was demolished between the wars. Like so many of the north Somerset gates, Buckland Gate was much concerned with the coal traffic: in a mining area, coal was the operative factor both in the condition of the roads and in the amount of traffic that used them. We have seen how the hostility of the colliers in the Bristol area delayed the provision of adequate roads under the earlier Acts by which the Bristol Trust was established; the incidents already quoted with reference to the Soho and Chew Stoke gates both link up with the coal trade, and Richard Wason's *Memoirs* give a further picture of the coal trade during the latter days of the turnpike era.

At one end of the farm was a turnpike gate, kept by a very bad-tempered and abusive old fellow. The road in those days was very largely used by coal-hauliers with whom he was always at feud, and they, on their part, did their best to make his life a burden. Tolls were fixed on a basis of number of wheels and weight. If the old fellow thought one of the hauliers had more than his allowed weight, he would make him drive on to his weighing-machine. In the early 1870s the first traction engine, then called a road-steamer, came his way. It was a weird object with an upright 'coffee-pot' boiler and either three or five wheels: at any rate there was an odd one in front. He was not going to be bested by this new-fangled invention, so he ordered the driver to go on the weighing-machine. In vain the man assured him that it would smash the machine: he had to go. Of course there was a frightful wreck which took a long time to repair, whilst the hauliers loaded their carts as much as they liked without his being able to check them, and greeted him with cheerful remarks such as, 'Who weighed the devil?'

Complaints are frequent about the road-conditions now, but let no-one imagine that was the golden age. There were many pleasanter jobs than driving that road on a dark night. Up to a late hour we were sure of meeting a procession of coal-carts, all without lights, many on the wrong side of the road and many of the drivers asleep or drunk, or both.

Special rates for coal carts were scheduled by certain Trusts; on the other hand, gates were from time to time re-sited in order to tap this lucrative traffic. Chilcompton gate, the outer gate of the Wells Trust on the road to Bath, was moved a quarter of a mile nearer Wells in 1835: since the erection of the original toll-house in 1767, Old Down Common had been enclosed, and the new gate could now control the junction with Coal Pit Lane, a narrow winding lane, sunk deep below the level of the fields, and clearly the old pack-horse trail leading away from the pits in the Nettle-bridge valley. The siting of gates in relation to the coal traffic was also apparent in the search for a group of Shepton Mallet gates in which I found myself absorbed a few years ago.

It all began with my buying a copy of Farbrother's *History of Shepton Mallet* in a second-hand bookshop. It was published in 1859, beautifully produced by a local printer, well illustrated, and lovingly and accurately annotated by some previous owner. But what made it worth far more to me than the few shillings I had to pay for it, was the turnpike ticket which I found between two of its pages. Was it merely a bookmarker, like today's bus ticket? Or was it some reader's gesture of farewell? For the year before the book appeared, the East Somerset Railway had reached Shepton Mallet amid 'the roar of cannon' and the inevitable 'dinners, dancing, illuminations, fireworks and promenading', and the days of the Shepton Mallet turnpikes were numbered.

The little ticket—oddly enough, the only one which I have ever seen except in a museum—measures four inches by two as illustrated on the following page.

This was clearly a challenge to my knowledge of Mendip: I would take the ticket, and clear the gates if they were to be found.

Cranmore Gate itself was easy to find, a familiar landmark to motorists streaming westwards from Frome along A.361. It was all that a turnpike cottage should be—neat and Gothick, 'one up and one down', with a later wing added. In the course of doing some interior decorations, the local builder, W. J. Trotman, had recently found the till where the takings were kept, built into the thickness of the wall below the window.* Another point of interest was that the gate was not on its original site, which was a few hundred yards farther to the east, where the line of an older

---

* The Stanton Drew toll-house (see p. 115) contains a built-in dresser with slots to receive the tolls taken at the gate.

road cuts down through the fields to pass close to the church and the Hall. This road must have been diverted when the Hall was rebuilt, and the park enclosed, by the Pagets, some time after the 1817 map was published.

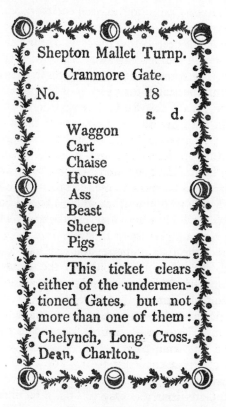

Shepton Mallet Turnp.
Cranmore Gate.
No.   18
                    s.   d.

Waggon
Cart
Chaise
Horse
Ass
Beast
Sheep
Pigs

This ticket clears either of the undermentioned Gates, but not more than one of them: Chelynch, Long Cross, Dean, Charlton.

Turnpike ticket issued at Cranmore Gate

Charlton Gate was also obvious, three miles farther west on the outskirts of Shepton Mallet, a square one-storeyed building with overhanging eaves—were these designed to give protection to the gate-keeper, in the absence of any form of porch?—and with a vast ammonite, nearly 18 in. across, built into the front wall. Here is an unobtrusive but historic crossing, for down from the north comes the Foss Way, no longer an arterial motorway, but a green lane striding down from the Beacon; in fact not even a green lane,

TOLL-HOUSES

28. (*above*) Stanton Drew (West Harptree Trust).
29. (*below*) Shipham (Wedmore Trust)

TOLL-HOUSES

30. (*above*) Kilmersdon (Radstock Trust). 31. (*below*) Chewton Mendip, the
site of Worberry Gate (Wells Trust)

HERE STOOD
THE
CHEWTON MENDIP
TURNPIKE
1753 - 1883

for the raised rampart of the Roman roadway is clearly visible in the fields close beside the modern lane.

Dean Gate was a much more difficult problem: Dean is only half a mile from Cranmore on the road to Charlton, yet the ticket categorically declared them to be alternatives: Dean or Charlton: Local memory denied all knowledge of a turnpike gate, and it appeared on no map; yet the minute book of the Shepton Trust showed that on 2 October 1820 it was resolved 'that a Gate or Chain be erected on the side of the Turnpike road at Dean leading from thence into a lane which runs into the Frome Turnpike road on Mendip'. The inhabitants of West Cranmore were exempted from paying toll at Dean Gate, but the following year this was hastily amended to apply 'only to those inhabitants who are not traders in coal, and all passage of coals to be paid for'. The lane was clearly being used as an uncontrolled southbound route from the Mendip pits across one of the main Shepton turnpike roads. The gate continued to appear in the Shepton returns until 1855, after which the gates were lumped together in groups; this makes it all the more surprising that no memory of it survives. The hamlet of Dean has been altered within the last few years almost beyond recognition, with the demolition of a number of houses and the widening of the main road; but the lane is still there, overgrown and rutted, with the naked rock scored deep by the drags on the wheels of the coal carts.

It is much less difficult to find Long Cross Gate, a lonely house at a five-pronged road junction on the very top of the Mendip ridge. The position of the house showed that it was not concerned with traffic along the Beacon road, which was the prerogative of the Wells and Frome Trusts, but with that coming across the ridge from Stoke Lane into Shepton territory. A carved stone dated the cottage: 1790. Above the door projected a bracket which must once have carried the lantern light, or held the gate firmly in its hinges against possible upheaval by recalcitrant road-users.

That left Chelynch, a hamlet off the main road, close to the Doulting quarries from which was hewn the stone for the great churches at Wells and Glastonbury. There was only one road junction, controlling yet another alternative route from the Mendip pits, past the Waggon and Horses. I asked an elderly man working in his garden, but he knew nothing of a turnpike gate at

Chelynch. He suggested that it might be where the road narrowed—he pointed to the place—and his friend who lived there might know. He began to walk down with me, and then said quite casually, 'Of course, in my house we've got the window where they used to take the money off the road.' There, just discernible in the wall of the corner cottage, was the filled-in outline of a little window. Inside, in the thickness of the wall, was a cupboard where the till must have stood; and outside, in the golden Doulting stone, I found the holes made by the hinges from which the gate once hung. My quest was at an end.

NOTE

In July 1964 the toll-board from the Blagdon Gate of the West Harptry (*sic*) Turnpike Trust was discovered during the rebuilding of a Cottage in Bell Square, close to the site of the gate. The tolls payable from 25 March 1854 included the sum of one shilling per wheel 'for every Carriage moved or propelled by Steam or Machinery'. (Cp. Wason's anecdote on p. 125.)

Part of another toll-board was also disinterred here—from a hitherto unrecorded gate at Emborough belonging to the same Trust.

CHAPTER TEN

From Bath to Wells

Get there if you can and see the land you once were
    proud to own
Though the roads have almost vanished and the
    expresses never run.

               w. h. auden: *Poems* 1930

I have lingered over my search for a small group of turnpike
gates: I now intend to trace in some detail the course of the
twenty-mile stretch of turnpike road from Bath to Wells. Both
these chapters describe pieces of purely local research, but I hope
that they are of more than purely local significance, if only they
serve to show how much history lies buried under our feet, and
how rewarding such field work can be: it is indeed the necessary
complement of the study of books, maps and documents. In comparison, for instance, with the recent interest shown in the early
history of canals and railways, our knowledge of the history of the
roads in our own area is often only rudimentary.

I have chosen the road from Bath to Wells for several reasons.
The first ten miles follow the Foss Way, and one can watch the
gradual adaptation of a Roman arterial highway to the needs of
later ages; at White Post the Wells road leaves the Foss Way and
strikes farther west across Mendip. In the Middle Ages there must
have been many ecclesiastical comings and goings, while the
monks of Bath and the canons of Wells disputed their title to the
Bishop's see, to say nothing of the great Abbey of Glastonbury
six miles farther to the south. The Wells Turnpike Act of 1753
referred to the Foss Way as 'the Great Western Road to the City
of Bath', and along this road poured a stream of travellers, some
of whom have left us descriptions of it. Later came the stage-
coaches and the mail-coaches; later still the torrent of holiday
motorists heading for the West, knowing little of the history of

the road that carries them to their destinations, or of the deviations and realignments of the last two centuries.

The Wells road for many centuries left Bath by the Old Bridge. There was a bridge here in 1304, though the familiar 'Old' Bridge, demolished in 1964, dated merely from 1754, its name serving to distinguish it from the New Bridge on the Bristol road. The Wells road climbs steeply up the Holloway, the traditional southern exit from the city, with its high raised pavement and general air of antiquity. (The present Wells Road from the Old Bridge to the top of Holloway was scheduled under the Act of 1829, and its continuation (A.367) was carried out between 1797 and 1806.) Where the Holloway emerges on to the Bear Flat, there was a toll-gate. The ascent to Odd Down was made, not by the modern Wells Road, but by Bloomfield Road: this was still in use when the Rev. Richard Warner of Bath set off on one of his excursions in September 1799. At the top of the hill he paused to admire the splendid view of what was to him 'the most beautiful city in the world', and to indulge in ponderous sarcasm at the expense of Cottage Crescent (now Bloomfield Crescent).[1] This poor relation of the crescents on the slopes of Lansdown still faces bleakly north, though no longer in the splendid isolation in which it appears on the 1817 map. Its architect was C. Harcourt Masters, whose map of the Bath turnpikes shows the layout of the roads at Burnt House, on the City boundary. The old road now comes to an abrupt end when it meets the modern road at a lower level and an acute angle. Here stood the Burnt House turnpike gate, and for half a mile or so the modern road follows the line of the Foss Way, before sweeping away from it on an easier gradient to cross the Dunkerton valley. At the very top of the hill a tell-tale double hedge on the right marks the line of the original road, and round the first bend the Foss Way is obvious to all, a green lane arrowing down the hillside.[2] There is a splendid stretch of the *agger* near Foss Farm, before the lane drops down to cross the Cam Brook and climb the opposite slope to Peasedown. Most of this section of road had been replaced by the date of Harcourt Masters' map (1787), but it still appears as a minor road on the 1817 map.

By this time a delightful little stone bridge had been built to carry the Foss Way across the recently opened Somersetshire Coal Canal, but this has now been destroyed and the canal filled in. The later sweep of the turnpike road also crosses the canal, and the parapets of the bridge are still visible on the section of road left as a lay-by after recent alterations. The steep climb to Peasedown also involved a series of realignments to ease the gradient: the old road plunged straight up the hill, its course still visible across fields beside another good piece of the Roman *agger*, in due course becoming a green lane which emerges close to the Prince of Wales Inn.

In 1827 the Bath Trust deposited a plan for a proposed diversion to avoid this hill altogether: a new road was to be driven through the villages of Dunkerton and Carlingcott to rejoin the Foss Way at the Red Post. This plan was never executed, but it would have served the community in the Cam valley, where coal-pits were now working, and the village of Peasedown would presumably never have come into existence. Apart from the Red Post Inn, not a single building is shown along the turnpike road on the 1817 map: astride an arterial road on a windy ridge, Peasedown is entirely a modern village, formed into a parish in 1874, with a present-day population of about 2,500. A toll-house was built at the Red Post in 1824, but the Red Post, whatever it may have been, was already there: Skinner in his *Journal* for January 1823 describes how Farmer Lippeatt, turned out of the Red Post Inn at midnight, dead drunk, missed his way, fell into a quarry and died of his injuries. The turnpike gate was put up in March 1824 on account of the damage done by carts from Clandown and Small-combe collieries, but it was removed in August of the same year because it was unprofitable.

Another diversion proposed in 1827 was put into effect, and completely altered the road system at Radstock. The Foss Way of course plunged on regardless, across two steep valleys, to rejoin the modern road at the Elm Tree in Westfield. It was still marked as a through road on the 1817 map, with a deviation to Small-combe colliery: the village of Clandown did not yet exist, but an old resident once told me that as a child he always used the track to reach Westfield or Norton Hill. It is just, and only just, possible to follow the road today, at times a stony lane, elsewhere a faintly surviving double hedge, elsewhere a hump that would test a scrambling motor cycle, and suddenly a magnificent stretch of the Roman *agger* running across the ridge in perfect condition. It was at this point, near the junction with a lane leading to Welton, that the Roman road was excavated and examined by James McMurtrie in 1884 and 1904. It was found to consist of the following layers: later metalling, 3 in.; paving of flat rubbly stones of irregular shape, 4½ in.; finer concrete bed for the paving, 5 in.; yellow con-

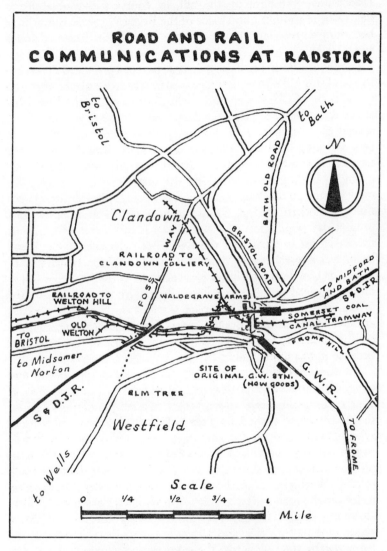

crete, 18 in.; rubbly stones lying on the subsoil, 6 in. The *agger* was 16 ft. wide at the base and 8 ft. at the top, where rut-marks, made presumably by the wheels of Roman vehicles, were visible, the width between the ruts being about 3 ft.[3]

The old Bath road into Radstock diverged from the Foss Way at the Camerton turning, close to the gates of Woodborough House, cut past the Round Hill and steeply down into the valley, emerging opposite the Waldegrave Arms. The new turnpike road swept round the slope of the hill above the village of Clandown, crossing the old Radstock–Bristol road, and easing down the hillside to join the older road at the bottom. Here, instead of the double level crossing, the road would have bridged a branch of the Somersetshire Coal Canal which was cut in 1799, but survived only a few years: the terminal basin, served by railroads from the collieries at Clandown and Welton, was situated behind the Waldegrave Arms, but in 1815 a railroad was substituted for the canal itself, and the line of this can still be seen as a footpath crossing the subway that passes underneath the Somerset & Dorset line, and indicating the original level of the valley at this point.

South of Radstock all is clear as far as White Post. At the Elm Tree, a landmark appearing on old estate maps when there was nothing else along the road except the West Field, the Foss Way reappears on a lane through a new housing estate, and at White Post the Bath Trust's jurisdiction ceased. In the wall at this point there is a beautifully lettered milestone, in the form of an iron plaque fastened to a large stone block and recording the distance 10 m. & 4 fur. to the Guildhall, Bath. There is a similar plaque on Rush Hill, 13 m. & 2 fur. from the Guildhall, marking another terminal point on the Bath roads.

It has been suggested that the original White Post marked the boundary between the Bath and Wells Trusts; but place names such as White Post, Red Post, White Cross and so on, are fairly widespread, and always precede the arrival of the turnpikes. Neither on Harcourt Masters' map nor on the 1817 map are any buildings marked at White Post, though it must always have been an important road junction, where ultimately no fewer than four Trusts converged—Bath, Wells, Shepton Mallet and Buckland Dinham.

A short distance north of White Post there is another pleasing relic of the Bath Trust, one of the parish boundary posts which the Trust erected in 1827. Several of these are still to be seen on the road from Bath, their faces neatly inscribed with the names of the parishes they divide; in this case Kilmersdon and Stratton. Like the old mileposts, relics such as these still give a touch of distinction to the stretches of road administered by individual Trusts. The Bath mileposts, for instance, merely reveal the distance to Bath, but south of White Post, the Shepton Mallet mileposts on the Foss Way gave the mileage to CHELTm as well as to Bath and Shepton; on the Wells road, the next milestone beyond White Post belonged to the Wells Trust, and stands, ostensibly, 9 miles from Wells and 11 miles from Bath, though it is only a hundred yards or so from the Bath boundary post, 10 miles and 4 furlongs from the Guildhall. The inconsistency must have arisen because the Wells Trust were primarily concerned to record the mileage from Wells; as we shall see, this milestone must have been pushed out towards White Post several times, as various cut-offs were built, and as vulgar fractions were impermissible, the distance to Bath could no longer pretend to be accurate except in the most general terms. There must have been many such vagaries at points where Trusts met.

Between White Post and Old Down, the Wells road has followed three different routes at different times. At first, the road turned sharply to the right across Norton Down, dipped steeply down into Chilcompton, and climbed the far side of the valley to rejoin the modern main road on Broadway: this is the through road marked on Greenwood's map in 1822 (and even on Walker's map of 1844 which shows the mail-coach routes). Greenwood actually marks the mileposts on the road as from Norton St. Philip, and also two proposed by-passes on the steep winding section of the road through Chilcompton. It is indeed almost unbelievable today that this narrow lane, with a gradient of 1 in 6 at one point, should have served as a link in a trunk route to the West, and for nearly forty years have carried the Royal Mail between London and Exeter.

Greenwood's by-passes were never realized: instead, another road was developed into the turnpike road. This turned off on Norton Down and kept along the south side of the valley, avoiding Chilcompton altogether. It was on this road that the lodge of Norton Hall referred to in Chapter Three was situated. The line of the road can still be followed, through the field beside the railway, as a deep ditch, with one or two fine beeches which must

32. The Somersetshire Coal Canal at Dunkerton about 1890; the bridge (now demolished) carried the Foss Way across the canal

33. Eastern Mendip in 1

from the Ordnance Survey

34. (*above*) Old Down in 1769—a copy of the painting by Ironside in the Blaise Castle Folk Museum. 35. (*centre*) Old Down Inn. 36. (*below*) Emborough Pool

once have been roadside trees. Close to the modern railway bridge the road turned south, climbing steeply past the Redan Inn, across present-day gardens and fields, to the inn at Naish's Cross, and then westwards again along what was then known as Broadway Lane. A dip in the field at Naish's Cross still marks the line of the road, very obviously when the field has recently been ploughed, and coal dust, that must have fallen from the packhorses or waggons stopping at the inn on their way down from the pits in the Moorewood valley, is brought to the surface. Near the Redan Inn, a very short strip of the road itself, only recently tarred, survives as a cul-de-sac that must have fallen out of use when the railway came in the 1870s. It was at this point—known as Fry's Well—that loungers used to wait, to watch the Wells coach make the sudden turn on the steep incline: as the driver made the turn, he would do fancy strokes with his whip, flicking out a penny from a certain crevice in the wall where the loungers had stuck it for their own entertainment in the exercise of his skill.[4]

The final alignment of the road eliminated this hazard. In 1822 and 1834 the Wells Trust produced plans for straightening out the winding course of the road, and Broadway Lane was extended north-eastwards, high above the Redan, and driving straight through to White Post. This is the road we know today as B.3139, but it might well never have been cut, and Broadway Lane might well have remained a purely local lane; for in 1815, the Wells Trust, realizing perhaps the hazards and difficulties of the Chilcompton–Radstock–Dunkerton section of the Great Western Road, had proposed a bold and entirely new route for a turnpike road to Bath. This was to leave the present road at Lynch Hill, half a mile east of Old Down, and to strike north and east, past the hamlets of Clapton, Radford and Tunley, to join the Foss Way at the top of Dunkerton Hill. A glance at the 1817 map shows that there was already an almost direct line of road throughout, only waiting to be turnpiked. The estimated cost was £7,395, but tolls were being lost because traffic was going to Exeter along the Foss Way through Ilchester and Honiton, and it was reckoned that the new cut-off would save three-quarters of an hour on the journey between Bath and Exeter. It would also have made a bid to tap some of the coal traffic which the Somersetshire Coal Canal, opened throughout in 1805, was now carrying away from the Camerton-Timsbury area. It would certainly have been a shorter and more easily graded through route, which still runs through some delightfully unspoiled countryside. But the motorists who used to wait in mile-long queues at the Radstock level-crossings on summer Saturdays were not likely to nose out what might have been one of the main holiday routes to the West.

The little toll-house near Old Down was erected there in 1835. The original gate, erected in 1754, was on a site nearer Chilcompton, at the foot of Lynch Hill, intriguingly described as 'in Broadway Lane, near Perry's Coffee House'. That at least was the intention, but a minute of 1767 is still dealing with estimates for the erection of the 'turnpike house at Broadway', which was to have a stone porch and to be roofed with tiles. The Wells minute books record the name of the first toll-gatherer on Broadway; he was Wm. Vagg, a member of a well-known local family.

And so to Old Down, the most important road junction between Bath and Wells, which demands a chapter to itself, together with Emborough Pool, half a mile farther west. From Old Down onwards, there is only one later deviation from the line of the original turnpike road, though when first made, the road must have run across open common for several miles. The enclosure of the Mendip common had begun in 1769, and by 1794 all the parishes through which the road passed had completed their enclosures, according to the list given by Billingsley.

The only deviation was near West Horrington, where the original road survives as a green lane curving round towards the village, where the modern road cuts straight down the hill. Outside the entrance to the Mendip Hospital, the road from the Beacon comes in on the left; half a mile farther on is the site of the East Wells Turnpike Gate, commemorated by a plaque at the end of Hawkers Lane; and round the next bend we are within sight of the cathedral at the heart of the city, and the twenty-mile journey is at an end. It is pleasant to recall that the Rev. Richard Warner, who left Bath at 5 a.m. on 2 September 1799, 'reached the Swan Inn to a late breakfast'.

CHAPTER ELEVEN

Old Down and Emborough

(1)

Gave the men on Old Down when the work was
measured, for beer. . . . 0 1 0

Wells Turnpike Trust accounts, 1756

In the opening paragraph of *The Woodlanders*, Hardy describes
'the forsaken coach-road running almost in a meridional line
from Bristol to the south shore of England'. This is the road
that crosses the Bath–Wells road at Old Down—A.37, no longer
a 'forsaken coach-road'.

Such a strategic crossroads was an obvious site for an inn from
the very earliest times: I have not been able to establish any
authority for the date 1640, now shown on the inn sign, but a
Hippisley map of the Ston Easton estate *c.* 1710 shows the house
as the 'Read Lyon' [*sic*], and a survey of the same date describes it
as 'a good house, an inn', occupied by Edward Gould. The map
also shows the curious kink in the road, which may have had
something to do with the fact that the inn stood on the edge of
Old Down Common. The recent alterations, however, have at
last eliminated what was a very dangerous road junction, though
in the process they have elbowed the inn off the historic trunk
road which it has so proudly fronted for several hundred years.
By the 1760s, at any rate, it had become a posting house, where
Woodforde used to take a fresh chaise on his journeys to and from
Oxford. On 1 February 1774 he had a rough passage over Mendip
on a return journey from Oxford:

> I got to Old Downe between 3 and 4 this afternoon where I stayed
> about a Quarter of an Hour, eat some cold rost Beef, drank a pint
> of Ale, and then got into a fresh Chaise for Ansford. It snowed all
> the way very thick from Bath to Old Downe.

At Bath for chaise pd.	o	10	6
Gave the Bath driver besides a dram	o	1	6
For a chaise at Old Downe to Ansford pd.	o	10	6
Eating etc., at Old Downe pd.	o	1	o

Eventually Woodforde reached home about 6 o'clock. It continued to snow all the way from Old Down to Ansford, and 'the wind blowed very rough and it was very cold indeed'. The Old Down driver was fortified with a dram at Cannard's Grave and another at home, as well as a tip of o.1.6. It was indeed an ill wind that blew nobody any good.[1]

By 1774 the inn was no longer the Red Lion, and we are luckily able to see exactly what it looked like in Woodforde's day, because in 1769 it was painted on a long wooden panel, about four feet by two, which is now in the Blaise Castle Folk Museum at Bristol, while a copy hangs in the hall of the inn itself. The painting actually poses certain rather awkward questions, but at first sight it is merely a somewhat crude representation of an ordinary country scene, by an otherwise unknown painter—one even hesitates to use the word 'artist'. It depicts a stage-waggon passing the Old Down Inn. The waggon is hauled by eight horses, and it has come to a halt outside the inn, just by the fifteenth milestone from Bristol. There is a man holding the leading horse, and under the enormous hood are various passengers, including a man who has put his arm round a young woman; there are other people in the road, with flagons and tankards, and behind them is the inn. There is a dog rubbing its behind against a post, and in the doorway, under a sign advertising Neat Wines, stands the landlady, with her arms akimbo; some of her regular customers are leaning out of the windows to have a look at what is going on.

The placard on the hood of the waggon reads:

> John Deane Wincanton
> Shaftesbury Sherborne
> & Bruton Common Stage
> Waggon to the 5 Kings
> Thos Street Bristol.

John Deane ought to have been easy enough to identify, but at museums, public libraries and record offices I drew a complete blank. I finally ran him to earth in Wincanton. He was one of the leading figures in the town at that time, and the owner of the

White Horse Inn in High Street. On the keystone of the arch over
the main door of the White Horse can still be seen the initials G.D.
and the date 1733. That was when the house was rebuilt by
Nathaniel Ireson, the well-known local architect, for George
Deane, John's father, whom he succeeded in 1746. Up behind the
inn are a lot of old stables where he must have kept his horses and
waggons. In the same year as the painting was done, a new Market
House and Town Hall were put up in Wincanton at a cost of
£400, and John Deane's name appears in the accounts: he was
paid £21 19s. 2½d. for the carriage of materials, including stone
from the quarries at Keinton Mandeville.[2]

The painter's name was Ironside. That is not a Westcountry
name, but there were Ironsides at Dorchester in the eighteenth
century—in particular one, Thomas Ironside, who is recorded in
the Dorchester archives as a painter and stainer; but he died in
1715. Perhaps another member of the family was a journeyman
painter who painted trade signs. The wooden panel looks as if it
was an advertisement for John Deane—even the horses' harness
is conspicuously marked J.D. Signs like this were perhaps put up
at points of call along his route, such as the Old Down Inn itself.
Only one other example of Ironside's work—a landscape dated
1767—has so far come to my notice.

But the more I think about it, the more I am convinced that
Ironside was not a local man, and did not really know the Bristol
side of Mendip. In fact he may have actually painted an entirely
imaginary background for John Deane's waggon. There are
some very puzzling things about the picture: first of all, the inn
stands entirely by itself in open country; but that is just possible,
as parts of Old Down remained unenclosed until nearly 1800. In
the distance there is what looks like a building with a spire, but
it is just possible that a brick-kiln is represented, as the 1817
O.S. map shows a brick-yard close by. Again, the inn itself is
painted red, with an undecipherable date on the gable. Behind the
present inn there is an earlier range of buildings; but they do not
look like the building in the picture, and anyhow they are built of
the local grey limestone. Is this a case of artistic licence? or does
the painting depict another earlier building that had disappeared?

A final point: the placard on the waggon states quite unmistak-
ably that John Deane plied to the Five Kings in Thomas Street,
Bristol. But the inn, as all older Bristolians will know, was called ·

the Three Kings. In 1606 it was one of the eighteen principal inns of the city; it survived until the early 1900s, and there is a photograph of its gabled exterior in one of Reece Winstone's books on *Bristol As It Was*. It was then in the last stages of dilapidation and served as a parcels depot for the Midland Railway.[3]

The main streets leading into Bristol from the south, like Redcliff Street and Thomas Street, were lined with inns where carriers put up. There is a list of them in Matthews's *Bristol Guide* for 1794. At the Three Kings there were waggons from Bath and Wells, and from places as far afield as Beaminster, Bridport and Crewkerne, as well as Wincanton. The Wincanton waggon came in on Mondays and went out on Tuesdays, and I have often wondered just how long the 40-mile journey took: even with eight horses it is a hard road all the way, and the pause for refreshment at Old Down must have been very welcome both to man and beast.

What the old painting depicts, in fact, is an almost timeless English roadside scene. Earlier in the eighteenth century the stage-waggon plying between Bath and Bristol took a whole day over the journey, with a pause for dinner at Keynsham, returning from Bristol to Bath the following day.[4] Wordsworth spoke of 'the slow-paced waggon', and a century later, Hardy, in *The Woodlanders*, described just such a carrier's cart with its 'varied freight of passengers and parcels'. Ironside's painting is in many ways a crude piece of work, but it is of considerable interest, because it gives us a vivid glimpse of what ordinary road travel was like 200 years ago. This was how ordinary folk travelled, the only alternative to Shanks' mare, unless you were well enough off to hire a chaise or to afford your own 'Phaeton, Curricle, Gig or other like Carriage'. When Billingsley engaged a young gardener from Kew, he gave careful instructions for his journey from London to Ashwick:

He can get on the outside of the Bath day coach any morning about half past four and he will arrive at Bath the same evening about 10. If he gets to Bath on Tuesday or Friday, he will have an opportunity of coming on the Wednesday or Saturday from the Full Moon Inn on the Bridge, Bath, by the Shepton Mallet Caravan* which passes my house on these days about 6 or 7 o'clock in the evening.[5]

* The O.E.D. defines *caravan* (a word deriving ultimately from the Persian, and now shortened to *van*) as a covered carriage or cart: in the seventeenth and eighteenth centuries it was applied to 'a private or public vehicle carrying passengers or a company of people together'.

Old Down and Emborough

Not all the traffic at Old Down, however, moved so slowly; much of the inn's fame derived from its connection with the mail-coaches. In the first issue of Bradshaw's *Railway Guide* in 1840, there is a map showing the railways then operating or planned: one single inn is marked on this map, the Old Down Inn—a reminder of its importance in the pre-railway era. The mail-coach service was inaugurated by a coach that ran from Bristol to London on 2 August 1784 in sixteen hours. In 1785 a London-Exeter coach began to run via Bath, Wells and Taunton. By 1797 the G.P.O. time-bills show that this coach was timed to leave London at 8 p.m. and to reach Bath at 10 a.m., where 30 minutes were allowed for breakfast: Old Down would have been reached at about 12.30 p.m. as three hours were allowed for the 19½ m. from Bath to Wells; Taunton was reached at 5.5 p.m. and Exeter at 10.40 p.m.—26 hours and 40 minutes in all for the journey of 196½ m., at an average of about 7¼ m.p.h. By 1836, at the end of the mail-coach era, these times had been greatly improved on, as the following tables show:

DOWN		UP	
London G.P.O.	8 p.m.	Exeter	10 a.m.
Bath	7 a.m.	Wells	4.55 p.m.
Old Down	8.50 a.m.	Old Down	5.35 p.m.
Wells	9.27 a.m.	Bath	7.30 p.m.
Exeter	3.57 p.m.	London G.P.O.	6.38 a.m.

The Bath–Wells stretch now only required 2½ hours, and the whole journey was accomplished in 20 hours at an average speed of almost 10 m.p.h.

While the horses were being changed at Old Down after the gruelling stages in either direction, much postal activity would be going on, with mail-bags being put down and taken up, and mail-carts or post-boys waiting to set off with the mail for neighbouring towns and villages. Old Down at different periods handled the mail for Shepton Mallet, Bruton and Castle Cary, as well as for surrounding villages.* The up mail-coach also dropped off letters from the west, including packet-boat letters from Falmouth: these were sent from Old Down to Bristol by mail-cart, for despatch thence to Wales or the north.

* The original address of the Benedictine community which settled at Downside in 1814 was 'Mount Pleasant via Old Down'.

Old Down was established as an official postal Receiving House in June 1798, as the result of an application by 'Mrs. Coxe' of Ston Easton. The Postmaster-General's minutes (11 June 1798) refer to the area surveyor's report:

> by which it appears that the amount of letters for Stone Easton, the residence of Mrs. Coxe, and which is about a mile from Old Down (a single house) would not justify the expense of establishing a Receiving House there, but as there are several other villages, the letters for which may be included in the same delivery, and which would derive great accommodation from the appointing Old Down a Receiving House, Mr. Lott (The Surveyor) proposes that measure at an expense of 20s. a year, which . . . with the pence on delivery will be an adequate compensation for the trouble of the Receiver.

Mrs Coxe was the widow of Henry Hippisley Coxe of Ston Easton Park, M.P. for Somerset, who had died in 1795. He left no heir, and his widow inherited his estate, which included Old Down Inn—hence her interest in getting the inn established as a Receiving House.

In this capacity it functioned as the equivalent of today's sub-post office, but because of its strategic importance on the London–Bath–Exeter route, it quickly assumed the importance of a 'post town', the equivalent of today's head post office; for 'post towns' were not always towns, but sometimes inns situated at focal points on the mail-coach routes. (Another example was the inn at Cross, at the western end of Mendip, on the Bristol–Bridgwater road.) Receivers (or sub-postmasters) were entitled to charge for delivering letters, except in 'post towns' which were in fact towns—hence the reference to 'the pence on delivery' in the Postmaster-General's minutes. Old Down continued to serve as a Receiving House until the early 1840s, when the railway reached Exeter, and the London–Bath–Exeter mail-coaches ceased running. Letters were franked at the inn, and from 1798 until about 1840 Old Down had its own postmark, OLD-DOWN, which is something of a collector's piece among postal historians. Through the generosity of E. H. Ford, whose *Postal History of Shepton Mallet* is a valuable source-book for our knowledge of the early postal services in North Somerset, I am now the possessor of a 'cover' bearing this rare postmark. The 'cover' is dated 10 November 1806, and was directed to Southampton, by the X (cross) Post, to ensure that it would not be sent via London, but via Devizes, Westbury and

Salisbury. But its real value and interest to me derives from the fact that it is an autograph of Sir John Coxe Hippisley of Ston Easton, who had by this time married Mrs Coxe and thus become the owner of Old Down.

By this time it is probable that the inn had been rebuilt with the fine façade which we see today, and equally probable that the rebuilding was due to its enhanced importance as a 'post town' on an important mail-coach route. The inn was within the manor and parish of Ston Easton, and held on lease from the Hippisleys, in whose possession it remained until 1938. Sir John obviously felt

Cover of a letter written by Sir John Coxe Hippisley of Ston Easton and postmarked at Old Down, 10 November 1806

proud of his inn, to judge by the sarcastic reference in Skinner's *Journal* to the 'two or three long speeches about himself and his inn at Old Down' to which he treated his fellow Commissioners at a meeting of the Bath Turnpike Trust.[6] It had certainly become a centre for a variety of local functions. Even before the turn of the century it had been a recognized place for meetings: on 22 August 1792, for instance, an important 'Agreement for the regulation of miners' wages' was negotiated there, after a successful strike for a wage increase made by about 4,000 colliers in the

Timsbury, Paulton and Radstock districts.[7] After its rebuilding the inn seems to have become a sort of rural Assembly Rooms. There were meetings of Turnpike Commissioners, assize dinners, and balls—upwards of 150 attended on New Year's Day 1828— and even a religious debate. Or rather there would have been a religious debate, if the ballroom had been larger and more convenient. A meeting of the British Reformation Society had been held at Old Down on 10 January 1834, and a series of 'discussion meetings', lasting for six days, between Protestant and Catholic representatives, with an impartial chairman, was finally held in the Old Chapel at Downside in February and March of the same year, before a numerous and rapt audience. The scene is described with gusto by Abbot Snow in his reminiscences of Old Downside.[8]

The coming of the railway marked the end of the old glories: the London–Bath mail-coach service was withdrawn in 1841, the Frome–Radstock branch was opened (for mineral traffic) in 1854, and the Somerset & Dorset Railway's Bath Extension from Evercreech in 1874. Sentence had been passed on Old Down, as on so many of the inns on the old coaching roads. On the night of 25 February 1885, a swift and terrible fire completely gutted the building. A sketch in an early issue of *The Downside Review* shows the melancholy ruin as it was in April 1885, its four walls standing naked to the sky.[9] The sketch is of interest as showing that when the inn was rebuilt—and only in the present Automobile Age has it regained its status as a popular port of call on two busy main roads—the exterior seemed unchanged, even to the little pillared portico protecting the front door. Recent alterations by the owners revealed a cobbled way underneath the hall and the bar: this suggests that at some stage, as at other coaching inns, there was a central archway and a passage through which the horses reached the stables. But this certainly did not exist at Sir John Hippisley's inn, nor at that depicted in Ironside's painting. There are two old wings jutting out behind the inn today: was it one of these which Ironside depicted, and was a larger block with a central archway then built in front of these at some date after 1769, to be replaced in turn by Sir John's façade? The problem seems insoluble, because no other picture of the inn appears to be known, which is indeed surprising, in view of its fame and importance over the last two or three centuries.

Old Down and Emborough

The visible scene
Would enter unawares into his mind,
With all its solemn imagery, its rocks,
Its woods, and that uncertain heaven, received
Into the bosom of the steady lake.

WORDSWORTH: *The Prelude,* Book V

Emborough Pool lies half a mile from Old Down on the road to Wells. According to the *Little Guide* to Somerset, it is 'a dismal sheet of water bordering the main road'. But on a grey day any sheet of water will appear uninviting. Dorothy Wordsworth could write of her beloved Grasmere: 'The lake looked to me . . . dull and melancholy, and the weltering on the shores seemed a heavy sound.' It is the same at Emborough, lying 700 ft. up on the northern slope of Mendip, when low clouds trail across the landscape, or a south-westerly gale slaps the little waves against the stone parapet that guards the sunken road.

The Rev. Richard Warner, on the other hand, touring the western counties in 1799 in search of The Picturesque, thought very differently. He saw the pool as 'a noble sheet of water flooding an area of ten acres, and surrounded by steep banks richly covered with sycamores, firs and beech trees. The spot is sequestered and pleasing, and possesses what the late Mr. Brown emphatically called "a capability" of being converted into a picture of very superior beauty.'[10] Collinson also admired the beauty of the wooded hillside slopes, the pleasant winding walks cut through the plantations, and the many curious ferns and mosses to be discerned among the rocks.[11]

But Emborough Pool is not, as would appear at first sight, a piece of eighteenth-century landscape gardening, a miniature Stourhead at the source of the little stream that carves out the Nettlebridge valley on its way to join the river Frome. There was a pool at Emborough long before the days of 'Capability' Brown. The tradition that here were fishponds belonging to Bruton Priory may derive from Bruton's ownership of one of the neighbouring manors of Ston Easton. Collinson says that the lake was granted by John Boteler, lord of Emborough, to the monks of Hinton Charterhouse. It is unlikely that either monastery needed fishponds high up on Mendip: perhaps they supplied the Carthusian settlement at Green Ore which was a cell of Hinton. At any rate, after the Dissolution, the lake came into the possession of the Hippisley family in whose hands it remained for 400 years. The late Commander R. J. Bayntun Hippisley, the last of his family to live at Ston Easton, told me an apocryphal story of how some Hippisley lads who lived at the Emborough manor house once broke open the head of the pond and let the water out, so that the monks were without fish from Emborough until the head was repaired. The monks were so indignant about this that they applied to some high authority to have the lads punished. I have never seen this story in print, but it was interesting to find a family tradition preserving the conjunction of monks and fish—especially in the light of the latter-day connection between Emborough and Downside.

If the origin of the pond is uncertain, so is its name. Today it is generally known as Emborough Pool (or Emborough Pond), but the 6-in. map marks it more romantically as Lechmere Water, as did the 1817 map, and both names were known to Collinson. To generations of Downside boys it was known familiarly as 'Sir John's', after its one-time owner, Sir John Coxe Hippisley.

Sir John was a notable personality in north Somerset. Skinner disliked him intensely and missed no chance of saying so—but then Skinner disliked so many people. He fell foul of 'this worthy baronet, as he is always denominated', at meetings of the Bath Turnpike Commissioners. On 1 January 1825 the question of the new alignment of the Bath road on Radstock Hill was debated, with Sir John in the chair, 'and such a chairman never before did I witness', Skinner wrote in his *Journal*. 'Instead of hearing calmly and impartially what each side of the question had to say, he got up and advocated the cause he had espoused. Indeed, that the said Baronet did not possess the same upper stowage as Solomon it would have been clearly ascertained at this one exhibition, when the worthy gentleman gave us all to understand that he was Asinus Maximus.' On another occasion, according to Skinner, he disclaimed 'all interested motives for what he did, at the same time shewing everyone present that this was his principal object'. Three months later, 'the Somersetshire orator', as Skinner styled him, was dead. '*De mortuis nil nisi bonum*' his old enemy carped; 'if I were called to write his epitaph, it should be as follows:

Old Down and Emborough

Hic saltem quiescit Sir John
Dominus de Ston Easton' [11]

There was obviously more to Sir John than this, even if one is
a bit overwhelmed by the 39 lines of pious eulogy which his
affectionate widow inscribed to his memory on a marble tablet in
Ston Easton church, 'near the Scenes He cherished in retirement
and where He was so long belov'd and respected'. He had certainly had a varied and distinguished career in his 79 years of life.
He was called to the Bar, and rose to be a Bencher of the Inner
Temple; he had been recommended to the East India Company by
Lord North, and had spent some years in India; he had on two
separate occasions resided in Italy while engaged on secret diplo-
matic missions and in negotiating with the Vatican, for which he
received high commendation from the government; in 1796 he
was rewarded with a baronetcy after negotiating the marriage between the Princess Royal and the Duke of Württemberg. For more
than 20 years he was M.P. for Sudbury in Suffolk, though his
home was at Warfield Grove in Berkshire, of which county he was
Sheriff in 1800. In the following year, however, he moved to
Somerset as a result of his marriage to the widow of Henry Hippisley Coxe of Ston Easton. Elizabeth Coxe Hippisley, as she
became by her second marriage, instead of Elizabeth Hippisley
Coxe, survived both her husbands and lived until 1843; she was
the daughter of Thomas Horner of Mells, so that Sir John
stepped straight into his place among the leading county families.
He looked after the estate he had inherited by his marriage, and
performed his duty to local society as Turnpike Commissioner
and Justice of the Peace:

In Discharging The Functions of Magistracy

he manifested (according to his marble memorial)

A Zealous Perseverance
to correct and meliorate the course of Public Justice
and During a long series of Parliamentary Labours....
a firm support of Liberal Principles
and Religious Toleration.

He was in fact a strenuous supporter of Catholic emancipation
(which may well be the reason for Skinner's violent antipathy towards him), writing many pamphlets and speeches to further this

cause (he is labelled a 'political writer' in the D.N.B.) and it is
therefore no surprise to find him in 1814 welcoming the Benedictine community to their new home at Downside in many practical
ways, including an invitation to skate at Emborough. For early
nineteenth-century winters brought skating as a matter of course.
Sometimes masters and boys would skate to Bath and back, which
involved a 6-mile walk to Paulton, 17 miles' skating into Bath
along the frozen Coal Canal, past ice-bound barges and an interminable series of locks, dinner in Bath, and then the arduous trek
home. But that was an expedition for heroes: ordinary mortals
were content with 'Sir John's', and early numbers of *The Downside Review* contain lyrical descriptions of the scene, and of the
multifarious activities enjoyed all over the ten acres of ice 'placidly
embosomed in trees'. There is a whole chapter devoted to the
exquisite pleasures of skating in Abbot Snow's *Sketches of Old
Downside*, and there was even a school skating song.

The scene can have changed little in the intervening years. In a
cold spell you can still hear the distant drone and the closer hiss of
skates on the polished ice, and watch the swiftly-changing pattern of dark figures, restlessly gyrating against a background of
naked trees. For them it is still 'Sir John's'. At midsummer, a
great peace falls upon the scene: the beeches fringe the water with
the cool mass of their foliage; not a breath of air disturbs the surface; a fisherman meditates his skill against the sudden tench or
pike; or a picnic party lies on the bank, pausing on their journey
in the heat of the day.

But Emborough appears at its best at mid-season: when the
russet and gold fires of autumn seem to cascade into the lake; or
when a pale spring sky is veined by the lattice work of boughs,
thrusting with sap; and a flush of bluebells under the trees, or a
cluster of marigolds at the water's edge, add their colour. A swan
moves slowly hither and thither, unconscious cynosure of every
eye; catspaws of wind ruffle the lake's surface, and water-fowl
scutter and echo among the reeds. On such a day as this, Emborough Pool is no longer 'a dismal sheet of water'; in another of
Dorothy Wordsworth's phrases, 'it calls home the heart to
quietness'.

CHAPTER TWELVE

The River Without a Name

Generations have trod, have trod, have trod.

G. M. HOPKINS: *God's Grandeur*

The outfall from Emborough Pool gurgles away across a meadow and then disappears underground: or rather the ground itself disappears, for large quarries gash the hill-side and, what with a railway embankment and a lofty viaduct, the natural lie of the land can only be guessed at. Half a mile down the valley the stream rather diffidently begins to flow again. These are the headwaters of a river that runs east towards Frome for about a dozen miles—a river without a name.

This was not always so: all the old map-makers, from Saxton in 1575 down to Bowen in the middle of the eighteenth century, mark it as the river Frome. Contemporary writers agreed: Drayton, in his great topographical poem *Polyolbion*, which was published in 1622, refers to the river Frome who 'scarcely ever wash'd the coal-sleck from her face'. There was never any mining in what is now known as the Frome valley, but all down the valley below Emborough, at Nettlebridge, Coleford and Vobster, there are remains of early workings, and on a map like Morden's (1695) the landscape is pock-marked with 'Cole Pitts'. Selden's note on Drayton's poem says that 'out of *Mendip* Hills *Froome* springeth, and through the Coalpits, after a short course Eastward, turns upward to *Bathe's Avon*'. So also Camden, who says that 'out of those *Mineral-mountains* arises the river *Frome*, which hastens eastward by these pits of coal . . . and before it has run any great way, (wheels) towards the north'.[1] Even as late as 1750, Dr Richard Pococke, travelling north from Wells, 'ascended the high Mendippe Hills and, crossing over the heath (i.e. the unenclosed common), came near the rise of the Frome, that falls into the Avon near Bath, where there are coal pits'.[2]

Against this, however, stands Leland, who visited Somerset about 1540, and wrote in his *Itinerary*: 'There cummith a broke from the cole-pittes in Mendepe, and strikith by south in the botom of Melles, and thens rennith into Frome ryver.'[3] This clearly gives the disputed title to the river on which the town of Frome stands, and the later topographers agree. According to Collinson, the principal source of the river is at Yarnfield Common, due south of Frome, and Phelps concurs. (This is certainly more precise than Leland who stalls with 'Frome water riseth at . . .', and less ambiguous than Lewis, whose *Topographical Dictionary* (1831) casually declares that the ironworks at Elm and at Nunney are *both* situated on the banks of the Frome, even though they are in completely different valleys.) In their first edition of the one-inch map, the Ordnance surveyors refused to commit themselves, and gave no name to either branch of the stream; but today the only official appellation that the Emborough stream has acquired is 'Mells River', in the last half-mile of its course above Spring Gardens, while the river Frome indubitably flows through the town on which presumably it originally bestowed its name.

For this is the really vital piece of evidence in the puzzle. The true names of almost all Somerset's rivers and streams are British in origin: Avon, Axe (which is identical with Esk, Exe and Usk and simply means 'water'), Brue, Cale, Cam, Chew, Parret and Yeo. So too is Frome, a river name that reappears in Dorset and Herefordshire, and twice in Gloucestershire, where it is responsible for the names of such settlements on its banks as Frenchay, Frampton, Framilode, and Frocester; and in Somerset too the settlement must have been named after the river.

The confusion arose, I imagine, because the two streams that meet near Spring Gardens are roughly equal in size, but the stream that rises at Emborough has the longer course and flows through a piece of country that in past centuries has been far more thickly populated and industrialized: it might thus claim to be the senior branch, and its description as 'the river that runs down the valley to Frome' might well in time be corrupted into 'the Frome river' or 'the river Frome'. I have never found any record of this name in use since the eighteenth century, but the old maps and books of travel show that until then it must have been accepted. Today nobody will give the stream anything more than a local name: Edford brook, Coleford brook, Mells brook or merely The

Brook. At Mells I was once told categorically that it was the river Cole.

Many of the streams in the broken hill country to the north of the main Mendip range appear at first sight to be called after the villages through which they pass—Winford brook, Cam brook, Wellow brook, Midford brook. But the word brook is in each case superfluous, for the names are in fact river names: Winford is identical with the Welsh Gwenffrwd, the 'white, holy, happy' stream; the Cam brook, like the Gloucestershire and Cumberland Cams, is the 'crooked' stream; the two villages of Wellow in Hampshire stand on the Blackwater, which was once itself called the Wellow, just as the Somerset stream has given its name to the villages of Wellow and Welton, while in Saxon times Radstock seems to have been described as 'aet Welewestoce', the place on the Wellow; Midford is the 'ford at the junction of streams', the streams being the Wellow and the Cam.

This is a very different story from the rivers which late in life have acquired names filched from settlements on their banks. There are two such back-formations in the Mendip country—the Sheppey and the Somer. Both are deplorable names. In Saxon times (705) the stream that flows through Shepton Mallet and Croscombe, and down to the moors beyond Wells, was known as the Doulting water, with reference to its source, the name Doulting itself deriving from a British river name. During the prosperity of Croscombe as a clothing town, the name was changed to Croscombe stream, but about 1884 Ordnance Survey officials arrived in Shepton Mallet and inquired the name of the stream. The late A. F. Somerville of Dinder records that when a non-resident told them that it had no particular name, they suggested that it must be Sheppey—and so it has remained. Such changes as this are unwarranted, because they destroy history, and as A. L. Rowse has observed, a country's history can be read in its place names.

The Somer is another recent and quite unjustifiable back-formation from Midsomer Norton through which it flows, as the town's name refers to the midsummer festival once held there on the day of St John, the patron saint of the parish church. John Wesley suggests that the name derived from the appalling roads in the district, which only allowed the village to be approached at midsummer, but the river Somer is just as much of a myth, though now accepted in the locality, and authorized by the Ordnance

Survey as the name of what was once a three-mile-long tributary of the Wellow. Better no name at all than such a name.

It is indeed strange that the very much larger and more significant stream that flows from Emborough down the Nettlebridge valley should have survived so many centuries of history as a river without a name, accepting, somewhat reluctantly, that it cannot really claim to be the river Frome. For all its thickly-populated reaches, and the frequent and varied signs of human activity that line its banks, it is a little-known stream, mentioned in no guide books (except perhaps for a passing reference at Vallis Vale), threading an unfashionable and unpublicized flank of Mendip. And yet a man who set himself to walk from the source to the confluence with the Frome would pass through a great deal of beautiful hill country on which many periods of history have left their mark.

A leisurely day's walk along the valley—not so leisurely, if one attempts to keep close to the water's edge, at times, in fact, almost impossible—would take one past mills recorded in Domesday Book; past the Fire Engine Inn; under the Foss Way; round the sweeping contours of Stratton Common where the wild daffodils flower in the early spring; past abandoned 'Cole Pitts'—Moorewood, Edford and Vobster, or the more romantically named Duck's Nest, Bilboa and Ringing Bell—and under the ruins of Stoke House and the pack-saddle bridge at Coleford. In Mells Park the stream slackens and broadens out into ornamental water before slipping down into the iron valley where the Fussells made their fortune, between the prehistoric promontory forts of Wadbury and Tedbury, and, flanked by railway sidings that serve the great limestone quarries—for this is the final eastward thrust of Mendip, where the mountain limestone plunges steeply out of sight beneath new geological deposits—it swirls under a fine Georgian aqueduct (built in 1800 to carry the Dorset & Somerset Canal down the valley from the Nettlebridge collieries), and out at last into the wider valley of the Frome, beneath the wooded slopes of Orchardleigh Park.

It is the first mile or so of the valley which is my favourite stretch, if only for the expectation that I shall be utterly alone there. But before we dip down, let us stand for a moment on the watershed at Emborough. From the field by the church, one looks down into the Chew valley, to Dundry on its high hill, and beyond to the mist-blue mountains of Wales; but from the ridge just across the pond, one is looking eastwards along the slowly falling flank of Mendip, across to the Westbury White Horse and the receding line of Wiltshire Downs, through which flow strange rivers like the Avon and the Kennet, that make their meeting with the sea at Southampton or at London, far beyond the bounds of the Westcountry.

The view is lost in a moment, as the valley curves down into the hills, out of sight of the railway and the quarry and the main road: Crock's Bottom according to the modern O.S. map, Shawcross Bottom in 1817, and the Romantic Valley to many generations of Downside monks and boys. By any name it is a secret sheltered place, where one can sprawl at ease in the warm sunshine, or wander all afternoon without meeting a soul. The tracks that once served the cottages in the valley are deserted, for the cottages lie in tumbled ruin, and the footpaths that thread the woods are hardly used, except by occasional children in search of primroses or nuts in season. Church Lane no longer echoes to the footsteps of the little community climbing up out of the valley on their weekly tramp to their parish church. High up on the hillsides on either side of the valley stand two farmhouses: Wintertop and Blacker's Hill, a fine seventeenth-century house, only spasmodically occupied of late years, staring across the tree-tops towards the Beacon on the far crest of Mendip. It is a stretch of countryside that must be lonelier now than it has been for centuries, for it is full of evidence of human activity from which life has ebbed away, leaving the valley to a quietness broken only by the song of birds and by the sound of wind and water.

Yet, standing in the utter quietness of the valley, it is hard to believe that in one direction one is within a mile of a main road and a railway—I have actually talked with a very old lady who lived alone in a cottage in the middle of the fields, called the Three Tunnys (once an alehouse?), and who remembered the cutting of the Somerset & Dorset in the 1870s; within a mile, too, of the clatter and dust of the stone-crushing plant at Emborough, and in the other direction less than a mile from the site of a Domesday mill and of a colliery which ceased work less than forty years ago. Crock's Bottom is, in fact, a scene of continuous human endeavour, and full of history for those who have eyes to see: not, of course, the world-shaking history of the captains and kings who

marched about the land with 'drums and tramplings', but the unobtrusive trend of local history that fashioned the countryside we
know for our own.

The crumbled cottages lie snugly under the northern slope of
the hill: here and there are traces of plaster on the walls, or smears
of smoke from the hearth. Scraggy elder trees grow inside gaping
walls which are bright with stone-crop and crane's-bill. The
abandoned gardens have long since reverted to wild. The shell of
Crock's Bottom Farm, with its outlying buildings and the ghost of
a garden, stands above the wood. A deserted track winds down
between grey stone walls, and thrusts up and over the opposite
hill towards unseen farms. In the open glade, where the buried
stream from Emborough has now come to light again, there are
ruined watercress-beds, long since untended. The dams are
broken and the shallow water is studded with the white stars of
water-fennel. Under a fallen mossy tree, where I have found the
rare and delicate Solomon's seal, the stream leaps and sparkles
away into the wood, which is misted with bluebells in the spring,
and loud with the startled flap of pigeons' wings. Abruptly the
valley merges with another valley where a larger stream comes
down from Gurney Slade, and here, until a few years ago, stood
the mill, silent and derelict: the dry leat was choked with nettles,
and the grindstones lay untidily among the rotting leaves where
they had fallen. Two hundred feet above, screened by the trees,
are the ramparts of Blacker's Hill Camp, the prehistoric earthwork that must have served to guard the Foss Way from the west.

There must be many valleys like Crock's Bottom, full of unrecorded history: every mile of the Mendip countryside poses
tantalizing questions to which no answer is forthcoming, or offers
half hints which a lucky strike may enable one to interpret cor-
rectly. Why, for instance, did the little community in Crock's
Bottom disappear? It is not as if there was an industry that decayed, as at Stoke Bottom, or in the valleys where there were
cloth mills. There were still quarries and coal-pits at work close at
hand; there was still good land to till. Yet the fact remains that less
than a hundred years ago there were between half a dozen and a
dozen inhabited houses in the valley, served by decent lanes. The
late Gilbert Fry of Stratton once told me how as a boy he was
sent on an errand to the last inhabited cottage: when he knocked
on the door, there was no reply, sudden premonition and panic

The River Without a Name

overtook him, and he ran all the way back to Stratton for a priest. The doctor came too, but when they broke down the door, the last inhabitant of the little hamlet was dead, and nobody cared to settle there again.

What superstitions were attached to the Fairey Slats on Blacker's Hill, which we now know are merely faulted strata? Who built the watercress-beds? They appear on the tithe map of 1841, but not in 1817: before the days of modern transport, watercress could hardly have been a commercial proposition like the present beds at Chilcompton. Were the ponds once the mill-ponds of an un-remembered mill? how many generations of millers ground their corn there? or were the dams to get a head of water for an iron mill that was never built?

We may never know: nor who Crock was. An old estate map, a parish register, a deed or a tax receipt in a lawyer's office or among a dusty bundle of public records might give a clue; but until then he survives as a mythical figure who gave his name to a beautiful and secluded mile of Mendip countryside.

CHAPTER THIRTEEN

The Little Railways

Who stands, the crux left of the watershed,
On the wet road between the chafing grass
Below him sees dismantled washing-floors,
Snatches of tramline running to the wood,
An industry already comatose,
Yet sparsely living.

W. H. AUDEN: *Poems* 1930

The peace and seclusion of Crock's Bottom might have
been broken once and for all a hundred years ago, if certain projected lines of railway had ever been carried out;
for, in the middle of the nineteenth century, for every line of railway that was built, there were probably half a dozen wildcat
schemes or alternative routes which were rejected or allowed to
fall into abeyance. The shelves of the Record Offices of both
Houses of Parliament, and of every county in England, are stacked
with the evidence of what might have been.

In 1862 the Somerset Central Railway and the Dorset Central
Railway amalgamated to form the Somerset & Dorset Railway,
though it was not until the following year that the immediate objective of a through route from Burnham to Poole, linking the
Bristol Channel and the English Channel, was achieved. It was an
over-optimistic venture from the start in view of the very limited
value of Burnham as a seaport: today, buffer stops block the approach to the little pier which sticks out into the mudflats of the
Parret estuary, from which the Somerset & Dorset once managed
to operate a cross-channel paddle-steamer service to Cardiff.
English to Bristol Channel traffic was likely to be even more
limited, seeing that the line traversed sparsely-inhabited country
and touched not even a moderate-sized town. It was not until 1874
that the north-south axis of the Somerset & Dorset was finally

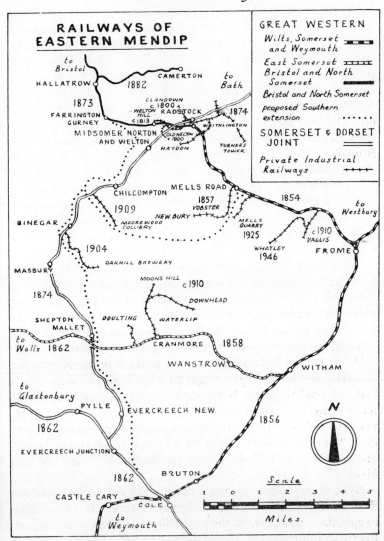

RAILWAYS OF EASTERN MENDIP

GREAT WESTERN

Wilts, Somerset and Weymouth

East Somerset

Bristol and North Somerset

Bristol and North Somerset proposed Southern extension

SOMERSET & DORSET JOINT

Private Industrial Railways

established, from Bath to Bournemouth, but from the earliest days the management had cast eager glances northwards towards the Somerset coalfield and the city of Bristol, dreaming of the through traffic that might be tapped from the Midlands and the north of England.

At this time, the coalfield which centred upon Radstock, with its collieries scattered about the hills and valleys to the north and south, was served by only one line of railway, a broad-gauge mineral branch from Frome to a terminal station near the site of the latter-day GWR goods station at Radstock. This line had been projected by the Wilts, Somerset & Weymouth Railway under an Act of 1845, but before it was built, the local company, whose independence was nominal, had been absorbed by the Great Western. The only other outlets from the coalfield were the Somersetshire Coal Canal in the Cam valley, which was opened in 1805 from Paulton to Limpley Stoke, where it joined the Kennet & Avon Canal; and its feeder, the Somersetshire Coal Canal Tramway from Radstock to Midford. The latter was laid on the towing path of a branch of the canal which had been very little used: it was opened in 1815, and along it horses drew trains of eight or nine tubs of coal which were off-loaded into canal boats at Midford wharf.

The mineral branch from Frome was opened in 1854, and the next twenty years saw the completion of the railway network to the north of Mendip (with the exception of the Hallatrow-Limpley Stoke branch which eventually replaced the Coal Canal). The promotion of the Bristol & North Somerset Railway in 1863 brought various proposals to develop railways to serve the coalfield.* It was by linking up with one of these proposals that the Somerset & Dorset hoped to get to Bristol, and so achieve solvency, if not prosperity. In the Parliamentary sessions of 1865–66 the B & NS Southern Extension scheme was proposed: this involved a main line from Farrington Gurney, over Mendip, to join the S & D near Evercreech, with a branch to serve the Nettlebridge valley and to link up with the Radstock–Frome line near Mells.

None of these plans came to fruition, and it was to Bath, and not to Bristol, that the S & D eventually gained access. It is interesting to speculate, however, on the possibility of a through route from Bristol to Bournemouth and to the south coast in general, though it is more to the immediate purpose to follow on the map the

* The standard-gauge B & NS was finally opened from Bristol to Radstock in 1873, with help from the GWR, by whom it was absorbed in 1884. Its name survives on the North Somerset Junction signal-box, about half a mile to the east of Bristol Temple Meads. The Radstock–Frome mineral line was converted to standard-gauge in 1874, and through passenger trains from Bristol to Frome began to run in 1875. The passenger service was withdrawn in 1959.

37. (*above*) 0–4–0 saddle-tank locomotive *Mendip* at the Oakhill Brewery.
38. (*below*) The Somerset & Dorset line: the abandoned quarries at Winsor
Hill, near Shepton Mallet. (BR 2–6–4 Class 4 tank on a Bath–Templecombe
stopping train)

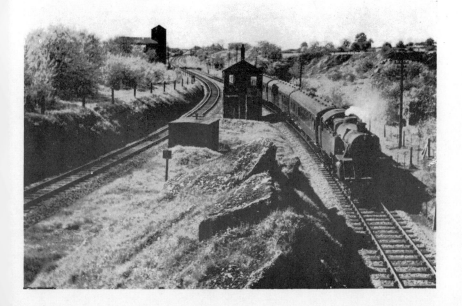

THE DORSET AND SOMERSET CANAL
39. (*above*) The 'noble and stupendous' aqueduct at Coleford
40. (*below*) Murtry aqueduct almost submerged in growth

proposed extension of the line from Bristol to its junction with the
s & D. In the deposited plan, it is marked on one of the later re-
prints of the 1817 Ordnance Survey map, and this gives a much
more vivid impression of its impact on the countryside than does
the modern map, where one is prejudiced by later roads and railways, and by the development of towns and villages in relation to
them.

Diverging from the Bristol–Radstock line near the site of the
Halt at Farrington Gurney, the Extension proceeded in a south-
easterly direction, climbing at 1 in 70, past Clapton and to the west
of Chilcompton, high up on the opposite side of the valley to the
s & D line, towards Old Down: instead of climbing over the
Mendip ridge at Masbury, the line swung to the east beyond Binegar, climbing on easier gradients of about 1 in 100, before plung-
ing into a 600-yard tunnel close to the Beacon, on a falling
gradient of 1 in 55: this was to be the ruling gradient all the way
down the southern slopes of the hill, where the line kept somewhat to the east of the later s & D line, past Shepton Mallet (where
there was to be a junction with the East Somerset Railway which
had been opened from Witham to Shepton Mallet in 1858, and
extended to Wells in 1862) and Evercreech village, to join the
Somerset & Dorset Railway near Lamyatt.

The Nettlebridge branch was to leave the main line near Old
Down, more or less opposite the latter-day s & D signal-box,
and slip down Crock's Bottom on a falling gradient of 1 in 60,
thereafter keeping along the bottom of the valley on easier
gradients, past Gurney Slade mill, past the Fire Engine Inn,
through Nettlebridge, and then along the line of the abandoned
Dorset & Somerset canal through Edford. To avoid the difficult
terrain in which the canal had been involved at Coleford, the railway was to keep to the south of the river, and then climb through
Vobster, to pick up the line of the canal until it reached the Radstock–Frome branch: there was to be a triangular junction close to
the site of Mells Road station. Presumably, since the B & NS was
a standard-gauge line, a third rail was to be laid in the GWR
broad-gauge track between Radstock and Frome. Perhaps, however, such mundane details had hardly yet been considered in this
chimerical scheme; which was, however, revived in 1872, when the
Somerset & Dorset Railway was building its Bath Extension, and
was not finally abandoned until 1878.

The Little Railways

It is hard to imagine the valley as it might well have been developed: intensively mined, with smoking chimneys, clutters of pithead gear, sprawling heaps of spoil, and the noise and smoke of mineral trains labouring on heavy gradients. Getting coal in the Somerset coalfield was difficult enough; getting it away was worse. There was still talk of a light railway down the valley when Wickham wrote his *Records by Spade and Terrier* about 1912, but only at the two extremities of the valley did any form of railway ever penetrate. When the Moorewood colliery was reopened in 1909 after being disused for a number of years, a 2 ft. gauge tramway was built to connect with the Somerset & Dorset line. On Stock Hill there was an inclined plane up which six trams at a time, containing 8–9 cwt. apiece, were hauled by cable: they were attached 'mane and tail', as an old miner put it, and there was a winding house at the bottom, and a drum at the top, of the incline. Here the trams were handed over to two small 0–6–0 saddle tank locomotives which were stabled in a wooden engine shed. These hauled the trams beside Coal Lane, where the packhorse was now superseded by the iron horse hauling fifteen or sixteen trams. It is still possible to trace the embankment, built of ashes and other spoil, and the abutments of the bridge that carried the line across Church Lane. Farther along the line there are more substantial remains of the embankment where the trams tipped their coal into the standard-gauge trucks at the Somerset & Dorset sidings controlled by Moorewood signal-box. The tramway was abandoned in the 1920s, when the colliery began to use road transport, before it finally closed in 1932.

Industrial remains such as these are often the only tangible relics of a particular stage in the economic development of some stretch of countryside, whose landscape was permanently affected by it, as well as the lives of the people who lived there. An obvious example of this, only a mile or two from the Moorewood valley, is the Oakhill Brewery railway, built in 1904 to transport the barrels of Oakhill stout to the Somerset & Dorset line at Binegar. With a peak output of 2,000–2,500 barrels a week, this was the heyday of the Oakhill Brewery, before the First World War, from which the stout trade never recovered. A traction engine had previously hauled the barrels of beer and stout to the station, making deep ruts in the roads in the process. A railway was accordingly built with a 2 ft. 6 in. gauge: this line struck south-west across the fields from the brewery to the Bristol–Shepton Mallet road, which it crossed on the level; it then kept alongside the main road, past the Mendip Inn, turned west along an old lane, and was finally carried across Binegar Bottom on a noble embankment and bridge, to a large shed in the goods yard at Binegar station. Two sturdy little saddle-tank engines, *Mendip* and *Oakhill*, hauled trains of long low trucks piled with barrels, on which the village children delighted to ride.[1] Photographs survive, and traces of the line can still be seen—the marks where the sleepers lay, an occasional level-crossing gate and so on; but here, too, the bulldozer is at work: where a year or so ago there were the stone abutment of the bridge and the embankment in Binegar Bottom, there is now a smooth and cultivated hillside.

Quite apart from the decline of the stout trade and the subsequent take-over of the Oakhill Brewery by larger and larger units, the little railway was quickly rendered obsolete by the development of the internal combustion engine. Motor lorries could deliver beer and stout far beyond the range of a two-horse waggon, and many a small local brewery saw the writing on the wall. In fact, the internal combustion engine put paid to many of the other little lines of railway all over Mendip, where coal and stone could now be hauled direct from pit and quarry, without having to be taken to railhead to begin a slow and circuitous journey to their destination. The quarries at Winsor Hill are silent, the sidings disused, and the signal-box an empty shell with shattered windows; the stone-crushing plant beside the line at Binegar has long since vanished (in fact two whole quarries have been filled up with spoil from the local pits); the aerial ropeway, which used to transport tiny swaying buckets of stone to the siding near Wookey station on the Cheddar Valley line, has been dismantled. Even the coal that was mined beneath my house, at New Rock colliery, went direct by road to the power station at Portishead, and stone-lorries make life precarious in many a narrow Mendip lane.

Some of the quarry lines are still traceable: the famous Doulting stone was moved from its beds along a horse tramway, across two turnpike roads, to a private siding on the East Somerset line; from Cranmore station a 2 ft. gauge line climbed over the ridge to serve Moon's Hill and Downhead quarries early in the present century, and beyond Long Cross the track formation is still clearly

The Little Railways

visible, although abandoned more than 40 years ago. This line was later replaced by a standard-gauge branch as far as Waterlip, now also abandoned, but 2 miles east of Cranmore a new 1½ mile branch was opened in 1970 to Merehead quarry, while another branch off the Radstock–Frome line winds up Vallis Vale past Bedlam and along Murder Combe to Whatley quarry. Neither of the two branches from Mells Road however has survived: Jericho siding was laid about 1925 to Beauchamp Bros' Mells quarry; the Newbury railway was originally a broad-gauge line, built by the Westbury Iron Co. in 1857 to serve their collieries at Coleford and their quarry at Vobster. Much of it was laid along the line of the abandoned Dorset & Somerset Canal. After the closure of Newbury colliery in 1927 it continued to serve Vobster quarry until 1966. It also served Mells colliery, who owned an historic locomotive, acquired from the GWR in 1931: this was an outside cylinder 0–6–0 tank engine No. 820, which had previously belonged to the Lambourn Valley Railway who had christened it *Ealhswith*.

Beyond Mells Road station one soon reached the complex of mineral lines which developed round the Radstock pits, linking individual collieries with one or other of the two through lines, or serving to haul coal up out of the steep-sided valleys to conveniently placed depots, from which it could be fetched by horse and cart in the days before motor transport. A 2 ft. 8½ in. gauge line from Foxcote, for instance, ran right out to the top of the ridge near Turner's Tower, while the standard-gauge branch at Kilmersdon colliery was still steam-operated in 1970 by a Peckett 0–4–0 saddle tank. The Clandown and Welton lines, long since closed, were of great historical interest, having been constructed about 1800 to feed the branch of the Somersetshire Coal Canal from Radstock to Midford. They appear as 'railroads' on the 1817 O.S. map and as such formed the southernmost extremity of the Coal Canal Tramway which was substituted for the canal in 1815 (cf. pages 134–5). Recent excavations by industrial archaeologists have uncovered a number of lengths of wrought-iron rails and stone sleepers still *in situ*, both in Radstock and on the Welton line, while the Coal Canal Tramway and other 'railroads' are now described in Kenneth Clew's recent book on *The Somersetshire Coal Canal and Railways*.

CHAPTER FOURTEEN

The Dorset and Somerset Canal

The bridges were unbuilt and trouble coming.

W. H. AUDEN: *Poems* 1930

The last few pages may seem to have moved some way away from Mendip, even if they were concerned with the industrial archaeology of the coalfield lying on the northern slopes of the range. One of the most remarkable survivals of this early industrial period, however, is to be found striking right up towards some of the highest parts of Mendip. Masbury in fact is only about three miles, as the crow flies, from the terminal basin of the ill-fated Dorset & Somerset Canal.

A few years ago I wrote a brief account of it,[1] but since then a lot more material has been unearthed, and a much more thorough exploration of its course has been possible. I have already referred to the interest of James Fussell IV in the canal (see p. 71), and it was an apparent misprint in my previous account which originally encouraged me to investigate the history of the Fussells and their ironworks. Charles Hadfield's *The Canals of Southern England* referred to 'a canal lift or balance lock . . . built by Mr Fussell, the patentee and an owner of ironworks at Wells.' I challenged this statement only to be confronted with the patent itself, 'granted to James Fussell, of Wells, in the County of Somerset, Iron Manufactor'. What could I do but climb down gracefully, and print 'James Fussell, of Wells', only to be reprimanded immediately by readers who wrote in to correct the 'misprint', and to let me know that the Fussells hailed from Mells, not Wells. I am now a good deal wiser about the Fussells, I know exactly where the balance lock was situated, and I also know that a Government office can make a mistake—in 1798, at any rate.

The Dorset & Somerset Canal was one of many abortive attempts to construct an inland waterway to link the Bristol Channel

A.D. 1798 . . . . Nº 2284.

Balance Lock for Raising or Lowering Boats &c., applicable to other Purposes.

FUSSELL'S SPECIFICATION.

TO ALL TO WHOM THESE PRESENTS SHALL COME, I, James Fussell, of Wells, in the County of Somerset, Iron Manufactor, send greeting.

WHEREAS His present Majesty King George the Third, by His Letters
5 Patent under the Great Seal of Great Britain, bearing date the Twenty-fourth day of December, One thousand seven hundred and ninety-eight, did give and grant unto me, the said James Fussell, my executors, administrators, and assigns, His Royal will and pleasure that I lawfully might make, use, and exercise and vend, during the term of years therein expressed, within that part of Great Britain called England, the Dominion of Wales, and Town of Berwick-upon-Tweed, my Invention of "A MACHINE OR BALANCE LOCK FOR RAISING BOATS FROM A LOWER LEVEL OF A CANAL TO AN UPPER, OR LOWERING THE SAME FROM AN UPPER TO A LOWER LEVEL OF A CANAL:" in which Letters Patent a proviso is contained that if I, the said James Fussell, should not particularly describe and
15 ascertain the nature of my said Invention, and in what manner the same is to be performed, by an instrument in writing under my hand and seal, to be inrolled in His Majesty's High Court of Chancery within one calendar month next after the date of the said Letters Patent, then such Letters Patent were to be void, as in and by the same, reference being thereto had, will more
20 fully appear.

NOW KNOW YE, that in compliance with the said proviso, I, the said James Fussell, do hereby declare that my said Invention is describeb in manner following that is to say:—

The first page of the patent for James Fussell's balance lock, designed for the Dorset & Somerset Canal in 1798

The Dorset and Somerset Canal

and the English Channel. It was authorized by an Act of 1796[2] to run for 40 miles, from the Kennet & Avon Canal at Widbrook near Bradford, through Frome and Wincanton, to end alongside the Poole road at Gains Cross beside the Dorset Stour near Sturminster Newton, with a branch from Frome to Nettlebridge, about 11 m. long. The course of the main line is actually marked on the map published in Nightingale's *History of Somerset* (1819), and on early editions of Cruchley's Railway and Telegraphic map of the county; but only the branch appears on the 1817 Ordnance Survey map, where it is recorded as 'unfinished'. The deposited plan of the canal was drawn on a scale of 3 in. to the mile by W. Bennett, Surveyor, of Beckington near Frome, in 1795. The outstanding feature of the main line was to have been a tunnel at the summit level near Brewham, 1,009 yards long; the estimate for the main line totalled £115,400 12s. 6½d., and for the branch, £30,583 19s. od. Subscriptions to the proposed Canal totalled £79,200 (only £58,000 was eventually received), of which James Fussell subscribed £1,000, and John Billingsley £3,500.

Work was begun on the branch, which under the terms of the Act the company was obliged to complete first; but by 1803 all the capital subscribed had been spent, and £10,000 besides, and 1¾ m. still remained to be cut. Costs had risen in the war years before the victory at Trafalgar had dissipated the threat of Napoleon's invasion, further capital was not forthcoming, and there was as yet no income from the Mendip coalfield, which the branch had been projected to tap as the most profitable source of traffic available. A pamphlet which was written about 1825 to revive interest in the canal, and to urge its completion (see page 71), gives a list of the works that had been completed:

13 Arched Bridges, built with excellent materials	6 Waste Weirs
5 Swivel Bridges	26 Culverts and Drains
5 Fixed Bridges	2 Tunnels
2 Draw Bridges	1 Tunnel, at a place called Goodeaves (only 90 yards complete)
11 Grooved Stop Gates	
9 Double Stop Gates	1 Balance Dock complete
19 Trunks	Two others partly finished

Besides a noble and stupendous Aqueduct at Coleford.

The '2 Tunnels' are a mystery: they do not figure on the deposited plan, and nowhere on the line of the canal is there any

ANNO TRICESIMO SEXTO

Georgii III. Regis.

C A P. XLVII.

An Act for making a Navigable Canal from or near *Gain's Cross*, in the Parish of *Shillingston Okeford*, in the County of *Dorset*, to communicate with the *Kennet* and *Avon* Canal, at or near *Widbrook*, in the County of *Wilts*, and also a certain Navigable Branch from the intended Canal.

[24th *March* 1796.]

HEREAS the making and maintaining a Navigable Preamble Canal for Boats, Barges, and other Vessels, from or near a Place called *Gain's Cross*, within the Parish of *Shillingston Okeford*, in the County of *Dorset*, to join and communicate with the *Kennet* and *Avon* Canal, at or near *Widbrook*, in the Parish of *Bradford*, in the County of *Wilts*; and also the Navigable Branch herein-after described, from the said intended Canal, will open an easy and convenient Communication with many considerable manufacturing Towns and Places in the Country through which the same are intended to pass, and also with the extensive Collieries near *Mendip*, in the County of *Somerset*; and will render the Conveyance of Goods, Wares, and Merchandize, Coal, Stone, Slate, Flags, Lime, Limestone, Timber, and other Things, less expensive than at present, and will be of great publick Utility: But the same

6 Z 2

cannot

Title-page of the Act of 1796 for the Dorset & Somerset Canal trace of tunnelling except at Goodeaves, in Highbury; the Balance Dock [*sic*] is obviously James Fussell's balance lock, which seems to have been doomed from the outset to be dogged by printers' errors.

The Act of 1796 authorized the branch to be built as far as Nettlebridge, where one of the properties to be acquired was the toll-house belonging to the Shepton Mallet Turnpike Commissioners, and the deposited plan shows the end of the canal abutting on the old Bath–Shepton Mallet turnpike road, just to the south of the George Inn. The last stretch to Nettlebridge, however, never seems to have been embarked upon; the 1825 pamphlet says that 'the works were commenced at Cote, in the parish of Stratton', by which the hamlet of Pitcot is presumably meant. As a matter of fact the terminal basin was about a mile from Pitcot, at the bottom of Stratton Common, and about half a mile west of Edford, at a point where a good stream of water comes down towards the river from the common. A parchment map of Stratton parish, dated 1824, marks this clearly—a rectangular basin, with the canal and tow-path. Until recently filled in by the bulldozer, this was indeed, one of the best remaining sections of the canal: there was a firmly embanked towpath, under which the stream was still carried by a culvert, and often after periods of heavy rainfall, especially in the winter, the old bed was satisfyingly full of water, though it is pretty certain that no boats except contractors' craft ever sailed along it. Work on the canal was obviously let out by contract in sections, some of which were finished and some were not, there being noticeable gaps where sections never joined up, though at other points the bulldozer and the hand of time have been at work, filling up the bed and obliterating every trace. Appropriately enough, the first bridge over the canal (one of the few survivors) was a packhorse bridge, carrying the old road from the coal-pits on Stratton Common down to Edford; for a brief moment old and new modes of transport confronted each other.

To the east of Edford the line of the canal is maintained by a series of stiles along what must once have been the towpath, though it is obliterated by a heap of spoil from the concrete works on the site of the abandoned Edford colliery. It is visible again at Ham, with another splendid stretch of towpath, and in a cutting near Bennett's Hill farm, and it then swung round the hillside to Coleford, where it would have crossed the road from Holcombe, near the site of the Greyhound Inn, to reach the 'noble and stupendous Aqueduct'. The aqueduct is not quite so noble and stupendous as it must have been before the parapet was removed for building stone, and the two arches bestriding the steep valley became smothered in ivy; nor is its nobility enhanced by its local appellation of the 'Hucky Duck'. At Chantry, however, there is part of an inscribed stone which was discovered, in a rockery, in the garden of the house which James Fussell V built himself in the 1820s. All that remains of the inscription reads:

AQUÆDUCT

ERE ANNO 1801

but above the break in the stone, the bottom of certain letters in another line of writing just allow one to guess at the name COLEFORD. I have sometimes wondered if, when work on the canal was finally abandoned, the proprietors were allowed to re-coup themselves from works that had been completed, and, if so, whether James Fussell V used some of the dressed stone to build his new house.* The stonework at Chantry looks very similar to the dressed stone which can still be seen here and there on the course of the canal, though only a geologist could determine its exact provenance. This suggestion would at least explain the complete disappearance of most of the completed works mentioned in the pamphlet.

The aqueduct stone, now preserved at 'The Chantry', is an intriguing link with the past; so is the Coleford mother, who was heard scolding her child for playing in 'the navvy', by which she meant the dried-up bed of the canal, used sporadically as a rubbish-tip. This almost amounts to a case of folk-memory, seeing that it is at least 160 years since the navigators, or navvies, left their mark on the hillside at Coleford. They may have intended to tunnel under the road here—there are some odd arches near the Wesleyan chapel; they certainly excavated the two cuttings leading to the proposed tunnel almost underneath Goodeaves Close. I have been told that there used to be a lot of dressed stone lying about there, before the cuttings were practically obliterated by rubbish-tips.

As far as Vobster, the canal was filled in to carry the branch

* In 1829, at any rate, John Fussell owned a quarry 'near the aqueduct'. This is mentioned in Hylton's *History of Kilmersdon* (p. 96), with reference to the supply of stone for the building of Coleford church.

line of railway to Newbury and Mackintosh pits, but just below Vobster Cross there is a good half-mile stretch of the bed, and a pleasant low-arched bridge under the road. At this point quarrying has destroyed the line, but on the branch line of railway from Vobster quarries to Mells Road station it appears again. Here we are close to Holwell farm where Richard White was born (see p. 78); in his autobiography he tells of going to Bristol with his uncle, and how they were delayed on the journey back and spent the night with relations, to avoid the long cross-country ride to Mells in the dark. His mother was dreadfully worried, and 'could not rest without someone going to see if we had met with an accident in the canal that ran through the farm'. This incident took place about 1840, forty years after the abandonment of the works.

From Mells Road station, the railway and the canal ran side by side towards Frome, but where the railway begins to descend a steep incline, the canal kept on along the slope of Barrow Hill, as shown on the 2½ in. map, just below the 450-ft. contour line. At this point comes a gap of more than a mile, before the line is picked up again at Elliotts, on the floor of the valley; almost at once, the bed of the canal plunges under the railway embankment and heads south up Vallis Vale. The reason for this sudden change of direction was the need to cross 'the river without a name', augmented since Mells by several streams, and by now a considerable body of water: this was negotiated by means of the splendid three-arched aqueduct (estimated to cost £317 13s. od.), which still stands, now used only as a farm track across the little valley, and almost hidden with ivy and undergrowth.[3] From now on, the canal kept to the south of the river, swinging round the hillside with the railway to Spring Gardens, above the ruins of Sheppards' cloth mills, to which it was planned to bring coal, and southwards beyond Whatcombe farm, where the junction with the main line of the canal was to have been made, according to the deposited plans, 'in Wm. Davis's field near Frome'. Here there is a long and spectacular piece of walling—'the Roman Wall' I have heard it called, with that delightfully vague sense of the past that attributes anything more than a century old to the Romans.

I have described the course of this little waterway in some detail, because the visible remains are disappearing all the time, and only at one point (near Vobster) is the line of the canal marked on the latest edition of the one-inch Ordnance Survey map, although there are plenty of other stretches which are equally clearly defined on the ground. It is also an excellent example of how much local history is still to be recovered and recorded by means of patient research, at the desk and in the field. Ten years ago, there was no accurate written account of the canal in existence, and only a few scattered references in old topographical works. When

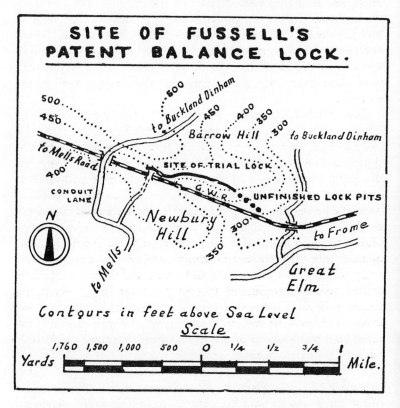

SITE OF FUSSELL'S PATENT BALANCE LOCK.

Contours in feet above Sea Level
Scale

Charles Hadfield wrote his account of the Dorset & Somerset Canal in 1955, he did not realize that the whole course could still be traced and the sites of most of the main features still be identified; nor did I—though living only a couple of miles from the terminal basin. A farmer's wife once firmly denied any possibility of there ever having been a canal past the house where she had lived for most of her life, although it was absolutely obvious to me that at that very moment we were standing talking in the bed of what was indubitably the canal, the whole canal and nothing but the canal. On the other hand, local memory has helped to fill in many of the details; in fact, a long and fruitless search for the site of its outstanding engineering feature was finally rewarded by a casual remark from one of my pupils at a W.E.A. class in Frome.

The Dorset & Somerset Canal achieved momentary fame—I hesitate to say 'immortality'—because of Fussell's Patent Balance Lock. The unfinished section of the canal extended from Barrow Hill nearly down to Murtry, involving a fall of about 210 ft. in little over a mile. The original plans provided for 207 ft. 9 in. of lockage between Frome and Vobster (with a further 56 ft. 6 in. of lockage between Vobster and Nettlebridge), but the words 'By Caissons' have been substituted for 'Lockage' by a later hand, and it would appear that the decision was made as a result of the successful exhibition of James Fussell's ingenious invention: no change apparently being made in the estimate. James Fussell's 'Machine or Balance Lock' was patented on 24 December 1798, and public exhibitions were held 'near Mells' on 6 September and 13 October 1800, and again 3 June 1802, and were fulsomely reported in the *Bath Chronicle*. The issue dated 16 October 1800, for instance, carried the following report:

A trial was made on Monday last according to notice on the Dorset and Somerset Canal of a Balance Lock, the invention of Mr. Fussell at Mells, near which place it is erected and to whom it is but justice to announce that it answered the design perfectly to the satisfaction of a great number of spectators: among them were many men of science, impartial and unprejudiced, who after its repeated operations and those without the least difficulty or mischance, and inspecting minutely every part of the machine, were unanimous in declaring it to the simplest and best of all methods yet discovered for conveying boats from the different levels and for public utility. –The expence of it exceeds but little that of the common lock, over which it has these advantages viz, it elevates a boat of ten tons burthen and sinks another of equal weight by the same operation 20 feet perpendicular in half the time that one boat passes the common lock and this with a trifling loss of water; a circumstance so valuable that it must render its use general. –The proprietors of the undertaking must be highly gratified to be in the hands of a gentleman whose first effort of the kind has been so fortunate and who has insured its success at the outset in a great measure by his superintendence and unwearied attention on the executive part of his machine and by giving every necessary instruction to its progress to the different workmen concerned.

After the first two trials, advertisements appeared in West-country newspapers inviting tenders for five additional balance locks, to be erected between Mells and Frome. The tenders were to be sent to W. Bennett of Beckington, now described as engineer to the canal company. It seems rather odd that Fussells, with their ironworks and forges only a mile or so away, did not undertake the construction themselves; one can only surmise that they were fully occupied with the production of edge-tools, and unwilling to branch out into a completely new line of production at a time when the nation's economy was anyhow under considerable strain owing to the prolonged war against Napoleon. It looked, however, as if James Fussell was destined to be second only in importance to James Brindley in the development of inland navigation. In the words of the *Bath Chronicle*, 'By this invention the difficulties which have so long existed of transferring boats on canals (sc. from one level to another) without loss of water are now fully removed and at less expense than by any scheme hitherto suggested and it is very probable that the necessity of tunnels will be thereby suspended.'[4]

At the trials, perpendicular lifts of 11 and 20 ft. were achieved, but the patent envisages lifts of 40, 50 or even 100 ft., as well as the adaptation of the machinery to an inclined plane. A fairly clear picture of the lock or canal lift, as it would be called nowadays, emerges from a careful reading of the patent. It was divided into two parallel pits by a broad buttress. The upper and lower levels of the canal were likewise divided into two channels. Barges were floated into large open watertight receptacles or caissons, made of iron or wood, which exactly fitted the channels of the canal and the lock pits. There were hatches at each end of the caissons, and stop-gates to control the water at either level of the canal. When these were closed, the caissons were simultaneously raised and lowered, like a pair of balance scales, by means of an arrangement of wheels and chains attached to a beam placed across the buttress which divided the lock into two. Additional motive power could also be supplied, when necessary, by admitting a small amount of water into a tank fixed underneath the descending caisson, which could be run off at the bottom.

Since the maximum lift achieved at the trials was 20 ft., it is not clear how six lifts (i.e. the trial lock and the five additional locks to be tendered for) were between them to cope with a rise of 207 ft. 9 in., though perhaps experience had given the proprietors enough confidence to plan for greater heights. But the visible remains do not seem to suggest this.

The site of these remains was the last problem to be solved, thanks to a young miner, Gerald Quartley, who heard me say at a lecture that nobody knew where the locks were to have been built, and came forward to say that he knew a series of large pits on a hillside, and had always wondered what they were. We went off together one afternoon to Barrow Hill, between Buckland Dinhorn and Great Elm. Barrow Hill is a lonely place, quite remote from any human habitation: the 2½-in. map marks an Anglo-Saxon burial ground on one flank, and farther over towards the railway there is a belt of scrub and trees striding down the hillside. One might walk past it again and again without realizing that one was descending the line of a flight of lifts; one might mistake the remains for a group of unfinished lime-kilns, but hardly for a canal. There are, of course, no traces of the actual machinery; only the lift pits—four great cavities in a descending line. The two middle ones are better preserved than the others: they are cut partly out of the naked oolite, in some places still faced with worked stone, and there are traces of the middle buttresses which separated their twin chambers.

It was tempting to believe that we were indeed standing on the scene of James Fussell's hour of triumph, 160 years before, where a large crowd of spectators, including the 'impartial and unprejudiced' men of science, had applauded the ingenuity and efficiency of his wonderful machine. But certain difficulties soon became apparent. The four pits that survive do not get the canal up to the summit level or down to the floor of the valley. It was hard to see how a successful demonstration could be given in an isolated lock not connected to any stretch of canal and with no apparent water supply. Furthermore, a newspaper advertisement early in 1801 spoke of Mr. Fussell's balance lock 'now in an actual State of work on the said canal, *in the Parish of Mells*',[5] whereas the Barrow Hill site lies in the parish of Great Elm.

Half a mile away, however, just beside the summit of the railway, there are the remains of yet another pit. This would have lifted the canal over the 425-ft. contour, where, incidentally, it managed to stay all the way to Stratton Common, through an extraordinarily difficult piece of country, a fine example of engineering by William Bennett. The site of this lift is 'in the Parish of Mells'; there is a clearly defined section of canal leading away from it in both directions; there is an old lane approaching from Mells, past Brickyard Cottages, giving access to the scene of the demonstrations, whereas the Barrow Hill site is almost completely inaccessible; and above all there is water; in fact, an excellent supply of water was piped from nearby Conduit Hill by the Horners to supply the Manor and the Rectory. The 1825 pamphlet refers to one complete balance lock and 'two others partly finished': to judge by the heaps of spoil, navvying had started on four of the other five proposed sites, but it is only reasonable to guess that the completed lock 'in an actual State of work' was the one whose remains are still to be seen today at the summit level.

We are unlikely now to know definitely: all we can be certain of is that the Dorset & Somerset Canal finally petered out on Barrow Hill. There can be no doubt that the heavy engineering works through Coleford, together with the vast amount of excavation required on Barrow Hill, whether for locks or for caissons, ate up the slender capital all too quickly at a time of rising costs, and in view of the uncertain outlook, the shareholders refused further calls on their shares, and the committee resolved 'to suspend the works until more auspicious times arrived', though a further Act was obtained in 1803 allowing the substitution of a railroad at any point to enable the line to be completed. The 1817 O.S. significantly marks the line of the canal along the side of Barrow Hill, and breaks off with four distant blobs which may or may not be intended to represent the four surviving lock-pits. But the 'auspicious times' never arrived, and work was never recommenced, though the anonymous author of the 1825 pamphlet pleaded eloquently for the raising of more funds and the completion of the design, at any rate as far as Frome and Bradford. Prosperity, apparently, was just round the corner: there was Mendip coal and Mendip limestone waiting to be transported; Fussells' ironworks and Sheppards' cloth mills were crying out for better transport facilities; there were potteries at Wanstrow and Crockerton; while Frome, Shepton Mallet and Wincanton were languishing in trade and 'not imbibing the spirit of progress', in danger of isolation

THE DORSET AND SOMERSET CANAL

41. (*above*) Edford bridge, carrying the old road from the coal-pits on Stratton common. 42. (*below*) Vobster bridge on the busy road between Coleford and Mells

43. Chew Valley lake from Knowle Hill, looking south towards Mendip

The Dorset and Somerset Canal

'for want of facilities of access and communication'. The days of the canal mania, however, were over and potential subscribers kept their hands firmly in their pockets; and nothing more was ever heard of Fussell's Patent Balance Lock, though similar lifts were later to be successfully operated on the Grand Western Canal between Taunton and Burlescombe.

NOTE

Since this chapter was first written in 1964, a lot more research has been carried out on the history of the Dorset & Somerset by Kenneth R. Clew. The results of this research and the whole story of the ill-fated waterway are now available in *The Dorset & Somerset Canal* (David & Charles 1971).

CHAPTER FIFTEEN

The Bull Pit

Some diversions, indeed, which were formerly in great
request, are now fallen into disrepute. . . . It is not needful
to say any more of these foul *remains of Gothic barbarity*,
than that they are a reproach, not only to all religion, but
even to human nature.

REV. JOHN WESLEY:
Sermon on *The More Excellent Way*

A piece of local research, such as that described in the last
chapter, disciplines one to scrutinize a map with the utmost care, even to the extent of using a magnifying glass,
if one has not got easy access to the 6-in. or 25-in. series, or if a
trip to the Somerset Record Office involves 75 miles of motoring.
It always surprises me how much one is apt to overlook on the
map of a piece of country with which one boldly claims to be
familiar. One cannot look too closely or too often.

When I was searching for the site of James Fussell's lift on
Barrow Hill, my eye was caught by the words 'Bull Pit', together
with the indication of an earthwork of some kind, which were
marked on the one-inch Ordnance Survey map, a mile to the
south-west of the village of Buckland Dinham, in the Gothic
lettering that denotes an ancient monument. Was this another survival, I wondered, from an older England, the England of Woodforde and Cobbett, in which bull-baiting was a recognized sport?
Perhaps not all that much older either, for the sport was not made
illegal until 1835. It was much the same with bear-baiting: even as
late as 1825, Parliament threw out a bill 'against Bear-baiting and
other cruel Practices'. Parson Woodforde thought it no shame to
go to a bear-baiting at Ansford in 1759.

Cock-fighting, too, was respectable enough: the Parson's
brother, John, went off to Bath to a Cock Match on 1 June 1772,

returning on 6 June with £50 he had won. On another occasion there was 'great cock fighting' at Ansford Inn, and a two-day county match between Wiltshire and Somerset, which Woodforde himself attended. Cock-fighting in fact outlasted the other 'cruel Practices', and still lingers on, to judge by the occasional prosecutions that are reported in the newspapers. The top storey of the Old Mill House in one Mendip village consists of a loft with gently sloping sides, framing a tiny arena which was ominously littered with feathers when the present occupants took over the house. There must be other such survivals, especially in remote areas, where the sport was carried on clandestinely.

Bull-baiting was less easy to conceal: many towns still have their Bull Rings—Birmingham, for instance, and Cirencester and Chapel-en-le-Frith, to take three random examples. In the Town Hall at Axbridge the bull anchor is preserved: an iron stake with five flukes, or barbed heads, which were embedded in the ground to defy the violence of the baited bull. The words 'Bull Pit' on my map naturally, therefore, suggested the survival of the old village bull pit at Buckland Dinham. My conjecture was corroborated by a reference in Skinner's *Journal*. In August 1819 he was archaeologizing near the mining village of Charterhouse-on-Mendip, and came across the prehistoric earthwork known as Gorsey-Bigbury: it was some forty paces in diameter and its banks were upwards of six feet high, but in the previous year the farmer had had them considerably lowered when preparing the ground for potatoes.[1] We now know that Gorsey-Bigbury is a Henge monument which was used as an early Bronze Age (beaker) living site.[2] In 1819, however, the inhabitants told Skinner that it was a 'bulpit', and it seemed to me to be significant that local people unhesitatingly identified the earthwork with something familiar, namely a village bull pit.

This comfortable theory of mine received a dash of cold water from a miner, who told me that the Buckland Dinham 'bull pit' was merely an abandoned coal-working, where mine-shafts had been sunk about 1880. In miners' parlance a 'bull pit' is one that has never produced any coal; 'bull' being good old English slang for 'dud' or 'useless', like Army 'bull'. When the Ordnance Surveyors asked what the old workings were, the inhabitants must have said that it was a 'bull pit', and the result was the Gothic lettering on my map. This, of course, would also account for

Gorsey-Bigbury being described as a 'bulpit'—an unproductive heap of spoil in the mining area round Charterhouse. Brian Vesey-Fitzgerald also told me that bull-baiting always took place in a bull-*ring* and never in a bull-*pit*, and furthermore that these were always situated in towns or big villages, and never in open country or in small hamlets.

It was all rather disheartening, until I did what I ought of course to have done long before: I went to look at the place for myself. I went with an old friend, Bill Gilling, who was born in the village, and farmed there, and we walked across fields which he had known all his life. There, in a little valley, was the abandoned coal-pit, with a dirt-batch (as a slag-heap is called in north Somerset), a brick-kiln, a very well-built chimney, and two mine shafts, lately sealed off afresh by the National Coal Board. Their records show that the shafts were sunk about 1880 to work coal seams in the Lower Series, and were abandoned in highly-inclined formations at a depth of about 420 ft.

But farther up the valley, on a steep hillside, was a tiny amphitheatre, open at one end where the ground fell away, its banks dotted with trees and shrubs. It might, of course, have been an old quarry or another abortive coal-working, but I myself feel convinced that it was the old village bull pit. What is more, the tithe map of 1841 records the name of the field as Bull Pit Ground, as does an estate map of 1813,[3] and that is seventy years before mining operations are known to have begun in the valley. A parish history of Buckland Dinham by a former vicar, Rev. J. D. D. Keilor, says that older generations knew the field as the 'Blood Field', and that there were even traces of an inhabited building where refreshments were sold on the occasion of a bull-baiting.[4]

My last lingering doubts about the authenticity of this bull-pit were dispelled when I found another example, quite by chance, as a result of looking at another tithe map for something quite different. This was about six miles away, at Stoke St. Michael, beside the road from Stoke to Oakhill, where the map marks a Bull Baiting Paddock; and there again I found a small amphitheatre, now largely filled with scrub and undergrowth. Again, it may well be the site of an old quarry, but the name of the field proves indubitably that it must at some period have been used for bull-baiting; it is quite distinct from the common use of the word bull in field names—there is a Bulls Close, for instance, on another Stoke farm, within half a mile of the Bull Baiting Paddock. It is also worthy of remark that both these bull-pits are right away from their villages, and indeed from any habitation except for an isolated farmhouse or two; both in fact are only just within their parish boundaries.* It is the same with cock-pits: there was a Cock Pit Ground at Buckland Dinham—a small enclosure of less than an acre among the meadow land on the western bank of the stream, once again well away from the village, as if it were something to be ashamed of and accepted surreptitiously, even if it were not actually illegal. There is still a cock-pit enclosure—a walled and hedged rectangle, 40 yd. long and 12 yd. wide—high up on the northern escarpment of the main Mendip range, more than a mile from the village of West Harptree, though somewhat closer to the old lead mines which were worked in the nineteenth century. Right in the south-east corner of Somerset, at Stoke Trister, another cock-pit is marked on the one-inch map in Gothic lettering, yet again on the parish boundary, and away from the village, in the little valley of a tributary of the river Cale.

How common were these village bull-pits and cock-pits? It would be interesting to know where they have authentically been identified and recorded, especially in purely agricultural areas as opposed to mining areas where the ground has so often been disturbed, and where an unidentifiable earthwork may misleadingly be called a bull-pit, just because it has never been known to produce any mineral. Many of the sites may originally have been the scene of quarrying or mining activity, but in many villages there would appear to be lingering memories of bull-baiting, as well as tell-tale names on tithe or estate maps.

I only know of two more such sites, one in Somerset, the other in Oxfordshire. The Somerset site is north of Mendip, at Hinton Charterhouse, close to the road from Norton St. Philip to Bath. Well away from the village, there is a vast pit, roughly circular in shape, with a diameter of about 50 yd. and a circumference of nearly a quarter of a mile: the bottom is more or less level, and both the bottom and the steep sides are now dotted with shrubs

---

* The Paulton tithe map also shows a field called Bull Pit on the west side of Old Mills Lane; here there is a small amphitheatre, again on the very edge of the parish.

and trees; in fact one might walk past and never realize that it was anything more than a small copse. At the south-west corner there is an entrance, with a ramp leading down to the floor of the pit. It does not look like a swallet, there is no record or tradition of its having been a gravel-pit or quarry; it lies very close to the line of the Roman road from Bath, but again there is no evidence available to prove that it was either an amphitheatre or a quarry for road metal, as has been sometimes suggested. Of one thing, however, we can be certain: that it was not built as a bull-pit, even though undocumented tradition links it with the age-old sport of bull-baiting.

It is the same at Wheatley near Oxford, where the parish stone-pit was used for bull-baiting. Though now situated in the middle of the village of Wheatley, the pit originally lay on the very edge of the parish of Cuddesdon, of which Wheatley was once a hamlet: it is now filled in, and serves the milder purpose of a recreation ground, though it still contains the village lock-up and the old stocks as reminders of a darker age; for Wheatley was a notoriously licentious place, and bull-baiting and cock-fighting are extensively recorded until well into the nineteenth century, and even later than that strangers to the village would remark on the number of bulldogs in Wheatley, the descendants of those which had been kept for the ancient sport. At Whitsuntide and at the October Feast, a bull was paraded through the streets, decked with ribbons, and on the following day, tied to a stake in the parish pit, was baited by everyone who had a savage dog to let loose at him.[5]

At Axbridge, the cruel spectacle was indulged in on Guy Fawkes' Day. After a service at the Parish Church (attended by the Mayor and Corporation), the bull was let loose in the Square and hunted through the town, windows being shuttered and barred to prevent damage, to a spot now called Outing Patch, above the Bristol road: here the bull was fastened to the 'anchor' and baited, and eventually carved up and the meat distributed to the poor.

Even though there was no bull pit at Axbridge, the scene must have been identical in many Mendip parishes where the pits have still to be identified and the traditions recorded. It is therefore all the more regrettable that on the seventh series O.S. one-inch map (1959) both the Cock Pit at Stoke Trister and the Bull Pit at Buckland Dinham have had their names deleted. I do not know whether the Ordnance Surveyor has doubts as to their authenticity, or refuses to recognize them as antiquities; but I do know that yet another piece of Old Mendip appears to have been obliterated.

CHAPTER SIXTEEN

The Art of Local Memory

> The iniquity of oblivion blindly scattereth her poppy,
> and deals with the memory of men without distinction
> to merit of perpetuity. . . . Who knows whether the best
> of men be known? or whether there be not more re-
> markable persons forgot than many that stand remem-
> bered in the known account of time?
>
> SIR THOMAS BROWNE: *Hydrotaphia* (1658)

I end as I began, searching for something that is lost—the
memory of the past. From books, from the face of the land itself, and from the lips of the people who live there, I have
attempted in this book to recover something of the living past
that surrounds us at every turn. Where we tread, 'generations
have trod, have trod, have trod'.

To know and to love one's countryside, one must be continually
asking questions, and, unlike jesting Pilate, one must stay for an
answer. 'This searching after antiquities is a wearisome taske,' as
Aubrey wrote. 'Though of all studies I take the least delight in
this, yet methinkes I am carried on with a kind of divine oestrum:
for nobody els hereabouts hardly cares for it, but rather makes a
scorn of it.'[1] Aubrey knew both the burden and the delight.
Heroic qualities are demanded of one—patience and pertinacity;
and these may well reap only scorn. Yet the 'divine oestrum'
goads the local historian to ask such apparently futile, and yet
utterly vital questions, if he is to fulfil his function:

> Old association—an almost exhaustive biographical or historical
> acquaintance with every object, animate or inanimate, within the
> observer's horizon. He must know all about those invisible ones of
> the days gone by, whose feet have traversed the fields which look so
> grey from his windows; recall whose creaking plough has turned
> those sods from time to time; whose hands planted the trees that
> form a crest to the opposite hill.[2]

So wrote Thomas Hardy, who above all other English writers seems to me to have been imbued with this sense of place.

One starts with one's own memories, and the memories of living people, or of people one has known in one's own lifetime. My father was born in 1854: the memories of his contemporaries carry us back a long way towards Old Mendip. Let us then progress, or rather regress, with jumps of approximately fifty years into the past. It is, say, 1910. The motor-car has just appeared on Mendip; it is the age of Genevieve in the first flush of her youth, strange and beautiful, as she still appears in the Age of Veteran Car Rallies; the hedges are white with dust; the tarring of Somerset roads began in 1913, but in 1923 the villages of Chantry and Whatley drew up a petition to their Rural District Council against the tarring of their roads—and the Council complied with their wishes. Not until the war did the motor-car become a reliable and normal method of transport: for people at large, transport was achieved by horse-drawn vehicles, by the safety bicycle, and by the railway. On August Bank Holiday, the Great Western Railway at Wells issued 250 tickets for day trips to Weston-super-Mare, Clevedon, Bristol and Weymouth.

1860: the railway is just beginning to penetrate the approaches to Mendip; coal is leaving Radstock by rail; the East Somerset Railway has reached Shepton Mallet. Wells, however, had been linked since 1859 with Burnham-on-Sea by the Somerset Central Railway. My grandfather was vicar of Somerton from 1857 to 1866, and my father used to tell me of day-trips to the sea-side: in a waggonette from Somerton to Glastonbury, and then by train (very nauseous) from Glastonbury to Burnham. Even if nauseating, the new form of locomotion was exciting: new horizons were opening up for the inhabitants of north Somerset, and the turnpike Trusts had begun to see the writing on the wall—the Highbridge and Frome Trusts were both wound up in 1870.

1810, however, was the heyday of the turnpikes: the mailcoaches were running at breath-taking speeds up and down the roads, and to get something of the exhilaration of this speed, one turns to de Quincey's account of 'Going Down with Victory' in *The English Mail-Coach*. It is the Canal Age, too; coal-barges are laboriously locked up and down the interminable flight of 22 locks at Combe Hay, but there is no movement on two waterways that reach out towards Mendip: this state of suspended animation, could the future but be foreseen, is the prelude to premature death. Mendip itself is all enclosed; but the woollen industry is on the decline, and mills are strangely silent; silent, too, many of the churches in their Georgian somnolence, with their galleries and box-pews and two- or three-decker pulpits. 'Pardi! On sert Dieu bien à son aise ici!' exclaimed Cobbett's Frenchman. 'Egad! they serve God very much at their ease here!' At Camely, or at Holcombe, one steps over the threshold into another age. But new chapels are being built with great energy and fervour, for Wesley has been a frequent visitor to the Somerset coalfield, inspiring men with new hope and new faith.

1760: everywhere the Turnpike Trustees are busy at work on the improvement of the roads along which Wesley is to ride so many hundreds of miles; coal is just about to be found at Radstock; Parson Woodforde has been made a Scholar of New College and expended 5s. 0d. on a copy of *Messiah*, 3s. 4d. on Two Bottles of Port Wine and 1d. on Nosegays. The Mendip commons are still unenclosed, for John Billingsley is only a boy of 13; lead-mining is on its way out.

1710: Queen Anne is not yet dead, and the best way to learn what Mendip was like is to read Dr Claver Morris's *Diary*, with its vivid day-to-day account of life in and out of Wells, the life of a sensitive, intelligent, cultured and public-spirited country physician, on his comings and goings, the length and breadth of Mendip.

For that is our problem: how to approach and understand that older Mendip that cannot be seen through any eyes into which we ourselves have looked. Rarely, very rarely, it is done for us, as in Hylton's *History of Kilmersdon*; but normally we must rebuild for ourselves. Beyond living memory we must look first at the tithe maps and schedules, one at each rectory or vicarage if we are lucky, and a complete series in the Somerset Record Office: here, at the beginning of the Victorian era, is a detailed close-up of the lay-out of the parish. For the Georgian era, we must go back to the Ordnance Survey of 1817, and learn to emulate the philosopher Hobbes, himself a Westcountryman by birth, who, according to Aubrey, 'tooke great delight to goe to the booke-binders' shops, and lye gaping on mappes'.[3]

There are three maps in particular on which I like to 'lye gaping'. The first is a map of my own parish, Stratton on the Foss [*sic*], 1824. I do not know its history, but it was given to me by a kind friend who thought it would be of more value to me than to himself. It is a thing of beauty, executed on parchment by P. Pilbrook of Horningsham, across the Wiltshire border: it measures 16 in. × 45 in. (for Stratton is a very elongated parish), and its scale is 110 yd. to the in. Each plot of land is delicately edged in green or yellow; each house is red, other buildings are grey, water is blue; the Foss road, and all the parish roads, are pale sepia. Each plot is numbered, but the numbers do not coincide with those of the tithe map of 1840. For whom the map was made, or why, or what is the significance of the different coloured plots, I do not know, and have not been able to discover. I only know that the map is to me a priceless possession, giving an exquisitely clear picture of the parish as it was almost a hundred and forty years ago. With such a map as this, and with the early census returns to help, the parish registers, and perhaps a volume of churchwardens' accounts, one can step boldly back into another world.

Above my desk hangs Morden's map of Somerset in 1695, extracted, perhaps (who knows?) from my own copy of Camden's *Britannia*. Here one is apt to be left stranded: the only road strikes south-west from Bristol, and peters out at Highbridge; many of the place-names, too, are unfamiliar from vagaries of spelling— Straton in the Vorsewey and Ligh Under Mendip are at least phonetic, but Bishopschue, Ochy Hole and Stoke Land are the older names for the villages which we are more familiar with as Chew Magna, Wookey Hole and Stoke St. Michael. Mendip has its Mineries and Cole Pitts, and the Axe, still a tidal river, boasts its two little ports of Ratclif (now Rackley) and Hyth. But conspicuous above all else, as it would have been to a traveller standing on the southern edge of Mendip and gazing down on to the moors, is a vast sheet of water, Meare Pool. Even in 1750 Dr Pococke could refer to the three streams which made Glastonbury almost an island, and met at 'Meer Poole, which is dry in summer', though making a fen which in winter is covered with water.[4] It was to be another fifty years before plans such as those by William White, which were described and illustrated in Billingsley's *Survey*, would drain the turf bogs and the flooded fields of the basins of the Axe and Brue, and produce the landscape we know today, in which Meare Pool is only a lingering memory.

It is a lake which also arrests the eye in the third of my three maps: the Chew Valley lake, which appears for the first time on the seventh series of the one-inch Ordnance Survey of 1959. When I arrived on Mendip in 1918, Blagdon lake had only been in existence for less than twenty years, but I never worried about what was hidden beneath its waters; in fact I cannot remember ever giving a moment's thought to the matter until the 1817 map came into my hands; and even then nothing very significant seemed to have happened: not even a road or a house seemed to have been drowned. But it was very different in the Chew valley, where a whole complex of lanes and hamlets, with which I had been familiar, had disappeared: there was Stratford mill—now re-erected in the grounds of Blaise Castle—where I used to cycle over to order corn for our chickens from Miss Hassell; there was the Roman road running down from the Blue Bowl; there was Walley Court, and Denny Farm, whose name survives in Denny Island; and above all there was Moreton, and as I compared the modern map with that of 1817, I noticed the words 'Powder Mill' at Moreton. Gunpowder? and if so, why in the remote hamlet of Moreton? I began to ask questions; the answer appeared simple and straightforward—'Powder Mill' meant a flour mill, as distinct from a grist mill: there it was, 'Flour Mill' on the 1886 six-inch Ordnance Survey. And then quite by chance I came across two entries in the parish register of Compton Martin, recording the burial on 15 December 1799 of Thomas Urch of Moreton, 'who died in consequence of having been burnt in a most dreadful manner at the Powder Mills', and of Joseph Gaskell, 'who was unfortunately blown to pieces by standing too near the fire with gun-powder in his pocket'.

Joseph Gaskell lies buried in Compton Martin churchyard; the site of Moreton mill lies drowned beneath the Chew Valley lake. Man and mill are both an essential part of Old Mendip. 'Methinks it shewes a kind of gratitude,' wrote Aubrey, 'to revise the memories and memorialls of the pious and charitable Benefactors since dead and gonne.'[5]

But 'the rude forefathers of the hamlet' are our benefactors in the sense that we are their heirs: for we have inherited the houses they built, the roads they made, the trees they planted and the churches they worshipped in. They are not, perhaps, famous men, but in one sense they are our fathers that begat us. Of Sir John Birkenhead Aubrey wrote: 'He had the art of locall memory.' It is an art which I too am well content to practise.

Up to Date

In the twenty-odd years that have elapsed since I wrote *Old Mendip*, a number of changes have taken place in some of the scenes I have described in the book, and it has seemed best to comment on some of these changes in an epilogue.

The Ministry of Works, for example, has become the Department of the Environment (page 15); the new owners of Gatcombe House, at the end of the lane in which I live, have turned their gateposts round and now live proudly in Lancet House, and thus help to preserve a piece of local history. Facing Lancet House across the lane are the remains of the parish "pound", and I was delighted to be told by the Post Office that I now lived in Pound Lane, which is the name on the 1887 Ordnance Survey map (page 47).

The lanes in the Chew Valley (page 116) are no longer alas! elm-studded, but where I now live, high up on the northern slope of Mendip, there never were elms. Ashwick and Oakhill: I suppose the oaks were felled hundreds of years ago to build our Navy, but the ashes you can see all round the parish, particularly if you walk down Ashwick Grove.

The turnpike roads seem hardly to have changed, though the road to the east of Cranmore (A361) has been widened to meet the demands of the stone lorries streaming out of Merehead quarry; the derelict toll-house at Leighton has been demolished in the interests of safety (page 117). In Wells the plaque at the bottom of Hawkers Lane (page 138) which commemorated the toll-house which once stood there, seems to have disappeared. It was identical to the plaque at Chewton Mendip, as shown in Plate 31.

I referred on page 155 to "the clatter and dust of the stone-crushing plant at Emborough", but the quarry at Emborough

— all 107 acres — is now worked out; quarrying stopped just before the Somerset & Dorset Railway was closed. The railway viaduct still bestrides the little valley: much of the quarry is now a placid sheet of water from which the rock-face rises abruptly, and the rest of the site is being developed by Blatcon Ltd. as a concrete works. It was strange revisiting a site that I had last seen in full working order, and seeing the strangely evocative quarry buildings emerging from the greenery that seems to be gradually smothering them. There was a date — 1876 — carved on a lintel and recording the first building, when Elijah John Barton started his "Somerset pipe, tile, pottery, terra & fine clay works" — I quote from Kelly's Directory for 1889. Quarrying did not start till the turn of the century, and considering the hundreds of thousands of tons of stone that were quarried, the site is amazingly invisible from any road: no motorist on his way to Wells or Shepton Mallet would have a clue to the great industrial site which he is passing.

Nearby, the Old Down Inn, stripped of its plaster front, now faces the road with its original stone facade neatly pointed. This males Plate 35 something of a period piece of historical interest, comparable to the sketch in the *Downside Review*, made soon after the fire of 1885, which I mention on page 146.

It is perhaps worth mentioning that you are no longer able to consult the Tithe Map of a parish by calling on the rector or vicar and examining the map at leisure spread out on his dining-room table or even on his study floor. All the Tithe Maps are now kept safely at the County Record Office at Taunton, and although this means a day's trip and 75 miles of motoring, it does enable me to consult a number of maps at a sitting, instead of having to make separate appointments with the incumbent of each parish.

The Little Railways

Since 1964, several more sections of railway around Mendip have been closed. Although the passenger service between Bristol and Frome via Radstock had been withdrawn in 1959, freight traffic on the Bristol — Radstock section continued until 1968. The Somerset & Dorset line was closed in 1966, except for the mile or so to Writhlington colliery: to serve this, a link line was brought into use at Radstock (where a proposal for a similar link between the GWR and the SDJR had been rejected as long ago as the 1870s), and coal trains continued to use this until the colliery was finally closed in 1973, when the little branch to Kilmersdon colliery, with its inclined plane which fed the Radstock—Frome line, was also closed.

Both the stations at Radstock have been completely demolished, and the motorist coming down the hill from Bath is now spared the problem of two sets of level crossing gates, and is confronted instead with an incredibly busy and complicated road junction where no fewer than eight roads converge. While he waits at the traffic lights — and one always has to wait — he can admire one of the pithead winding wheels that has been put up on the site of the Somerset & Dorset line to commemorate Radstock's industrial past.

Several of the S&D station buildings have survived: Midsomer Norton has been used by local schools as a field study and project centre; Masbury is almost intact, except for the removal of the signal box, and makes a delightful residence with the addition of a new wing. The bay window is still surmounted by the fanciful stone carving of a medieval castle, complete with crenellations and portcullis and the Gothic legend "Maesbury Castle" — but you will be disappointed of a castle if you labour up the hill to what is generally called Maesbury Camp, where a ring fortifications guard the Iron Age camp 950 feet above sea level. Between Masbury and Shepton Mallet there are several splendid viaducts, and another at Prestleigh on the long bank down to Evercreech; here at the Junction the station buildings are all inhabited, but the *Silent Whistle* no longer guards the crossing. The old *Railway Hotel* now masquerades as the *Natterjack Inn*.

Two branches to quarries still survive. The branch which once followed the circuitous course of the Mells river through Vallis Vale to reach the quarry at Whatley has now been realigned: it leaves the Radstock line half a mile further from Frome, and runs through a couple of tunnels, more or less straight up Murder Combe, to the quarry. This avoidance of the tortuous curves of the wooded gorge of the Mells river

191

enables large diesels to work through to Whatley and bring away full train-loads of stone.

The most interesting developments are over the hill at Cranmore, on the former GWR branch from Witham to Wells. Passenger services were withdrawn in 1963, but the line stayed open to serve Foster Yeoman's quarry Dulcote; it was then cut back as far as Cranmore, where the Merehead quarry had been opened in 1958. This is served by a long siding which leads to the Torr Works, where trains are assembled and loaded, before setting off down the fearsome gradients of the branch — the ruling gradient is 1:47 — to join the main line at Witham.

Cranmore station survives almost intact as the Headquarters of the East Somerset Railway. This Company, under the chairmanship of David Shepherd, takes its name from the original Company which completed its line from Witham to Shepton Mallet in 1858, and on to Wells in 1862, before it was absorbed by the GWR. The station is beautifully done up and cared for: there is a signal box, used as a small museum and for a display of David Shepherd's paintings and prints; and a purpose-built engine-shed designed by a local architect, Robin Butterell, to a standard GWR design. This houses David Shepherd's stud of steam locomotives which include a BR 2-10-0, "Black Prince", a class 4MT 4-6-0, "Green Knight" (now owned by the East Somerset) and several vintage specimens.

From March to the end of October, the East Somerset now runs a regular service of steam-hauled trains on Sundays (and on Wednesdays during the summer months) along the mile of track as far as Merryfield Lane Halt. (This is the point where the tramway from Chelynch quarries used to bring stone down to the works, which had a siding of their own at a time when the finished article was sent away by rail.) The East Somerset owns another half-mile or so of track, running down the hill on a gradient of 1:56 towards Shepton Mallet, along which it is now planned to extend the passenger service. During the last year for which figures are available (1983), over 18,000 passengers were carried on over 350 trains. It is indeed good to hear that steam-hauled trains are once again on a line which I first travelled on in 1933 — more than 50

192

years ago.

Wookey Hole

In Chapter Five I have given some account of the paper-mills which used to flourish all round Mendip until the middle of the nineteenth century. Only the mill at Wookey Hole survived into the twentieth century. It was owned by the Hodgkinsons for a hundred years until it was sold by Guy Hodgkinson to the Inveresk Paper Co. in 1951. With the decline in demand for hand-made paper, they gradually closed down the mill, transferring the last two vats to St. Cuthbert's Mill, half a mile down the valley.

Wookey Hole Mill, where the making of paper had flourished for more than 350 years, was offered for sale in 1972, and in the following year Mrs. Olive Hodgkinson decided to sell the Caves which her husband, Wing-Commander Gerard Hodgkinson, had been developing for many years. Madame Tussaud's bought the Mill *and* the Caves, and they have proceeded to develop the property as a whole. A new tunnel has been cut, opening up to the public another cave, and leading out on to the opposite side of the valley to the original entrance, and a footpath alongside the leat now leads down to the east side of the Mill. Here hand-made paper is once again being made, for sale to tourists and for a limited number of export sales.

When visitors have passed through the caves, and watched the skill of the paper makers at work, they have still to see Lady Bangor's Fairground Collection of objects made between 1870 and 1939, which was acquired by Madame Tussaud's and first exhibited at Wookey Hole in 1974. There is also Madame Tussaud's Storeroom — one of the old drying lofts in the Mill — where more than 2000 moulds, from which the casts are taken, have been sent down from London for safe keeping.

It is strange to realise that in 1933, when I came to live in the village of Wookey Hole, many of the items in Lady Bangor's Collection were still in daily use, and that it was not until thirty years later that she began to assemble her Collection, and that Madame Tussaud's moulds were still stored in cramped and vulnerable quarters in the cellars of Baker Street. Stranger still, perhaps, that along with 38,000 visitors I was able to enjoy the splendours of Wookey Hole at the cost of one shilling.

Fussells of Mells

Fussells ironworks were established at Mells in 1744 and they continued working until they were closed down in 1894 — a period of 150 years. From Mells they expanded their business downstream to Great Elm, and into the neighbouring valleys: Railford, Little Elm and Nunney. Rather surprisingly, on the First Edition of the Ordnance Survey, published in 1817, Nunney is the only place where Fussells Edge Tool Mill is marked. The Mells works are of course shown on the Tithe Map c.1840, and a large scale plan of "The Mells Iron Works the property of Messrs James Fussell sons and Company", dating from the late 1840s, has recently been discovered.

A splendid photograph of the "old Iron Works", taken from the south bank of the river, has now come to light. This must date from c.1900: it shows a scene of complete dereliction, with the buildings stripped of roofs and windows, but with most of the walls still standing to their full height, and the office block intact, just as it is today. The general lay-out of the works is quite clear.

In the late 1950s, when I first visited the site, things were very different. Beyond the office block there was an indescribable jumble of broken walls, with great mounds of rubble and earth, from which large trees were growing — "the ruins of a derelict industry". But in 1974 B.I.A.S. (the Bristol Industrial Archaeological Society) arrived on the scene. Under the direction of John Cornwell, they explored and excavated the site, whenever the weather allowed, helped by a number of local friends, including boys from Downside School. They moved hundreds of tons of rubble, cut down large trees, excavating deep below the surface to reveal the remains of furnaces, a large number of forges, the framework of an 11ft wrought-iron water-wheel, and the whole ground plan of the works, with the network of channels through which came the water which was for so long the source of power — and the source of the wealth which the Fussells accumulated.

The climax was, perhaps, April 1983. At the conclusion of

194

Daffodil Week in Mells, about 200 people assembled in the Village Hall to hear a talk on the iron industry, followed by a walk down the valley to the site of the works, where a descendant of the Fussells explained to the assembled company the lay-out of what was once a large and complex industrial set-up, going back 250 years.

The future remains uncertain. B.I.A.S. have finished their excavations, but great interest has been stimulated, and it is difficult for the present owners to prevent all access. It is going to be impossible to keep down the vegetation which is even now beginning to spring up again. At least there is a public footpath running down the valley from which one can get an impression of what was once a large industrial complex in this remote and silent Mendip valley.

APPENDIX I

Note on Chantry Church

The design of Chantry church has by tradition been attributed to Sir Gilbert Scott: the earliest evidence for this, however, is the entry in Morris's *Directory* for 1871, twenty-five years after the church was built. I have been unable to find any newspaper account of the opening of the church in 1846, nor any mention of the architect in diocesan or ecclesiastical building records. In the possession of Ronald Vallis, the Frome architect, there are drawings of Chantry church dated 1844-5 and signed William George Brown. Browns were a firm of Frome builders and surveyors who specialized in ecclesiastical repairs. Laverton, Beckington and St. John Baptist, Frome are examples of their restoration work. John Betjeman considers that for its date Chantry seems an unexpectedly advanced Tractarian building to emanate from the office of a Frome surveyor. It looks as if young William George Brown (he was born in 1827) made copies of Scott's plans which his firm were executing: at any rate details such as the edge-tool angels may well have been left to the initiative of the local firm, just as the painted panels on the reredos were later executed by W. L. T. Collins, an art master from Frome, who taught at the school at Chantry founded by the Fussells.

NOTES

Chapter One (*page* 13)

1. A. L. Humphreys, *Somersetshire Parishes*, 1906, s.v. Ubley.
2. C. 2. Elizabeth, B. 18/36; C. 3/149/12.
3. J. Collinson, *History of Somerset*, 1791, ii, 134.
4. J. W. Gough, *The Mines of Mendip*, 1930, reprinted 1967, pp. 14–16, 187–90.

Chapter Two (*page* 19)

1. W. Cobbett, *Rural Rides*, 31 October 1822.
2. M. W. Beresford, *The Lost Villages of England*, 1954, includes a list of the sites of deserted medieval villages which have so far been identified in Somerset.
3. C. & J. Greenwood, *Somersetshire Delineated*, 1822.
4. Ethelbert Horne, 'A Legend of Holcombe', *The Downside Review*, 1916; see also Horne, *Somerset Folk*, 1938.
5. Sheet XIX (29 in. by 23 in.) shows the whole of Mendip; it more or less follows the eastern boundary of Somerset from Bath to Stourhead, and covers about two-thirds of the area shown on Sheets 165 and 166 of the Seventh Series One-Inch O.S. Photocopies of this sheet are obtainable from the British Museum, and it is available as Sheet 76 in the David & Charles reprint of the first edition of the One-Inch O.S.

Chapter Three (*page* 25)

1. A. W. Coysh, E. J. Mason and V. Waite, *The Mendips*, 1954, pp. 129–33.
2. N. Pevsner, *The Buildings of England (North Somerset and Bristol)*, 1958, s.v. Camerton.
3. H. Coombs and A. N. Bax, *Journal of a Somerset Rector*, 1930, *passim*.
4. Pevsner, op. cit., p. 163.
5. J. Collinson, *History of Somerset*, 1791, ii, 120. Jenkins (later Jenkyns) came of a wealthy family connected with the north Wiltshire woollen trade. He died in 1806, aged 71, and was buried at Melksham. He was a cousin of John Jenkyns, vicar of Evercreech, whose son, Richard, became Dean of Wells (1845–54).

6. Oswald Wyndham Hewett, *Strawberry Fair*, 1956, *passim*.

7. Hylton, *History of Kilmersdon*, 1910, pp. 21–3, 37.

8. Hylton, op. cit., pp. 59–60.

9. J. D. C. Wickham, *Records by Spade and Terrier*, *c.* 1912, pp. 243–4.

10. *The Downside Review*, 1884, pp. 101–2.

11. J. Collinson, *History of Somerset*, 1791, ii, 129.

  The Werrets (of Shepton Beauchamp) left £100 in 1681 for apprenticing poor boys of the parish of Chilcompton; their names are found in the Chilcompton parish registers between 1603 and 1669 (Bishop's transcripts).

12. Wickham, op. cit., p. 379.

13. Wickham, op. cit., p. 97.

14. J. Leland, *Itinerary* (1535–1543), ed. Toulmin Smith, 1907, V. 84–6, 104.

15. F. B. Kettlewell, *Trinkum-Trinkums of Fifty Years*, 1927, pp. 26–7.

16. The Scrope surveys, together with the later Waldegrave Estate maps, have been deposited with the Waldegrave papers at the Somerset Record Office.

17. L. S. Palmer and H. W. W. Ashworth, 'Four Roman Pigs of Lead from the Mendips', Somerset Arch. Soc. Procs., Vol. 101–2, 1956–7.

18. Ethelbert Horne, 'A Patriarch of Mendip', *The Downside Review*, 1904; see also Horne, *Stories of West Country Folk*, 1948.

19. J. W. Gough, *The Mines of Mendip*, 1930, reprinted 1967, p. 44.

Chapter Four (*page* 45)

1. J. Collinson, *History of Somerset*, ii, 449.

2. J. Murch, *Presbyterian and General Baptist Churches in the West of England*, 1835, pp. 155 ff.

3. J. Billingsley, *General View of the Agriculture of the County of Somerset*, 1797, 2nd ed., 1798.

4. T. F. Plowman, *Edmund Rack*, 1914, pp. 35–7. (Reprinted from the Bath and West and Southern Counties Society's *Annual Journal*, Vol. VIII, Fifth Series.)

Chapter Five (*page* 55)

1. J. Collinson, *History of Somerset*, 1791, ii, 484.

2. *Bonner and Middleton's Bristol Journal*, 31 July 1784.

3. A. H. Shorter, 'Paper and Board Mills in Somerset', *Notes and Queries for Somerset and Dorset*, XXV, March 1950, pp. 245–57.

4. P.R.O. I.R.I. 70/177 (1802).

Notes

5. J. Rutter, *Delineations of the North Western Division of Somersetshire*, 1829, p. 137.
6. A delightful account, almost contemporary with Evelyn, of a mill at Canterbury, is to be found in *The Journeys of Celia Fiennes*, ed. Morris, 1947, p. 124.
7. *The Wells Journal*, 6 October 1904.
8. *The Bristol Mirror*, 26 May 1832, 2 June 1832.
9. Act of 1846; described in *The Illustrated London News*, 23 April 1853.
10. Ethelbert Horne, 'The Waters of Stoke Lane', *The Downside Review*, 1905.

Further sources consulted:

D. C. Coleman, *The British Paper Industry 1495–1860*, 1958.
W. W. Jervis and S. J. Jones, 'The Paper-making Industry in Somerset', *Geography*, 1930, pp. 624–9.
A. H. Shorter, *Paper Mills and Paper Makers in England 1495–1800*, 1957.

Chapter Six (page 68)

1. *The Somerset Year-Book*, 1935, pp. 43-4.
2. Hubert van Zeller, *Willingly to School*, 1952, pp. 37-8; see also Ethelbert Horne, *Somerset Folk*, 1938, 'An Old Iron Mill'.
3. J. Collinson, *History of Somerset*, 1791, ii, 461.
4. Horner MSS. 484.
5. *Bristol Times and Mirror*, 6 August 1903.
6. The architect has not been identified, but it has been pointed out that the same architect almost certainly designed Parish's House, Timsbury, about 1816, the entrance fronts showing a marked similarity with many identical features. See *Country Life*, 1 June 1961, 2 November 1961, article and letter by Mark Girouard.
7. H. Coombs and A. N. Bax, *Journal of a Somerset Rector*, 1930, p. 179.
8. L. S. Pressnell, *Country Banking in the Industrial Revolution*, 1956 p. 28.
9. Minutes of Committee of Council, tabulated reports on schools inspected in the counties of Cornwall, Devon, Dorset and Somerset by the Rev. E. Douglas Tinling and assistant Inspectors, 1860.
10. A. Raistrick, *Dynasty of Ironfounders*, 1953, p. 17.
11. Raistrick, op. cit., p. 272.

Main sources consulted:

Edward Tylee, 'An Old Somerset Industry', *The Somerset Year-Book*, 1934.
Horner MSS. at Mells.

Notes

Daniel MSS. at Frome.

MS. Autobiography of Richard White, belonging to A. J. S. White.

Chapter Seven (*page* 95)

1. J. Collinson, *History of Somerset*, 1791, iii, 473.
2. W. Phelps, *History and Antiquities of Somersetshire*, 1836, Vol. I (General Introduction), pp. 105–7.
3. Hylton, *History of Kilmersdon*, 1910, pp. 132, 275.
4. *The Somerset Year-Book*, 1929, p. 38.
5. Collinson, op. cit., ii, 105.
6. Collinson, op. cit., ii, 5.
7. See frontispiece to J. W. Gough, *The Mines of Mendip*, 1930, r/p 1967.
8. For a description of Monmouth House (later Soho House) see J. T. Smith, *Nollekens and his Times*, ed. G. W. Stonier, 1949, p. 15; Marcus Whiffen, *Thomas Archer*, 1950, frontispiece and p. 34.

Main sources consulted:

R. Evans, 'The Defence Forces of Somerset', Somerset Arch. Soc. Procs., Vol. 105, 1961.

Emanuel Green, *Somerset and the Armada*, 1888.

Bryan Little, *The Monmouth Episode*, 1956.

Chapter Eight (*page* 104)

The documents relating to the Wells Turnpike Trust (1753–1883) are now in the Somerset Record Office: the collection comprises 27 volumes of MSS. and 9 maps, together with a miscellaneous mass of papers, bills, receipts, lawyers' opinions, copies of Acts of Parliament, etc. These have all been worked through by Dr R. D. Reid of Wells, a pioneer in the study of the local turnpike system, who has published a number of articles on the Wells Turnpike roads.

All the other original documents quoted or referred to in Chapters Eight to Ten are in the Somerset Record Office.

A complete survey of all the material available has been made by Sir R. de Z. Hall, who has deposited with the Record Office a handlist covering the turnpike legislation and records for the whole of Somerset, with details of the dates at which turnpiking of various routes was authorized: these have also been coloured in on a one-inch map.

The Somerset Record Office holds a fairly complete set of returns of annual statements of accounts for all Trusts from 1822; a volume of returns, made in accordance with an Act of 1820, giving details of the mileage and limits of the roads maintained by each Trust; a number of deposited plans of alterations or improvements either proposed or

200

Notes

carried out; and the following volumes relating specifically to Mendip —Frome Trust Order Book 1772-1790; Shepton Mallet Trust Minute Books from 1776; Bath Trust Minute Books (not complete) 1759-1878.

1. G. M. Trevelyan, *English Social History*, 1944, pp. 382-4.
2. Diary of a West Country Physician, ed. Hobhouse, 1934, p. 73.
3. H. Coombs and A. N. Bax, *Journal of a Somerset Rector*, 1930, pp. 90, 92.

Chapter Nine (*page* 120)

1. *Diary of a West Country Physician*, ed. Hobhouse, 1934, p. 105.
2. J. Billingsley, *Survey of Somerset*, 1798, p. 308.
3. Billingsley, op. cit., pp. 159, 260.
4. John Wood, *An Essay towards a Description of Bath*, 1749, Vol. II, pp. 354-65.
5. J. D. D. Keilor, *A Study of Our Somerset Village*, reprinted from *The Somerset Standard*, 1924.

   For further accounts of travelling in North Somerset in the eighteenth century see *passim*, *Diary of a West Country Physician*, ed. Hobhouse, 1934, and *Diary of a Country Parson* (James Woodforde), ed. Beresford, 1924, Vol. I (1758-1781).

   The MS. Memoirs of Richard Wason belong to his granddaughter, Mrs F. W. Widgery.

Chapter Ten (*page* 131)

1. R. Warner, *A Walk through some of the Western Counties of England*, 1800, pp. 4-6.
2. J. McMurtrie (Somerset Arch. Soc. Procs., 1884, Vol. 30 (2), p. 76), refers to another turnpike gate at this point, but this is not confirmed on any known map or by any other reference.
3. J. McMurtrie, Somerset Arch. Soc. Procs., 1884, Vol. 30 (2), p. 76; and 1904, Vol. 50 (2), p. 108.

   J. McMurtrie, Bristol and Gloucestershire Arch. Soc. Trans., Vol. 26, p. 326.

   I. D. Margary, *Roman Roads in Britain*, 1955, i, 116.
4. *The Downside Review*, 1903, p. 180.

Chapter Eleven (*page* 139)

1. *Diary of a Country Parson*, ed. Beresford, 1924, i, pp. 123-4.
2. G. Sweetman, *History of Wincanton*, 1903, p. 189.
3. Reece Winstone, *Bristol as it was* 1914-1900, Plate 71.
4. *Kilvert's Diary*, ed. Plomer, 1944, p. 265 (2 November 1874).

5. Letter dated 30 March 1802 in the possession of E. H. Ford.
6. H. Coombs and A. N. Bax, *Journal of a Somerset Rector*, 1930, pp. 92–3.
7. Somerset Arch. Soc. Procs., 1953, Vol. 98, p. 39.
8. Snow, *Sketches of Old Downside*, 1903, 'In the Lists', pp. 44–57.
9. *The Downside Review*, 1886, pp. 160–3.
10. R. Warner, *A Walk through some of the Western Counties of England*, 1800, p. 11.
11. J. Collinson, *History of Somerset*, 1791, ii, 135.
12. Coombs and Bax, op. cit., pp. 90, 92–3, 98.
Further sources consulted:
Hippisley MSS. at the Somerset Record Office.
E. Vale, *The Mail Coach Men*, 1960.
E. H. Ford, *Postal History of Shepton Mallet*, 1958.

Chapter Twelve (*page* 151)

1. W. Camden, *Britannia*, 1695, p. 69.
2. R. Pococke, *Travels through England* (Camden Soc. 1888), i, 153.
3. J. Leland, *Itinerary* (1535–1543), ed. Toulmin Smith, 1907, v. 105.

Chapter Thirteen (*page* 158)

1. *The Story of Our Village*, Ashwick and Oakhill Women's Institute, 1953.
Main sources consulted:
Bristol and North Somerset Southern Extension and Nettlebridge Branch, Deposited Plans, 1865, in the House of Lords Record Office.
D. S. Barrie and C. R. Clinker, *The Somerset and Dorset Railway*, 1948 and 1959 (revised edition).
D. St. J. Thomas, *A Regional History of the Railways of Great Britain*, Vol. I, *The West Country*, 1963 (revised edition).

Chapter Fourteen (*page* 165)

1. Robin Atthill, *The Curious Past*, 1955, p. 8.
2. 36 George III, cap. 47.
3. Bryan Little, 'Frome's Forgotten Bridges', *The Somerset Countryman*, Vol. 18, No. 11, July 1956.
4. *Bath Chronicle*, 11 September 1800.
5. *Aris's Birmingham Gazette*, 26 January 1801.
Main sources consulted:
Deposited Plans of the Dorset & Somerset Canal in the House of
N*

Lords Record Office and the Somerset Record Office.

The Dorset and Somerset Navigation, c. 1825. B.T.C. Archives (GWR Canal Relics Book No. 16 HRP 6–3), and also at the Dorset County Record Office.

Patent No. 2284 (1798): Balance Lock for raising or lowering boats, etc.

Charles Hadfield, *The Canals of South West England*, 1967, pp. 191–4.

Chapter Fifteen (*page* 178)

1. B.M. Add. MSS. 33653 f. 182, quoted by J. W. Gough, *The Mines of Mendip*, 1930, reprinted 1967, pp. 38–9.
2. E. K. Tratman, Bristol University Spelaeological Soc. Procs., 1938.
3. Strachey papers at Somerset Record Office.
4. J. D. D. Keilor, *A Study of Our Somerset Village*, reprinted from *The Somerset Standard*, 1924.
5. *Wheatley Records*, Oxfordshire Record Soc., 1956, ed. Dr. W. O. Hassall.

Chapter Sixteen (*page* 184)

1. John Aubrey, *Brief Lives*, ed. Powell, 1949, p. 12.
2. Thomas Hardy, *The Woodlanders*, Chapter XVII.
3. Aubrey, op. cit., p. 241.
4. R. Pococke, *Travels through England* (Camden Soc. 1888), i, 145, 150.
5. Aubrey, op. cit., p. 13.

Acknowledgements

Thanks are due to the following for permission to make use of copyright material: W. H. Auden and Faber & Faber Ltd. for extracts from *Poems* (1930); T. S. Eliot and Faber & Faber Ltd. for extracts from *Four Quartets*; the Executors of the Robert Frost Estate and Jonathan Cape Ltd. for an extract from *Collected Poems*; the Trustees of the Hardy Estate and Macmillan and Co. Ltd. for an extract from *The Woodlanders*: C. Day Lewis and Jonathan Cape Ltd. for extracts from *Word Over All*; the Oxford University Press for an extract from *The Poems of Gerard Manley Hopkins*, and for an extract from *Diary of a Country Parson* by James Woodforde.

I am grateful to the Editors of *Country Life*, *The Countryman*, the Bristol *Evening Post*, *Somerset Countryman*, and *The Western Gazette*, in whose pages some of my material first appeared in article form, and who have kindly allowed me to reprint it here.

I should like to acknowledge the kindness of the following who generously allowed me to make use of private material in their possession: the Marquess of Bath; the Bath and West and Southern Counties Society; Brades Skelton and Tyzack Ltd.; Mr Peter Coombs; the Bishop of Clifton; Mr Hilary M. Daniel; the Abbot of Downside; Mr E. H. Ford; the Earl of Oxford and Asquith; the Postmaster-General; Mr Ronald Vallis; Mr A. J. S. White; Mrs F. W. Widgery; and many incumbents who have allowed me to examine their church records, especially the Rev. R. P. Cavendish, formerly of Mells, and the Rev. A. F. Dobbie Bateman of Chantry.

I must also thank many people in official positions who have helped me with my researches, and who have answered my numerous and often tiresome queries—in particular the Director of the Victoria Art Gallery and Municipal Libraries of Bath (Mr Peter Pagan); the City Librarian of Bristol (Mr W. S. Haugh); the

Acknowledgements

Curator of the Curtis Museum at Alton; the Archivist of the Dorset County Record Office, Dorchester; the Librarian of the Ministry of Education; and above all the Somerset Archivist, Mr Ivor P. Collis, and his indefatigable and ever courteous staff at the Somerset Record Office, Taunton.

Many different people have advised me about particular areas of research: Sir R. de Z. Hall gave me the full benefit of his own wide knowledge of the turnpike roads of Somerset, and kindly read Chapters Eight to Ten in typescript; Dr A. H. Shorter read Chapter Five on the paper mills—both of them thereby saving me from making a number of gratuitous mistakes. Dr R. D. Reid supplied me with information on many matters relating to Wells; and Mr Charles Hadfield advised me where to glean information about the Dorset & Somerset Canal.

To many members of my W.E.A. classes in north Somerset, and to members of the Frome Society for Local Study to which I am proud to belong, I owe an incalculable debt. Among the latter I wish to record particularly the names of Mr H. J. Norville and Miss E. D. Overend. It would be impossible to put on record the names of all my friends, up and down Mendip, who, often unwittingly, have provided me with information without which this book could hardly have been begun. I only hope it will not seem invidious if I acknowledge a special debt of gratitude to the late Mr Leonard Dunford of Chilcompton, the late Mr Evan Robbins of Ston Easton, Mr Tom Payne of Chew Stoke and Mr Austin Wookey of Coley. My son, Mr Charles Atthill, very kindly undertook the compilation of the index.

A large number of the photographs were specially taken for me by Mr K. F. Marchant whose tireless and enthusiastic co-operation over a considerable period of time I most gratefully acknowledge. Other photographs were taken for me by Mrs E. L. Green-Armytage (Plates 16 and 17); Bolwell Studio, Bath (Plate 9); Mr Stephen Green-Armytage (Plate 10); and Mr J. McDonnell (Plates 12 and 13)—to all of whom I am most grateful.

Plate 33 is reproduced by courtesy of the Trustees of the British Museum who also supplied the photograph: Plate 9 by permission of the Victoria Art Gallery, Bath; Plate 37 by permission of the Locomotive Publishing Co. Ltd. who also supplied the photograph.

The following individuals kindly allowed me to make use of

private material in their possession: Mr C. Burge of Chilcompton (Plate 7); Mr A. W. Dibble of Old Down (Plate 34); Mrs Olive Hodgkinson of Wookey Hole (Plate 12); Mr A. J. S. White (Plate 18); Mrs Wood of Dunkerton (Plate 32). The line-drawing on p. 98 is reproduced by permission of Earl Waldegrave.

Index

Agricultural reforms, 48–53, *see also* Enclosures
Ammerdown Park, 29, 115
Ansford, 112, 124, 139–40, 178–9
Armada, Spanish, 97–8, 100
Ashwick Grove, 45–7, 48, 53
Axbridge, 58, 179, 182
Axe, R., 17, 50, 56, 61, 118, 187

Babington, 22
Bampfylde family, 22, 35, 116
Banwell, 59, 62
Barrow Hill, 171, 173–6
Batcombe, 113, 117–18, 122–3
Bateman, Richard, 42
Bath, 131–2, *see also* Turnpike Trusts
Bath and West Society, 48, 52, 53
Beacon Hill, 96–7, 99, 100, 110, 113, 161
Beacons, 95–100
    Crook Peak, 96, 97
    Dundry, 97
    Dunkery, 98, 99
    Rybury, *see* Beacon Hill
Beauchamp family, 27, 33
Bennett, William, canal engineer, 167, 174, 176
Billingsley, John, 17, 48–54, 55, 57, 68, 104, 110, 118, 120, 121, 125, 138, 142, 167, 186
Billingsley, Nicholas, 47, 48
Binegar, 162–3
Bisse family, 21, 64
Black Death, 20, 21–2
Blacker's Hill, 155, 156, 157
Blagdon Lake, 14, 63, 188
Bleadney, 61, 112
Bristol, 141–2, *see also* Turnpike Trusts
Bristol and Exeter Railway, 119
    Cheddar Valley line, 62, 163
Bristol and North Somerset Railway, 160–1
Brown, W. G., architect, 189
Bruton, 122, 143, *see also* Turnpike Trusts

Bruton Priory, 147
Buckland Dinham, 125–6, 178, 179–80, 181, *see also* Turnpike Trusts
Bull-baiting, 178–83
Bull pits, 178–83
Buonaparte, Napoleon, 71, 95, 97, 174

Cam, R., 138, 153, 160
Canals, Dorset and Somerset, 48, 68, 71, 114, 154, 161, 164, 165–77
    Glastonbury, 118
    Kennet and Avon, 48, 160, 167
    Somersetshire Coal, 32, 48, 132, 135, 137, 150, 160, 164, 185
Cannard's Grave, 112, 123, 140
Chantry, 74–6, 87, 89, 91, 185, 189
Chantry ironworks (Little Elm), 73, 74, 81, 92
Chantry School, 88–9, 91
'Chantry, The', 72–4, 87, 91, 170
Charlton House, 29–30
Charlton Gate, 128–9
Cheddar, 56, 57, 62, 118, 119
Chelynch, 129–30
Chew Stoke, 108–9, 125–6
Chewton Mendip, 27–9, 63
Chewton Priory, 27–9
Chew Valley Lake, 63, 108, 187–8
Chichester family, 64–6
Chilcompton, 30–3, 68, 112, 121, 127, 136–8, 157
    Manor Farm, 30–1
    Norton Hall, 31–2, 136
Churchill, 106–8, 116, 121
Coal industry, 22, 27, 50, 83, 114–15, 145, 151, 159–60, 162, 179–80, 186
Coal, transport of, 104, 114, 115, 117, 120, 121, 125–7, 129, 133, 160, 162, 163, 164, 185, *see also* Canals and Railways
Cobbet, William, 20, 25, 26, 120, 186
Cockfighting, 178–9, 181
Coleford, 83, 104, 114, 151, 154, 161, 164, 169–70, 176

207

Index

Index